Dictionary of IT Terms

DICTIONARY OF IT TERMS

Piyush Sen

CYBER TECH PUBLICATIONS
4264/3, Ansari Road, Daryaganj New Delhi - 110002 (India)
Phone : 011-23244078, 011-43559448, Fax : 011-23280028
Email : cybertechpublications@gmail.com

CYBER TECH PUBLICATIONS
4264/3, Ansari Road, Daryaganj
New Delhi - 110002 (India)
Phone : 011-23244078, 011-43559448,
Fax : 011-23280028
E-mail : cybertechpublications@gmail.com
Website : www.cybertechpublications.com

2nd Edition : 2018

ISBN 81-7884-018-9

Rs. 3000.00

Printed at :

New Green Print Solutions, New Delhi 110078

A

Abandoned Well
An oil or gas well not in use because it was a dry hole originally, or because it has ceased to produce in paying quantities. State statutes and regulations require the plugging of abandoned wells to prevent oil, gas or water seeping from one stratum of underlying rock to another.

Available Transfer Capability (ATC)
The measure of the transfer capability remaining in the physical transmission network for commercial activity beyond already committed uses

Abandonment
Termination of a sale or interstate transportation of natural gas. Abandonment of a service that is subject to FERC jurisdiction requires some type of advance determination by the FERC under Section 7 (b) of the NGA that the "present or future public convenience and necessity" requires termination.

Abandonment, Pregranted
A provision of a FERC certificate of public convenience and necessity that authorizes abandonment on a future condition subsequent or on a date certain.

Absolute Pressure
See PRESSURE.

Absorbers
Dark-colored objects that soak up heat in thermal solar power collectors used to produce heat energy. The component of a solar thermal collector that absorbs solar radiation and converts it to heat, or, as in a solar photovoltaic device, the material that readily absorbs photons to generate charge carriers (free electrons or holes).

Absorption Chiller
A type of air cooling device that uses absorption cooling to cool interior spaces.

Absorption Coefficient
In reference to a solar energy conversion devices, the degree to which a substance will absorb solar energy. In a solar photovoltaic device, the factor by which photons are absorbed as they travel a unit distance through a material.

Absorption Cooling

A process in which cooling of an interior space is accomplished by the evaporation of a volatile fluid, which is then absorbed in a strong solution, then desorbed under pressure by a heat source, and then recondensed at a temperature high enough that the heat of condensation can be rejected to a exterior space.

Absorption Refrigeration

A system in which a secondary fluid absorbs the refrigerant, releasing heat, then releases the refrigerant and reabsorbs the heat. Ammonia or water is used as the vapor in commercial absorption cycle systems, and water or lithium bromide is the absorber.

Absorptivity

In a solar thermal system, the ratio of solar energy striking the absorber that is absorbed by the absorber to that of solar energy striking a black body (perfect absorber) at the same temperature. The absorptivity of a material is numerically equal to its emissivity.

Access

The legal right to use an electrical or gas transmission and /or distribution system as a means of transferring electrical energy or natural gas as set forth in the contract.

Access Charge

A charge levied on power supplied, or its customer, for access to a utility's transmission or distribution system. It is a charge for the right to send electricity over another's wires.

Account No. 191

Tracking system established by the FERC for unrecovered gas supply costs incurred by interstate pipelines, to be eliminated once pipelines sell gas at market-based rates under blanket sales certificates pursuant to Order No. 636.

Account No. 858

Tracking system established by the FERC used by interstate pipelines for costs incurred transporting sales gas on upstream pipelines.

Accredited

Generating capability recognized as meeting MAPP requirements to satisfy a portion of a MAPP member's generating capacity obligation.

Accumulator

A component of a heat pump that stores liquid and keeps it from flooding the compressor. The accumulator takes the strain off the compressor and improves the reliability of the system.

A.C. (Alternating Current)
Type of electrical current, the direction of which is reversed at regular intervals or cycles.

Ace
See AREA CONTROL ERROR.

Acid Rain
Also called acid precipitation or acid deposition, acid rain is precipitation containing harmful amounts of nitric and sulfuric acids formed primarily by nitrogen oxides and sulfur oxides released into the atmosphere when fossil fuels are burned. It can be wet precipitation (rain, snow or fog) or dry precipitation (absorbed gaseous and paniculate matter, aerosol particles or dust). Acid rain has a pH below 5.6. Normal rain has a pH of about 5.6, which is slightly acidic. The term pH is a measure of acidity or alkalinity and ranges from 0 to 14. A pH measurement of 7 is regarded as neutral. Measurements below 7 indicate increased acidity, while those above indicate increased alkalinity. Active Solar Heater A solar water or space-heating system that moves heated air or water using pumps or fans.

Actual Unit Starts
Number of times the unit was synchronized.

Acquired Capacity Agreement
Under capacity release, an agreement between a gas pipeline and an acquiring shipper which establishes the terms and conditions for the acquiring shipper using firm capacity rights from a releasing shipper.

Acquiring Shipper
In the context of capacity release, a shipper who acquires firm capacity rights from a releasing shipper (also known as "replacement shipper").

Acre-Feet
The amount of water it takes to cover one acre to a depth of one foot. This measure is used to describe the quantity of storage in a hydrosystem reservoir. An average household of four will use approximately one acre foot of water per year.

Active Power
The power (in Watts) used by a device to produce useful work. Also called input power.

Active Solar Heater
A solar water or space-heating system that use pumps or fans to circulate the fluid (water or heat-transfer fluid like diluted antifreeze) from the solar collectors to a storage tank subsystem.

Actual Interchange
Metered electric power that flows from one control area to another.

Actual Peak Reduction
The actual reduction in annual system peak load (measured in kilowatts) achieved through consumer's participation in a utility DSM (see DEMAND SIDE MANAGEMENT) program. It reflects the changes in the demand for electricity resulting from a utility DSM program that is in effect at the same time the utility experiences its annual system peak load, as opposed to the installed peak load reduction capability (i.e. potential peak reduction).

Actuals
In the context of futures trading, actual cash commodities in contrast to futures commodities. In the context of ratemaking, actual costs and throughput data relating to a given time frame.

Adapter
Typically a non-attenuating fiber optic connector, for example a zero buildout. (Formerly called a coupler)

Adapter Panel
Bulkhead, sometimes modular, used to mount adapters and buildouts. Usually means the part unequipped with adapters or buildouts. (Formerly called a coupler panel)

Adequacy
A bulk electric power system's ability to supply the aggregate electrical demand and energy requirements of customers at all times.

Adequate Regulating Margin
The minimum on-line capacity that can be increased or decreased to allow the system to respond to all reasonable demand changes in order to be in compliance with the NERC Control Performance Criteria. See also SPINNING RESERVES.

Adjacent System or Adjacent Control Area
Any system or control area either directly interconnected with or electrically close to (so as to be significantly affected by the existence of) another system or control area.

Adjustable Speed Drive
An electronic device that controls the rotational speed of motor-driven equipment such as fans, pumps, and compressors. Speed control is achieved by adjusting the frequency of the voltage applied to the motor.

Adjustment Clause on Provision (Rate Adjustment, Fuel Adjustment, Purchased Gas Adjustment, Tax Adjustment, Commodity Adjustment)
A provision in a utility tariff that provides for changes in rates or total charges with changes in specified items of cost, such as No. 2 or 6 fuel price, purchased gas, tax, etc.

Administrative and General Overhead (A&G) Costs

See COSTS, ADMINISTRATIVE AND GENERAL.

Ad Valorem Tax
Tax imposed at a percent of a value. Local property taxes are often ad valorem taxes.

Aerial
Above ground installation for power lines or telephone lines or cables are installed on a pole or overhead structure.

Age
The number of years the unit(s) has been in commercial service.

Agency Service
An arrangement which allows a gas buyer to give an agent authority to act on the buyer's behalf to arrange or administer pipeline transportation and/or sales services.

Aggregative Schedule
A coordination requirement which calls for identification of the purchasing-selling entities that "aggregate" an interchange schedule.

Aggregator
A company that consolidates a number of individual users and/or supplies into a group.

AH
Ampere-Hours - The current x duration of current flow, usually used to denote capacity flowing from a battery.

Air Conditioner
A device for conditioning air in an interior space. A Room Air Conditioner is a unit designed for installation in the wall or window of a room to deliver conditioned air without ducts. A Unitary Air Conditioner is composed of one or more assemblies that usually include an evaporator or cooling coil, a compressor and condenser combination, and possibly a heating apparatus. A Central Air Conditioner is designed to provide conditioned air from a central unit to a whole house with fans and ducts.

ir Conditioning
The control of the quality, quantity, and temperature-humidity of the air in an interior space.

ir Conditioning Cycling Program
A demand-side management program in which the utility remotely controls customers' cooling equipment and periodically interrupts power to the equipment during times of high power system demands.

Air Diffuser
An air distribution outlet, typically located in the ceiling, which mixes conditioned air with room air.

Air Infiltration Measurement
A building energy auditing technique used to determine and/or locate air leaks in a building shell or envelope.

Air Register
The component of a combustion device that regulates the amount of air entering the combustion chamber.

Air Retarder/Barrier
A material or structural element that inhibits air flow into and out of a building's envelope or shell. This is a continuous sheet composed of polyethylene, polypropylene, or extruded polystyrene. The sheet is wrapped around the outside of a house during construction to reduce air in-and exfiltration, yet allow water to easily diffuse through it.

Air-Source Heat Pump
A type of heat pump that transfers heat from outdoor air to indoor air during the heating season, and works in reverse during the cooling season.

Air-to-Air Heat Pump
see Air-Source Heat Pump.

Air-to-Water Heat Pump
A type of heat pump that transfers heat in outdoor air to water for space or water heating.

Alliance
An agreement among businesses, organizations or groups to work cooperatively toward a common purpose.

Allowance for Funds Used During Construction (AFUDC)
A non-cash accounting convention of regulatory utilities that represents

the estimated composite interest costs of debt and a return on equity funds used to finance construction. The allowance is capitalized in the property accounts and included in income.

Alkaline Batteries
Batteries that can last for a long time because they do not corrode easily.

Alternate Firm Receipt/Delivery Point
Firm receipt or delivery point, not including primary points designated in a gas contract, at which a firm shipper may schedule gas receipt or delivery with a priority above that of interruptible service.

Alternate Fuel Capability
The ability of any user such as an industrial facility to use more than one fuel, whether or not the facilities for such use have actually been installed.

Alternating Current (AC)
A periodic current, the average value of which over a period is zero. Unless distinctly specified otherwise, the term refers to a current that reverses its direction at regularly recurring intervals of time and that has alternately positive and negative values. Almost all electric utilities generate AC electricity because it can easily be transformed to higher or lower voltages. That form of electric current that alternates or changes in magnitude and polarity (direction) in what is normally a regular pattern for a given time period called frequency. An electric current with its direction reversed at regular intervals, used to send high voltage electricity over long distances. The current is then lowered by a transformer so that it can be used by regular households. A periodic current, the average value of which over a period is zero. Unless distinctly specified otherwise, the term refers to a current that reverses its direction at regularly recurring intervals of time and that has alternately positive and negative values. Almost all electric utilities generate AC electricity because it can easily be transformed to higher or lower voltages. A current that flows alternately in one direction and then in the reverse direction. In North America, the standard for alternating current is 60 complete cycles each second. Such electricity is said to have a frequency of 60 hertz. Alternating current is used in power systems because it can be transmitted and distributed more economically than direct current.

Alternating Current Distribution
The supply of electrical energy from one or more major receiving stations to the point of ultimate utilization. The energy is generally supplied at a voltage that can be directly utilized by large rotating machinery and step-down transformers are utilized to reduce the voltage for most commercial or residential utilization.

Alternative Delivery Procedure (ADP)
A futures contract provision in which buyers and sellers make and take delivery under terms and conditions which differ from those imposed in the futures contract.

Alternative Fuel Capacity
The on-site availability of apparatus to burn more than one fuel.

Alternator
A generator producing alternating current by the rotation of its rotor, and which is powered by a primary mover.

American National Standards Institute (ANSI)
The coordinating organization for U.S. federated national standards system. The ANSI federation consists of 1400 company, organization, government agency, institutional and international members.

Amorphous Silicon
Sometimes abbreviated as "a-Si", amorphous silicon is used as a disordered semi-conductor material in the plasma-enhanced chemical vapor deposition (PECVD) process used to create thin-film solar cells on a stainless-steel substrate

Ampacity
Current carrying capacity expressed in amperes.

Ampere (AMP)
The unit of current flow of electricity. It is to electricity as the number of gallons per minute is to the flow of water. One ampere flow of current is equal to one coulomb per second flow. A unit of measure of electric current. The unit of measurement of electrical current produced in a circuit by 1 volt acting through a resistance of 1 ohm. The measure of the rate of flow of electrons past a given point in an electric conductor such as a power line. A unit of measurement for electrical current or rate of flow of electrons (coulombs per second). If a group of electrons whose total charge is 1 coulomb passes a point in a conductor in 1 second, the electric current is 1 ampere. Its mathematical symbol is "I" the term is often shortened to "amps". A unit of measure for an electrical current; the amount of current that flows in a circuit at an electromotive force of one Volt and at a resistance of one Ohm. Abbreviated as amp.

Amp-Hours
A measure of the flow of current (in amperes) over one hour.

Ammeter
An instrument for measuring the strength of an electric current. Electrical

test instrument used to measure current in a circuit.

AMR
Automated Meter Reading.

Ancillary Services (Ancillaries)
Those services from electric generating resources necessary or beneficial to support the transmission of capacity and energy from resources to loads while maintaining reliable operation of a transmission system in accordance with good utility practice. Ancillaries include: spinning reserve (.hot stand-by.), non-spinning reserve, regulation, replacement reserves and operating reserves.

Anthracite
'Hard coal', appearing bright and shiny, generally found deeper in the Earth than bituminous coal. It produces no smoke when burnt. A form of coal often referred to as "hard coal," which is generally used in the production of steel, characterized by low volatile matter, low sulfur, low ash, low Hargrove index (indicating a hard coal) and high heating value. Sometimes blended with bituminous coal in sized coal cargoes to increase heating value. Heating value is often at or above 13,500 Btu/lb.

Ancillary Services
Interconnected Operations Services identified by the Federal Energy Regulatory Commission (Order No. 888 issued April 24, 1996) as necessary to effect a transfer of electricity between purchasing and selling entities and which a transmission provider must include in an open access transmission tariff. Services necessary to support transmission of capacity and energy from resources to load while maintaining reliable operation of the transmission system.

Annual Effects
The total effects in energy use (measured in kilowatt-hours) and peak load (measured in kilowatts) caused by all participants in the DSM programs that are in effect during a given period.

Annual Solar Savings
The annual solar savings of a solar building is the energy savings attributable to a solar feature relative to the energy requirements of a non-solar building.

Anode
The positive pole or electrode of an electrolytic cell, vacuum tube, etc. (see also sacrificial anode).

Anthracite (coal)
A hard, dense type of coal, that is hard to break, clean to handle, difficult

to ignite, and that burns with an intense flame and with the virtual absence of smoke because it contains a high percentage of fixed carbon and a low percentage of volatile matter.

Apparent Power

For single phase, the current in amperes multiplied by the volts equals the apparent power in volt-amperes. This term is used for alternating current circuits because the current flow is not always in phase with the voltage; hence, amperes multiplied by volts does not necessarily give the true power or watts. Apparent power for 3 phase equals the phase to neutral volts multiplied by ampere multiplied by 3. The product of voltage and current in a circuit.

APA

Alaska Power Administration. A power marketing and electric transmission agency of the United States government with headquarters in Juneau, Alaska.

APPA

American Public Power Association. The trade association of publicly-held power entities.

Apparent Power

For single phase, the current in amperes multiplied by the volts equals the apparent power in volt-amperes. This term is used for alternating current circuits because the current flow is not always in phase with the voltage; hence, amperes multiplied by volts does not necessarily give the true power or watts. Apparent power for 3 phase equals the phase to neutral volts multiplied by ampere multiplied by 3. The product of voltage and current in a circuit.

Application Service Provider (ASP)

A company that provides businesses with access to application programs via the Internet. The application resides on the ASP's site and the user organization pays a license fee or some other usage charge.

Arbitrage

Trading the same security, currency or commodity in two or more markets in order to profit from differences in prices. The simultaneous or near simultaneous purchase of one commodity against the sale of similar or identical commodities in order to profit from fluctuations in the usual price relationships. By its nature, arbitrage generally has little to no risk with relatively minimal reward.

Arbitrageur

An arbitrageur takes advantage of momentary disparities in prices between markets. Arbitrageurs make markets more efficient by bringing the prices in line with each other.

ARC

Sparking that results when undesirable current flows between two points of differing potential. This may be due to leakage through the intermediate insulation or a leakage path due to contamination.

Area Control Error (ACE)

The instantaneous difference between actual and scheduled power flow between two entities.

Armature Coil

A winding that develops current output from a generator when its turns cut a magnetic flux.

Array (Solar)

Any number of solar photovoltaic modules or solar thermal collectors or reflectors connected together to
provide electrical or thermal energy.

Asynchronous Generator

A type of electric generator that produces alternating current that matches an existing power source.

Automatic Damper

A device that cuts off the flow of hot or cold air to or from a room as controlled by a thermostat.

Automatic (or Remote) Meter Reading System

A system that records the consumption of electricity, gas, water, etc, and sends the data to a central data accumulation device.

Auxiliary Energy or System

Energy required to operate mechanical components of an energy system, or a source of energy or energy supply system to back-up another.

Availability

Describes the reliability of power plants. It refers to the number of hours that a power plant is available to produce power divided by the total hours in a set time period, usually a year. Time that a generating unit, transmission line or other system is capable of providing service, even if it isn't actually providing service all the time. It is expressed as a percentage of a specific time period.

Available Heat
The amount of heat energy that may be converted into useful energy from a fuel.

Average Demand
The demand on, or the power output of, an electrical system or any of its parts over an interval of time, as determined by the total number of kilowatt-hours divided by the units of time in the interval.

Average Cost
The total cost of production divided by the total quantity produced.

Average Wind Speed (or Velocity)
The mean wind speed over a specified period of time.

Avoided Cost
The incremental cost to an electric power producer to generate or purchase a unit of electricity or capacity or both.

Axial Fans
Fans in which the direction of the flow of the air from inlet to outlet remains unchanged; includes propeller, tubaxial, and vaneaxial type fans.

Axial Flow Compressor
A type of air compressor in which air is compressed in a series of stages as it flows axially through a decreasing tubular area.

Axial Flow Turbine
A turbine in which the flow of a steam or gas is essentially parallel to the rotor axis.

B

Backfill
A term used in surface mining to reflect the practice of placing overburden behind the location where the coal seam has been removed, typically using a long reach dragline. The intent is to move the overburden as little as possible to reduce cos

Backhaul
A "paper transport" of natural gas by displacement against the flow on a single pipeline, so that the natural gas is redelivered upstream of its point of receipt. See also DISPLACEMENT.

Back-Stopping
Arranging for alternate supplies of gas in the event a user's primary source fails to be delivered.

Backup Energy System
A reserve appliance; for example, a stand-by generator for a home or commercial building.

Back-up Power
Power which a wheeling utility must provide by contract to another utility or by virtue of its control area responsibility to a customer when that customer's normal source of power is not available. Power provided by contract to a customer when its normal sources are unavailable

Back-Up Protection
Protection equipment or system which is intended to operate when a system fault is not cleared in due time because of failure or inability of the main protection to operate or in case of failure to operate a circuit-breaker other than the associated circuit-breaker.

Backup Supply Service
Capacity and energy provided to a transmission customer to replace the loss of its generation sources and to cover that portion of demand that exceeds the generation supply. The interconnected operations service that provides the needed capacity and energy to transmission customers to replace the loss of generation and to cover the portion of demand that exceeds generation supplies for more than a short period

Backwardation
In the context of futures trading, a market condition in which futures prices are gradually lowered in the future months of delivery.

Balanced Load
An equal distribution of current on all phases of an AC circuit. An alternating current power system consisting of more than two current carrying conductors in which these conductors all carry the same current.

Balance-of-System
In a renewable energy system, refers to all components other than the mechanism used to harvest the resource (such as photovoltaic panels or a wind turbine). Balance-of-system costs can include design, land, site preparation, system installation, support structures, power conditioning, operation and maintenance, and storage.

Balancing
Equalizing the volumes of gas withdrawn from a pipeline system with he volumes of gas injected into the pipeline. Penalties may be assessed

for transportation imbalances beyond specified tolerances. A process that compares actual customer gas use with the amount of natural gas delivered to a local distribution company during a special time period (e.g., daily or monthly). The differences (either over or under) between these two amounts are called imbalances.

Ballast
A device used to control the voltage in a fluorescent lamp.

Ballast Efficacy Factor
The measure of the efficiency of fluorescent lamp ballasts. It is the relative light output divided by the power input.

Ballast Factor
The ratio of light output of a fluorescent lamp operated on a ballast to the light output of a lamp operated on a standard or reference ballast.

Balun Filter
Input line filter often used on DC-DC converters that include a differential wound transformer. Balun filters present a low impedance to differential mode signals and a high impedance ot common mode signals.

Band Pass
The frequency range over which an inductor or capacitor exhibits a low impedance.

Band Stop
The frequency range over which an inductor or capacitor exhibits a high impedance.

Banking
Energy delivered or received by a utility with intent to return it in the future.

Baseline Performance Value
Initial values of Isc, Voc, Pmp, Imp measured by the accredited laboratory and corrected to Standard Test Conditions, used to validate the manufacturer's performance measurements provided with the qualification modules per IEEE 1262.

Base Load
The minimum demands of electricity on a power station over a given period of time. Muja is a base load power station. The minimum amount of electric power delivered or required over a given period of time at a steady rate. The minimum continuous load or demand in a power system

over a given period of time. The minimum level of electric power demand of a utility, region, or utility customer, generally expressed in units of kilowatts or megawatts. The minimum continuous load over a given period of time. Base load generating stations operate essentially at full output whenever possible. The minimum amount of electric power or natural gas delivered or required over a given period of time at a steady rate. The minimum continuous load or demand in a power system over a given period of time usually not temperature sensitive.

Baseload Capacity
The power output of a power plant that can be continuously produced. The generating equipment normally operated to serve loads on an around-the-clock basis.

Baseload Demand
Minimum demand experienced by a generating plant. The minimum demand experienced by a power plant.

Baseload generating plant
A baseload generating unit is normally used to satisfy all or part of the power demand that generally exist all of the time within the system and, as a consequence, produces electricity at an essentially constant rate and runs continuously.

Base Load Plant
A plant which is normally operated to take all or part of the minimum continuous load of a system, and which consequently produces electricity at an essentially constant rate. These plants are operated to maximize system mechanical and thermal efficiency and minimize system operating costs. A base load plant is typically characterized by relatively high fixed costs and low unit operating costs. Traditionally, coal and nuclear plants and some high efficiency steam electric plants have been considered as base load plants.

Base-Load Unit
An electric power plant, or generating unit within a power plant, that is normally operated continuously to meet the base load of a utility or of a larger area operated by an ISO. California Independent System Operator (CAISO) or (ISO) The Independent System Operator operates the transmission systems owned by Pacific Gas and Electric (PG&E), Southern California Edison, and San Diego Gas & Electric (SDG&E). The abbreviation ISO sometimes refers to the California ISO, and sometimes to refers to any Independent System Operator (also see Independent System Operator).

Baseload Power Plant
A power plant that is normally operated to generate a base load, and that

usually operates at a constant load; examples include coal fired and nuclear fueled power plants.

Base Plate

Substrate to which circuit components are mounted or, a metal plate to which the converter is attached. Normally used to draw heat away from critical circuit components. Also see Heat Sink.

Base Power

Power generated by a power generator that operates at a very high capacity factor.

Base Rate

A charge normally set through rate proceedings by appropriate regulatory agencies and fixed until reviewed at future proceedings. It is calculated through multiplication of the rate from the appropriate electric rate schedule by the level of consumption. It does not include components that may vary from billing cycle to billing cycle, such as fuel.

Basis

The difference between the spot or cash price of a financial instrument or commodity and the price of the futures contract or a related derivative instrument. A seller is "short of the basis" if selling spot goods hedged by the purchases of futures. Someone who is "long of the basis" has bought spot goods and hedged them by the sale of futures. A basis point is one percent of one percent. The difference between the prices of a commodity at two different locations or at two different times, e.g., between the cash (or .spot.) price and the price of the nearest futures contract for the same or a related commodity.

Base Resistance

The resistance of a PolySwitch device under specified conditions (e.g., 20jC), before connection into a circuit. Devices of a particular type will be delivered with a range of resistances; therefore, a minimum value, Rmin, and/or a maximum value, Rmax, are often given.

Basis

In the context of futures trading, the difference between the futures price for a given commodity and the comparable cash or spot price for the commodity.

Basis Swap

A basis swap involves swapping one floating rate index for another. An interest rate swap in which payments are on a different floating-rate basis, e.g., three-month versus six-month. Also known as a floating/floating swap. A basis swap enables the user to lock in a differential between two grades, two product types or two locations of a commodity. This tool is used to fine-tune energy price risk management. (A swap on the differential between a petroleum product and crude oil is often referred to as a "crack spread" swap.)

Battery

A device which stores energy by converting electrical energy into chemical energy. This energy can be reconverted to electrical energy by the reversal of the chemical reactions. A collection of cells, grouped together to provide higher voltage and/or higher current than a single cell.

Battery:

For off-grid systems a battery is used to provide energy storage. Nearly all batteries used for PV systems are of the lead-acid type (with a small quantity of antimony to reduce self-discharge). Nickel-cadmium batteries are also suitable and have the advantage that they cannot be overcharged or discharged, but are considerably more expensive. All PV batteries are deep-cycle i.e. designed to be discharged down to 50% or more without damage so that they can supply power over a long period of time (in contrast to a car battery, for example, which is usually only discharged down to 3 to 5 %).

The lifetime of a battery varies depending on factors such as how it is used, how it is maintained and charged, and temperature, but is typically between 5 and 10 years.

Battery Backup

Subsystem for electronic equipment that provides power in the event of input power loss. Battery backed systems are a common application are for DC-DC converters.

Battery Disconnect Switch

Master switch that disconnects a battery reservoir from a UPS. Provides personnel protection when batteries or UPS require service.

Battery energy storage

The three main applications for battery energy storage systems include spinning reserve at generating stations, load leveling at substations, and peak shaving on the customer side of the meter. Battery storage has also been suggested for holding down air emissions at the power plant by shifting the time of day of the emission or shifting the location of emissions.

Battery Reservoir

A combination of cells or batteries used to power a UPS's system inverter when it is in the emergency mode.

Bayonet Coupling
A quick coupling device for plug and receptacle connectors, accomplished by rotation of a cam operating device designed to bring the connector halves together.

Bcf
The abbreviation for 1 billion cubic feet of natural gas.

Bedrock
The part of the Earth's crust that is almost unbroken rock, and is relatively unaffected by the process of erosion.

Beryllium Copper (BeCu)
A relatively expensive contact material with properties superior to brass and phosphor bronze. It is recommended for contact applications requiring repeated extraction and reinsertion because of its resistance to fatigue at high operating temperatures.

Best Efforts Service
Service offered to customers under rate schedules or contracts that anticipate and permit some interruption on short notice, generally in peak-load seasons, by reason of the claims of firm service customers.

Beta particle
A particle emitted from an atom during radioactive decay. Beta particles may be either electrons (with negative charge) or positrons.

BHMAX (Maximum Energy Product)
Indicates the maximum energy that a magnetic material can supply to an external magnetic circuit when operating at the Bd, Hd point on its demagnetization curve, measured in megaGauss-Oersteds (MGOe) or kilo Joules per cubic meter (kJ/m3).

Bid
An offer to pay an asking price in an over-the-counter or commodity market. It is the average price of those people recently willing to purchase. Bid is the purchase price and asked is the selling or offer price.

Bidding Shipper
A natural gas shipper bidding for capacity released by a firm capacity holder.

Bid-Offer Spread
The fixed rate at which a dealer will take either the pay- or the receive-fixed side of a swap transaction.

Bilateral Contract
A direct contract between the power producer and user or broker outside of a centralized power pool or POOLCO.

Billing Cycle
The regular periodic interval used by a utility for reading the meters of a customer for billing purposes. Usually meters are scheduled to be read monthly or bimonthly.

Billing Demand
The demand charge that a customer actually pays for the reservation of capacity or facilities used, regardless of consumption. Billing demand may be based on a contract maximum, a contract minimum or a previous peak or maximum demand and, therefore, may not necessarily coincide with the actual measured demand for the billing period. Also referred to as Ratchet, or Ratcheted Demand Charge.

Binary Cycle
Combination of two power plant turbine cycles utilizing two different working fluids for power production. The waste heat from the first turbine cycle provides the heat energy for the operation of the second turbine, thus providing higher overall system efficiencies.

Binary Cycle Geothermal Plants
Binary cycle systems can be used with liquids at temperatures less than 350 F (177 C). In these systems, the hot geothermal liquid vaporizes a secondary working fluid, which then drives a turbine.

Bin Method
A method of predicting heating and/or cooling loads using instantaneous load calculation at different outdoor dry-bulb temperatures, and multiplying the result by the number of hours of occurrence of each temperature.

Binned
Binned refers to resistance-matched devices, which are supplied such that all parts in one particular package (or reel) are within 0.5 ohms of each other (1.0 ohms for TR250-080T devices). Individual matched packages are supplied from the full resistance range of the specified device. The benefit is that resistance-matched devices reduce the tip-ring resistance differential, reducing the possibility of line imbalance. Sorted devices are those that are supplied with resistance values that are within specified segments of the device's full range of resistance, giving greater design flexibility.

Biological shield

A mass of absorbing material (e.g., thick concrete walls) placed around a reactor or radioactive material to reduce the radiation (especially neutrons and gamma rays respectively) to a level safe for humans.

Biomass

The total amount of biological material in a given area, including material from plants and animals, as well as bacteria, fungi, and plant and animal organisms.

Biomass Conversion

The process by which organic materials, such as wood waste or garbage, are burned for direct energy or electrical generation, or by which these materials are converted to synthetic natural gas.

BJPV (Building-Integrated Photovoltaic)

A term for the design and integration of Photovoltaic into the building envelope, typically replacing conventional building materials. This integration may be in vertical facades, replacing view glass, spandrel glass, or other facade material; into semitransparent skylight systems; into roofing systems, replacing traditional roofing materials; into shading "eyebrows" over windows; or other building envelope systems.

Bituminous Coal

'Soft coal', containing between 15 and 50 percent volatile matter. It is 'younger' and of lower heat value than anthracite. It is the chief fuel in power plants that generate electrical energy with steam. Older geologic age than subbituminous coal, with higher heating value, lower sulfur, typically higher volatile matter and ash than subbituminous coal. Used for both steam and electricity production, as well as for production of steel. Metallurgical coal is typically bituminous coal, with a free swelling index of over 4.5 and with "dial divisions per minute" (a measure of "fluidity") of over 1,500 and sometimes over 20,000. Heating value of bituminous coal typically ranges from 10,000 to 13,000 Btu/lb.

Blackout

A total power failure caused unintentionally by storm damage, equipment failure or overloading power supply equipment. The emergency loss of the source of electricity serving an area caused by failure of the generation, transmission or distribution system. A total loss of commercial power.

Black Start

A rapid start up of an off-line, idle, non-spinning electric generation source. Equivalent to the starting up of a car after it has not been used for a while. Some power stations have the ability to start-up independently of a power grid. This is an essential prerequisite for system security as these plant can be called on during a blackout to repower the grid.

Blade
The part of a wind generator rotor that catches the wind.

Blocking diode
A diode used to restrict or block reverse current from flowing backward through a module. [UL 1703] Alternatively, diode connected in series to a Photovoltaic string; it protects its modules from a reverse power flow and, thus, against the risk of thermal destruction of solar cells.

Blower
The device in an air conditioner that distributes the filtered air from the return duct over the cooling coil/heat exchanger. This circulated air is cooled/heated and then sent through the supply duct, past dampers, and through supply diffusers to the living/working space.

Blower Door
A device used by energy auditors to pressurize a building to locate places of air leakage and energy loss.

Blown In Insulation (see also Loose Fill)
An insulation product composed of loose fibers or fiber pellets that are blown into building cavities or attics using special pneumatic equipment.

Bobbin Core(CoEv)
A core with the shape of a bobbin or spool which contains flanges. Bobbin cores are available with and without leads and in the axial and radial form.

Boiler
A device for generating steam for power, processing or heating purposes, or for producing hot water for heating purposes or hot water supply. Heat from an electrical combustion source is transmitted to a fluid contained within the tubes in the boiler shell. This fluid is delivered to an end-user at a desired pressure, temperature and quality. Boilers are often classified as steam or hot water, low pressure or high pressure, capable of burning one fuel or a number of fuels. A vessel or tank where heat produced from the combustion of fuels such as natural gas, fuel oil, or coal is used to generate hot water or steam for applications ranging from building space heating to electric power production or industrial process heat.

Boiler Feedwater
The water that is forced into a boiler to take the place of that which is evaporated in the generation of steam.

Boiler Fuel
Fuels suitable for generating steam or hot water in large industrial or electrical generating utility applications.

Boiler Fuel Gas
Natural gas used as fuel for the generation of steam or hot water.

Boiler Horsepower
A unit of rate of water evaporation equal to the evaporation per hour of 34.5 pounds of water at a temperature of 212 degrees Fahrenheit into steam at 212 degrees F.

Boiler Pressure
The pressure of the steam or water in a boiler as measured; usually expressed in pounds per square inch
gauge (psig).

Boiler Rating
The heating capacity of a steam boiler; expressed in Btu per hour (Btu/h), or horsepower, or pounds of steam per hour.

Boiling water reactor (BWR)
A common type of light water reactor (LWR), where water is allowed to boil in the core thus generating steam directly in the reactor vessel, (cf PWR)

Bonding
Deliberate connection of two or more points to reduce any difference of potential (voltage).

Bonding Jumper
A bare or insulated conductor used to ensure the required electrical conductivity between metal parts required to be electrically connected. Frequently used from a bonding bushing to the service equipment enclosure to provide a path around concentric knockouts in an enclosure wall - also used to bond one raceway to another.

Book Cost
The amount at which property or assets are recorded in a company's accounts without deducting depreciation, amortization or various other items.

Book Transfer
Transfer of title without a physical movement.

Boost Charge
The process of charging a battery at an elevated voltage for a prescribed

period - typically 2.50 Volts in the case of flooded cells.

Boost Regulator

A basic DC-DC switching converter topology that takes an unregulated input voltage and produces a higher regulated output voltage. The higher output voltage is achieved by storing energy in an input inductor and then transferring the energy to the output by turning a shunt switch (transistor) on and off at a fast rate.

BOS or Balance of System (photovoltaic)

The parts of a photovoltaic system other than the array. For instance: switches, controls, meters, power conditioning equipment, supporting structure for the array, storage components, etc.

Bottleneck Facility

A point on the system, such as a transmission line, through which all electricity must pass to get to its intended buyers. If there is limited capacity at this point, some priorities must be developed to decide whose power gets through. It also must be decided if the owner of the bottleneck may, or must, build additional facilities to relieve the constraint.

Bottom Ash

Slag or other residue remaining in the boiler after coal is burned.

Bottoming-cycle

A means to increase the thermal efficiency of a steam electric generating system by converting some waste heat from the condenser into electricity. The heat engine in a bottoming cycle would be a condensing turbine similar in principle to a steam turbine but operating with a different working fluid at a much lower temperature and pressure.

Boule

A sausage-shaped synthetic single-crystal mass grown in a special furnace, pulled and turned at a rate necessary to maintain the single-crystal structure during growth.

Braking System

A device to slow a wind turbine's shaft speed down to safe levels electrically or mechanically

Brayton Cycle

A thermodynamic cycle using constant pressure, heat addition and rejection, representing the idealized behavior of the working fluid in a gas turbine type heat engine

Bread Box System
This simple passive solar hot water system consists of one or more storage tanks placed in an insulated box that has a glazed side facing the sun. A bread box system is mounted on the ground or on the roof (make sure your roof structure is strong enough to support it). Some systems use "selective" surfaces on the tank(s). These surfaces absorb sun well but inhibit radiative loss. Also known as batch heaters or integral collector storage systems.

Breakdown Voltage
The voltage at which an insulator or dielectric ruptures, or at which ionization and conduction take place in a gas or vapor. Maximum AC or DC voltage that can be applied from the input to output (or chassis) of a converter without causing damage.

Breakover Current
Instantaneous current flowing at the breakover voltage, VBO.

Breakover Voltage
Maximum voltage across a SiBar device at breakdown measured under a specified voltage rate of rise and current rate of rise.

Breed
To form fissile nuclei, usually as a result of neutron capture, possibly followed by radioactive decay.

Breeder reactor
see Fast Breeder Reactor and Fast Neutron Reactor.

Bridge Converter
Switching converter topology that employs four switching elements (full bridge) or two switching elements (half-bridge). This topology is more often used in off-line supplies rather than DC-DC converters. Bridge converters provide high output power and low ripple, but are significantly more complex than other types of converter topologies and thus are more expensive and prone to failure. Also see Boost Regulator, Buck Regulator, Flyback Converter, Foward Converter, Push-Pull Converter and Resonant Converter.

British Thermal Unit (BTU)
The amount of heat energy necessary to raise the temperature of one pound of water one degree Fahrenheit.

British Thermal Unit (Btu), Dry
A measure of the heating value of natural gas that is free of moisture, or contains less that 7 pounds per Mcf of water vapor. Condition under

which natural gas is usually delivered for first sales.

British Thermal Unit (Btu), Saturated
A measure of the heating value of natural gas that is fully saturated with water vapor under standard temperature, pressure and gravity conditions. This standard of measure usually has little or nothing to do with the state in which the natural gas is actually delivered for first sales.

Boyle's Law
The volume of gas is inversely proportional to the pressure on it if the temperature is unchanged. That is, the more pressure, the smaller the volume of a gas.

Branch Circuit
A division of a load circuit with current limited by a fuse or circuit breaker.

Break-Before-Make
Operational sequence of a switch or relay where the existing connection is opened prior to making the new connection.

Brown Coal
Brownish-black coal that is about 50 percent water.

Brown out
The partial reduction of electrical voltages caused by customer demand being higher than anticipated or by the failure of the generation, transmission, or distribution system. A brownout results in lights dimming and motor-driven devices slowing down. A low voltage condition lasting longer than a few cycles. "Brownouts" differ from "sags" only in duration. A system voltage reduction in response to a shortage of power relative to demand. Although service is not disrupted completely, a brownout will cause a dimming of lights and may result in a loss of load.

Brushes
Devices for transferring power to or from a rotating object. Usually made of carbon-graphite. Found in electric motors, alternators and generators.

BTU
British Thermal Unit. Energy required to raise one pound of water one degree Fahrenheit. One pound of water at 32 degrees F requires the transfer of 144 BTUs to freeze into solid ice.

Bubble Point
The temperature and pressure at which a liquid begins to convert to a gas.

Buck-Boost Transformer
A small, low voltage transformer placed in series with the power line to increase or reduce steady state voltage.

Buck Regulator
A basic DC-DC switching converter topology that takes an unregulated input voltage and produces a lower regulated output voltage. The lower output voltage is achieved by chopping the input voltage with a series connected switch (transistor) which applies pulses to an averaging inductor and capacitor.

Buck Regulator (DC-DC)
A basic DC-DC switching converter topology that takes an unregulated input voltage and produces a lower regulated output voltage. This output voltage is achieved by chopping the input voltage with a series connected switch (transistor) which applies pulses to an averaging inductor and capacitor.

Buckets
In an impulse hydro turbine, the buckets are attached to the turbine near the runner, and used to 'catch' the water. The force of the water hitting the buckets turns the runner, which turns the alternator drive shaft, causing the alternator to generate power.

Buildout
Attenuation inserted into a transmission/signal path (for example, order wire buildout or fiber optic buildout). Fiber optic buildout is an adapter with attenuation.

Bulb
The transparent or opaque sphere in an electric light that the electric light transmits through.

Bulb Turbine
A type of hydro turbine in which the entire generator is mounted inside the water passageway as an integral unit with the turbine. These installations can offer significant reductions in the size of the powerhouse.

Bulge
A rapid increase in futures prices.

Bulk Electric System
The aggregate of electric generating plants, transmission lines and related equipment. The term may refer to those facilities within one electric utility

or within a group of utilities in which the transmission lines are interconnected.

Bulk Electricity
Large amounts of electric power at transmission voltages, generally to run industrial plants and operations.

Bulk Power
Preferred DC power architecture in which one set of rectifiers and batteries is shared by an entire structure, as distinguished from *Distributed Power,* sometimes meant as including ***Bulk Ringing.***

Bulk Power Supply
Often this term is used interchangeably with wholesale power supply. In broader terms, it refers to the aggregate of electric generating plants, transmission lines, and related equipment. The term may refer to those facilities within one electric utility, or within a group of utilities in which the transmission lines are interconnected.

Bulk Power System
A term describing all electric generating plants, transmission lines and equipment. See also BULK ELECTRIC SYSTEM.

Bundled Sales Service
The sale and/or transportation of natural gas or electricity under one rate, which does not differentiate separate rate components for the sale, transportation, storage or gathering services associated with such sale or transportation.

Burnable poison
A neutron absorber included in the fuel which progressively disappears and compensates for the loss of reactivity as the fuel is consumed. Gadolinium is commonly used.

Burner Capacity (Burner Rating)
The maximum Btu per hour that can be released by a burner while burning with a stable flame and satisfactory combustion.

Bulk Ringing
Preferred ringing power architecture in which one set of ring generators is shared by many transmission equipment modules; using implied as part of *Bulk Power.*

Burner Tip
The end of the transportation of natural gas from the wellhead, and the

point of consumption.

Burn In

Operation of newly manufctured converters for some period of time prior to shipment. The intent is to stabilize the converter and eliminate infant mortality by aging the device. The time period and conditions (input power cycling, load switching, temperature, etc.) varies from vendor to vendor. However, the less stringent the conditions, the less likely it is that potential problems will be caught by the vendor.

Burnup

Measure of thermal energy released by nuclear fuel relative to its mass, typically Gigawatt days per tonne (GWd/tU).

Bus

An electrical conductor that serves as a common connection for two or more electrical circuits.

Busbar

The point at which power is available for transmission. A conductor, or group of conductors, that serve as a common connection for two or more circuits, generally in the form of insulated cable, rigid rectangular or round bars or stranded overhead cables held under tension. The equivalent, in electric power terms, of the gas plant tailgate. A heavy, rigid conductor used for high voltage feeders.

Busbar Cost

The cost of producing one kWh of electricity delivered to, but not through, the transmission system.

Bus Support Insulators

These are porcelain or fiberglass insulators that serve to isolate the bus bar switches and other support structures and to prevent leakage current from flowing through the structure. These insulators are similar in function of other insulators used in substations and transmission poles and towers.

Bushing

An insulating structure, including a through conductor or providing a passageway for such a conductor, with provision for mounting on a barrier, conducting or otherwise, for the purposes of insulating the conductor from the barrier and conducting current from one side of the barrier to the other.

Butane ($C4H10$)
A hydrocarbon substance consisting of molecules composed of four atoms of carbon and ten atoms of hydrogen, used primarily for blending in high-octane gasoline, for residential and commercial heating and in manufacture of chemicals and synthetic rubber.

Butylene ($C4H8$)
A hydrocarbon substance consisting of molecules composed of four atoms of carbon and eight atoms of hydrogen, used primarily for blending in high-octane gasoline, for residential and commercial heating and in manufacture of chemicals and synthetic rubber.

Buyout
A swap is closed and settled at current price.

Buy/Sell
An arrangement whereby a party sells gas at the wellhead to a party with priority space in the pipeline queue, and then repurchases the gas downstream, paying transmission costs and any prearranged differentials.

Buy Through
An agreement between utility and customer to import power when the customer's service would otherwise be interrupted.

Bypass
The action of a retail customer to obtain power or natural gas directly from a wholesale supplier or transporter, thus eliminating any utility charges applicable to distribution. This term is also sometimes applied when an end-user closes down operations, installs alternate fuel capability or moves its operations to the service area of another natural gas supplier, thereby curtailing its purchases from its traditional supplier.

Bypass diode
A diode connected across one or more solar cells in a photovoltaic module such that the diode will conduct if the cell(s) become reverse biased. [UL 1703] Alternatively, diode connected anti-parallel across a part of the solar cells of a Photovoltaic module. It protects these solar cells from thermal destruction in case of total or partial shading of individual solar cells while other cells are exposed to full light.

C

Cable
A conductor with insulation, or a stranded conductor with or without

insulation and other coverings (single-conductor cable), or a combination of conductors insulated from one another (multiple-conductor cable).

Cable Assembly
A cable with plugs or connectors on each end.

Cable sheath
A conductive protective covering applied to cables. Note: A cable sheath may consist of multiple layers of which one or more is conductive.

Cadmium (Cd)
A chemical element, atomic number 48, used in making certain types of solar cells and batteries.

Cadmium telluride (CdTe)
A polycrystalline thin-film photovoltaic material

Cage
The component of an electric motor composed of solid bars (of usually copper or aluminum) arranged in a circle and connected to continuous rings at each end. This cage fits inside the stator in an induction motor in channels between laminations, thin flat discs of steel in a ring configuration.

Capability
The maximum load that a generating unit, power plant, or other electrical apparatus can carry under specified conditions for a given period of time, without exceeding its approved limits of temperature and stress.

Capability Margin
The difference between net electrical system capability and system maximum load requirements (peak load); the margin of capability available to provide for scheduled maintenance, emergency outages, system operating requirements and unforeseen loads.

Capacitance
That property of a system of conductors and dielectrics that permits the storage of electricity when potential difference exists between the conductors. Its value is expressed as the ratio of quantity of electricity to a potential difference. A capacitance value is always positive.

Capacitor
A transmission element designed to inject reactive power into the transmission network. Also utilized to increase voltages, reduce loadings,

and increase available kW output from generators. Capacitor ratings are typically given in Megavars. Two plates or conductors separated by an insulator. Applying a voltage across the plates causes current to flow and stores a charge. Capacitors resist changes in voltage.

Capacitor Bank

An array of capacitors connected into a circuit. Capacitors are used to control voltages supplied to the customer by eliminating the voltage drop in the system caused by inductive reactive loads.

Capacity

The number of amperes of electric current a wire will carry without becoming unduly heated; the capacity of a machine, apparatus or device, is the maximum of which it is capable under existing service conditions; the load for which a transformer, transmission circuit, apparatus, station or system is rated; for a generator, turbine, the URGE rating. Ampere-hours that can be discharged from a battery. The load for which a generator, turbine, power plant, transmission circuit, or power system can supply under specified conditions for a given time interval without exceeding approved limits of temperature and stress, a) With respect to pipelines, the maximum volume of liquid or gas that can be transported.through a pipeline; (b) with respect to electricity generation, the maximum load that a generatingunit or station can carry under specific conditions for a given period of time; (c) with respect to storage, the total storage space or volume of a warehouse or storage container or tank farm.

Capacity (Condensing Unit)

The refrigerating effect in Btu/h produced by the difference in total enthalpy between a refrigerant liquid leaving the unit and the total enthalpy of the refrigerant vapor entering it. Generally measured in tons or Btu/h.

Capacity (Effective, of a motor)

The maximum load that a motor is capable of supplying.

Capacity (Heating, of a material)

The amount of heat energy needed to raise the temperature of a given mass of a substance by one degree Celsius. The heat required to raise the temperature of 1 kg of water by 1 degree Celsius is 4186 Joules.

Capacity Factor

A measure of the degree to which the capacity of a generating unit is being used during a specified period of time. Expressed as a ratio of the electric energy produced during the specified period to the electric energy the unit could have produced if it operated at full capacity during the entire period. The ratio of the average load on (or power output of) a generating unit or system to the capacity rating of the unit or system over a specified period of time.

Capacity Peaking

The capacity of facilities or equipment normally used to supply incremental gas or electricity under extreme demand conditions. Peaking capacity is generally available for a limited number of hours per day at a maximum rate.

Cap Rock

The solid, dense layer forming the barrier above a gas or oil deposit. Shale is one example.

Carbon Zinc Ceil Battery

A cell produces electric energy by the galvanic oxidation of carbon; commonly used in household
appliances.

Cascade Failure

A failure mode wherein the failure of one component of a complex system causes other components of that system to fail; for example, in a system of standby emergency diesel generators that must be synchronized in AC parallel to operate, a failure mode on one generator could cause all of the other generators in parallel to fail.

Cascading

An uncontrolled successive loss of system elements triggered by an incident at any locale which typically results in widespread service interruptions and cannot be restrained from spreading ("cascading") beyond an area predetermined by appropriate studies

Cathodic protection

A method of preventing oxidation (rusting) of exposed metal structures, such as bridges and pipelines, by imposing between the structure and the ground a small electrical voltage that opposes the flow of electrons and that is greater than the voltage present during oxidation.

Cavitation

Air bubbles in a closed water system. Greatly reduces efficiency in a hydro turbine generator system, and can damage water pumps and pipes in a home water supply system.

cf/s

A unit of measurement for water flow. Flow equals the volume of water (cubic feet) passing through an area in a given time period (per second). 1 cf/s = 7.48 gallons per second.

Cell
The basic unit of a photovoltaic system.

Cell barrier
A very thin region of static electric charge along the interface of the positive and negative layers in a photovoltaic cell. The barrier inhibits the movement of electrons from one layer to the other, so that higher-energy electrons from one side diffuse preferentially through it in one direction, creating a current and thus a voltage across the cell. Also called depletion zone, cell junction, or space charge.

Cell junction
The area of immediate contact between two layers (positive and negative) of a photovoltaic cell. The junction lies at the center of the cell barrier or depletion zone.

Central power
The generation of electricity in large power plants with distribution through a network of transmission lines (grid) for sale to a number of users. Opposite of distributed power.

Central Power Plant
Large facility that generates power for distribution to multiple customers. A large power plant that generates power for distribution to multiple customers.

Central Receiver Solar Power Plants
Also known as "power towers," these use fields of two-axis tracking mirrors known as heliostats. Each heliostat is individually positioned by a computer control system to reflect the sun's rays to a tower-mounted thermal receiver. The effect of many heliostats reflecting to a common point creates the combined energy of thousands of suns, which produces high-temperature thermal energy. In the receiver, molten nitrate salts absorb the heat energy. The hot salt is then used to boil water to steam, which is sent to a conventional steam turbine-generator to produce electricity.

Centrifugal Pump (rotating pump)
A water pump using a rotating element or screw to move water. The faster the rotation, the greater the flow.

Ceramic Cores
One of the common materials used for inductor cores. Its main purpose

is to provide a form for the coil. In some designs it also provides the structure to hold the terminals in place. Ceramic has a very low thermal coefficient of expansion, which allows for relatively high inductance stability over the operating temperature ranges. Ceramic has no magnetic properties. Thus, there is no increase in permeability due to the core material. Ceramic core inductors are often referred to as Oair coreO inductors. Ceramic core inductors are most often used in high frequency applications where low inductance values, very low core losses, and high Q values are required.

Chain reaction
A reaction that stimulates its own repetition, in particular where the neutrons originating from nuclear fission cause an ongoing series of fission reactions.

Charge carrier
A free and mobile conduction electron or hole in a semiconductor.

Charge Controller
A component of a photovoltaic system that controls the flow of current to and from the battery subsystem to protect batteries from overcharge, overdischarge, or other control functions. The charge controller may also monitor system operational status. Charge controllers are typically used in off-grid photovoltaic power systems. The primary function of a charge controller (or regulator) is to maintain the battery at the highest possible State Of Charge (SOC) and provide the user with the required quantity of electricity, while protecting the battery from deep discharge (by the loads) or extended overcharge (by the PV array). Most charge controllers operate via voltage regulation set points. However, as voltage is not representative of the true SOC, new algorithms are being developed to evaluate the state of the battery, based on Ah or combined VAh monitoring. Additional features such as battery temperature or wire compensation, meters and alarms can enhance the ability of the charge controller to meet the load demand and extend battery lifetime. Other functions such as MPPT, d.c./d.c. conversion, anti-theft protection, load management, prepayment and data logging can also now be built into the charge controller.

Charge Regulator
A device that controls the changing rate and/or state of charge for batteries. Wired between a photovoltaic array and a battery bank, its main job is to prevent the battery from being overcharged from the PV array, while monitoring the array and/or battery voltage.

Charger
An AC-to-DC converter which powers a UPS inverter and maintains the battery reservoir charge.

Chemical vapor deposition (CVD)
A method of depositing thin semiconductor films. With this method, a substrate is exposed to one or more vaporized compounds, one or more of which contain desirable constituents. A chemical reaction is initiated, at or near the substrate surface, to produce the desired material that will condense on the substrate.

Chlorofluorocarbon
A family of chemicals composed primarily of carbon, hydrogen, chlorine, and fluorine whose principal applications are that of refrigerants and industrial cleansers and whose principal drawback is the tendency to destroy the Earth's protective ozone layer.

Choke
An inductor which is intended to filter, or OchokeO, out unwanted signals.

Circuit
A conducting path through which an electric current is intended to flow. The complete path electricity takes. A conductor/system of conductors through which electric current flows. A device, or system of devices, that allows electrical current to flow through it and allows voltage to occur across positive and negative terminals.

Circuit Breaker
A device which shuts off electricity, or breaks its path, if there is a problem. A device for interrupting a circuit between separable contacts under normal or fault conditions. A device used to interrupt or break an electrical circuit when an overload condition exists; usually installed in the positive circuit; used to protect electrical equipment.

Circuit Lag
As time increases from zero at the terminals of an inductor, the voltage comes to a particular value on the sine function curve ahead of the current. The voltage reaches its negative peak exactly 90 degrees before the current reaches its negative peak thus the current lags behind by 90 degrees.

Circuit Switchers
Circuit switchers a a set of switches for redirecting current in a substation. Circuit switchers provide equipment protection for transformers, lines, cables, and capacitor banks. They also are used to energize and deenergize capacitor banks and other circuits.

CISPR
The International Special Committee on Radio Interference.

Cladding

The metal tubes containing oxide fuel pellets in a reactor core.

Clamp-On CT

A current transformer which clamps around a current-carrying conductor so the conductor does not have to be opened for insertion of the transformer primary. Particularly suited for monitoring where current must be sensed at many points for relatively short periods.

Classes of Electric Service

Residential - A customer, sales, and revenue classification covering electric energy supplied for residential (household) purposes. The classification of an individual customer's account where the use is both residential and commercial is based on principal use.

Other Public Authorities - A customer, sales, and revenue classification covering electric energy supplied to municipalities or divisions or agencies of federal or state governments (as ultimate customers) under special contracts or agreements or service classifications applicable only to public authorities, except such items included in the classifications Public Street and Highway Lighting, Sales to Railroads and Railways, and Sales for Resale. Excludes Department of Energy sales which are classified as Industrial.

Clearance (between objects)

The clear distance between two objects measured surface to surface.

Clearance (for work)

Authorization to perform specified work or permission to enter a restricted area.

Cleavage of lateral epitaxial films for transfer (CLEFT)

A process for making inexpensive GaAs photovoltaic cells in which a thin film of GaAs is grown atop a thick, single-crystal GaAs (or other suitable material) substrate and then is cleaved from the substrate and incorporated into a cell, allowing the substrate to be reused to grow more thin-film GaAs.

Close Coupled

An energy system in which the fuel production equipment is in close proximity, or connected to, the fuel using equipment.

Closed Cycle

A system in which a working fluid is used over and over without introduction of new fluid, as in a hydronic heating system or mechanical refrigeration system.

Closed-Loop Geothermal Heat Pump Systems
Closed-loop (also known as "indirect") systems circulate a solution of water and antifreeze through a series of sealed loops of piping. Once the heat has been transferred into or out of the solution, the solution is recirculated. The loops can be installed in the ground horizontally or vertically, or they can be placed in a body of water, such as a pond.

Closed Entry Contact
A female contact designed to prevent the entry of a pin or probing device having a cross-sectional dimension (diameter) greater than the mating pin.

Coal
A solid, combustible, organic hydrocarbon formed by the decomposition of vegetable material without free access to air. A black, solid fossil fuel found in the Earth. Coal is often burned to make electricity. A black or brownish solid combustible substance formed by the partial decomposition of vegetable matter without free access of air and under the influence of moisture and often intense pressure and temperature. The rank of coal (anthracite, bituminous, subbituminous, and lignite) is determined by its heating value.
Anthracite - Hard and jet black with a high luster, it is the highest rank of coal.
Bituminous - The most common coal - soft, dense, black with well-defined bands of bright and dull material. Bituminous is ranked between anthracite and subbituminous.
Lignite - A brownish-black coal of the lowest rank, it is mined in North Dakota, Montana and Texas.
Subbituminous - A dull black coal ranking between lignite and bituminous.

Coal Gasification
The process of making a gaseous fuel from coal.

Coal Seam
A bed of coal usually thick enough to be mined with profit.

Coaxial Cable
A high-band width cable consisting of two concentric cylindrical conductors with a common axis that is used for high-speed data communication and video signals.

Cogeneration
The production of heat and electrical energy from the same fuel source. (Combined Heat and Power) is the sequential use of a primary energy source to produce two useful forms of energy... heat and power. The

simultaneous production of both useable heat or steam and electricity from a common fuel source. The process in which fuel is used to produce heat for a boiler-steam turbine or gas for a turbine. The turbine drives a generator that produces electricity, with the excess heat used for process steam. The use of a single prime fuel source to generate both electrical and thermal energy to optimize fuel efficiency. The dominant demand for energy is usually thermal with excess electrical energy, if any, transmitted into the local power supply companies' lines. Energy system that consumes a fuel, usually natural gas, to produce electricity and thermal energy in the form of steam or hot air. Cogeneration systems use heat energy that otherwise would be wasted.

Cogenerator
A generation facility that produces electricity and another form of useful thermal energy (such as heat or steam), for industrial, commercial, heating, or cooling purposes.

Combined collector
A photovoltaic device or module that provides useful heat energy in addition to electricity.

Combined-cycle system
Energy system that takes the heat produced by the generation of electricity in a high-temperature gas-fired combustion turbine or other prime mover to create steam that generates additional electricity in a steam turbine.

Combined Cycle Unit
An electric generating unit that consists of one or more combustion turbines and one or more boilers with a portion of the required energy input to the boiler(s) provided by the exhaust gas of the combustion turbine(s).

Combined Cycle
An electric generating technology in which electricity is produced from otherwise lost waste heat exiting from one more gas (combustion) turbines. The exiting heat is routed to a conventional boiler or to a heat recovery steam generator for utilization by a steam turbine in the production of electricity. This process increases the efficiency of the electric generating unit.

Combined-Cycle Power Plant
A power plant that uses two different thermal cycles for producing electricity. The first cycle burns a fuel inside a gas turbine, and the gas turbine drives an electric generator. The hot air coming out of the gas turbine is used to turn water into steam, and the steam turns a second electric generator. Combined cycle power plants are the most efficient

technology currently available for turning a fuel into electricity. They can use a wide variety of liquid and gaseous fuels, but almost all of the combined cycle power plants in the United States burn natural gas.

Combined-Cycle Gas TurbinePlant

Power plant which combines gas and steam turbines in the same operation. The gas turbine produces mechanical power to drive the generator and heat in the form of hot exhaust gases which are fed to a boiler, where steam is raised to drive a conventional steam turbine also connected to the generator.

Combined Heat & Power

Simultaneous generation of useable heat and electrical power in a single process. A generating facility that produces electricity and another form of useful thermal energy (such as heat or steam) used for industrial, commercial, heating or cooling purposes. Power station technology which generates heat and power from a single operation.

Combustion

A complex series of chemical reactions in which substances combine with oxygen and release heat energy,

Combustion Turbine

A fuel-fired turbine engine used to drive an electric generator. Combustion turbines, because of their generally rapid firing time, are used to meet short-term peak demands placed on power distribution systems. An electric generating unit in which the prime mover is a gas turbine engine.

Combustion Turbine Power Plant

A combustion turbine burns a fuel to produce a large volume of hot air, which then goes through a series of precision fan blades, which convert the energy of the hot air into rotation of a shaft. The shaft, in turn, is connected to an electric generator. The technology is closely related to the jet engines used on airplanes. Combustion turbine power plants can be built at a lower cost than other large power plants, but they are relatively inefficient in converting fuel into electricity.

Common Mode (CM)

The term refers to electrical interference which is measurable as a ground referenced signal. In true common mode, a signal is common to both the current carrying conductors.

Common Mode Noise

An undesirable voltage which appears between the power conductors and ground.

Compound
A substance containing more than one element.

Concentrating (Solar) Collector
A solar collector that uses reflective surfaces to concentrate sunlight onto a small area, where it is absorbed and converted to heat or, in the case of solar photovoltaic (PV) devices, into electricity. Concentrators can increase the power flux of sunlight hundreds of times. The principal types of concentrating collectors include: compound parabolic, parabolic trough, fixed reflector moving receiver, fixed receiver moving reflector, Fresnel lense, and central receiver. A PV concentrating module uses optical elements (Fresnel lense) to increase the amount of sunlight incident onto a PV cell. Concentrating PV modules/arrays must track the sun and use only the direct sunlight because the diffuse portion cannot be focused onto the PV cells. Concentrating collectors for home or small business solar water heating applications are usually parabolic troughs that concentrate the sun's energy on an absorber tube (called a receiver), which contains a heat-transfer fluid.

Condenser
The device in an air conditioner or heat pump in which the refrigerant condenses from a gas to a liquid when it is depressurized or cooled.

Condenser Coil
The device in an air conditioner or heat pump through which the refrigerant is circulated and releases heat to the surroundings when a fan blows outside air over the coils. This will return the hot vapor that entered the coil into a hot liquid upon exiting the coil.

Condensing Furnace
A type of heating appliance that extracts so much of the available heat content from a combusted fuel that the moisture in the combustion gases condenses before it leaves the furnace. Also this furnace circulates a liquid to cool the furnace's heat exchanger. The heated liquid may either circulate through a liquid-to-air heat exchanger to warm room air, or it may circulate through a coil inside a separate indirect-fired water heater.

Condensing Unit
The component of a central air conditioner that is designed to remove heat absorbed by the refrigerant and transfer it outside the conditioned space.

Conductor
A material capable of carrying an electrical current. A substance or body, usually in the form of a wire, cable or busbar that allows a current of electricity to pass continuously along it. The material through which

electricity is transmitted, such as an electrical wire, or transmission or distribution line.

Conduction

The transfer of heat through a material by the transfer of kinetic energy from particle to particle; the flow of heat between two materials of different temperatures that are in direct physical contact.

Conduction Band

An energy band in a semiconductor in which electrons can move freely in a solid, producing a net transport of charge.

Conductivity (Thermal)

This is a positive constant, k, that is a property of a substance and is used in the calculation of heat transfer rates for materials. It is the amount of heat that flows through a specified area and thickness of a material over a specified period of time when there is a temperature difference of one degree between the surfaces of the material.

Conduit

A tubular material used to encase and protect one or more electrical conductors. A tubular raceway for data or power cables. Metallic conduit is common, although non-metallic forms may also be used. A conduit may also be a path or duct and need to be tubular.

Congestion .

Condition where the transmission system has more scheduled load or supply than it is capable of carrying at a given point in time, resulting in application of administrative procedures to allocate available capacity. Congestion solutions or responses may include curtailment of transmission service, redispatch of generation resources, reconfiguration of the transmission grid, and/or shedding load. See Curtailment, FTRs, LMP.

Connected Load

The sum of the ratings of the electricity consuming apparatus connected to a generating system.

Connection

The physical junction (e.g., transmission lines, transformers, switch gear, etc.) between two electric systems permitting the transfer of electric energy.

Connection Charge

Fee paid by a customer for a connection to an electricity utility's distribution system. An amount paid by a customer for being connected to an electricity supplier's transmission and distribution system.

Connection Conditions
Portion of the Grid Code identified as the Connection Conditions.

Conserve
To manage or use wisely.

Control Area
A control area is an electrical system bound by interconnect (tie- line) metering and telemetry and regulating its generation in order to maintain its interchange schedule with other systems, contributes to frequency regulation of the Interconnection and fulfills its obligations and responsibilities in accordance with NERC and reliability region (such as MAPP) requirements. An electric system or systems bounded by interconnection metering and telemetry that controls generation to maintain its interchange schedule with other areas and the frequency regulation of its interconnection .An electric power system or combination of electric power systems to which a common automatic control scheme is applied in order to: (1) match, at all times, the power output of the generators within the electric power system(s) and capacity and energy purchased from entities outside the electric power system(s), with the load in the electric power system(s); (2) maintain, within the limits of Good Utility Practice, scheduled interchange with other Control Areas; (3) maintain the frequency of the electric power system(s) within reasonable limits in accordance with Good Utility Practice; and (4) provide sufficient generating capacity to maintain operating reserves in accordance with Good Utility Practice.

Control Area Load
Control area load is the entire demand for energy within a specified control area.

Control Center
A location used for the purpose and operation of the transmission system or a user system other than a generator's system or an external system.

Conventional Generation
Electricity that is produced at a generating station where the prime movers are driven by gases or steam produced by burning fossil fuels. Power generation from sources such as petroleum, natural gas, or coal. In some cases, large-scale hydropower and nuclear power generation are considered conventional sources.

Conventional Thermal Power Station
Power station generating electricity by burning fossil fuel to produce heat to convert water into steam, which then powers steam turbines.

Converter
A device which changes alternating current to direct current.

Cooling Pond
A body of water used to cool the water that is circulated in an electric power plant.

Cooling Tower
A structure used to cool power plant water; water is pumped to the top of the tubular tower and sprayed out into the center, and is cooled by evaporation as it falls, and then is either recycled within the plant or is discharged.

Copper Loss(CoEv)
The power lost by current flowing through the winding. The power loss is equal to the square of the current (I) multiplied by the resistance (R) of the wire (I2R). This power loss is realized in the form of heat.

Copper Loss(Raychem)
The power lost by current flowing through the winding. The power loss is equal to the square of the current multiplied by the resistance of the wire (1^2*R). This power loss is transferred into heat.

Core
The ferrous center part of a transformer or inductor used to increase the strength of the magnetic field.

Core Losses
Core losses are caused by an altering magnetic field in the core material: The losses aer a function of the operating frequency and the total magnetic flux swing. The total core losses are made up of three main components: Hysteresis, eddy current and residual losses. These losses vary considerably from one magnetic material to another. Applications such as higher power and higher frequency switching regulators require careful core selection to yield the highest inductor performance by keeping the core losses to a minimum.

Core Saturation
Condition when an inductor or transformer core has reached maximum magnetic strength.

Cogeneration
The concurrent production of electricity and heat, steam or useful work from the same fuel source.

Cost of Service

The total amount of money - including return on invested capital, operation and maintenance costs, administrative costs, taxes, and depreciation expense - to produce a utility service. The total amount of money - including return on invested capital, operation and maintenance costs, administrative costs, taxes, and depreciation expense - to produce a utility service.

Closed Transition Transfer

In this scheme, a customer's source of power is transferred from Xcel Energy to its own generation and vice-versa while momentarily connecting the two systems together. Here, the Customer's load is not interrupted at all during the transfer process. The time duration of the momentary parallel (connection) of the two systems together is only long enough to safely start and bring the Customer's generation into synchronization or to safely shut down the generation. The parallel is typically completed within 30 seconds.

Compact fluorescent lights

Lights that use a lot less energy than regular light bulbs. We can use compact fluorescent lights for reading lights and ceiling lights.

Component Lead

The solid or stranded wire or formed conductor that extends from a component and serves as a readily formable mechanical or electrical connection or both.

Compressed-air energy storage (CAES)

CAES plants use off-peak electrical energy to compress air into underground storage reservoirs for storage until times of peak or intermediate electricity demand. Wind power offers a good opportunity for charging CAES storage. The storage is typically underground in natural aquifers, depleted oil or gas fields, mined salt caverns, or excavated or natural rock caverns. To generate power, the compressed air is first heated by gas burners, then passed through a turbine.

Concentrator

A Photovoltaic module that uses optical elements to increase the amount of sunlight incident on a Photovoltaic cell.

Concentrating

arrays must track the sun and use only the direct sunlight because the diffuse portion cannot be focused onto the Photovoltaic cells.

Concentrate

See Uranium oxide concentrate (U_3Og).

Concentrator (module, array, or collector)
An arrangement of photovoltaic cells that includes a lens to concentrate sunlight onto small-area cells. Concentrators can increase the power flux of sunlight hundreds of times.

Concentricity
In a wire or cable, the measurement of the location of the center of the conductor with respect to the geometric center of the surrounding insulation.

Control Area
An electric power system (or combination of electric powersystems) to which a common AGC scheme is applied in order to: i) match, at all times, the power output of the Generating
Units within the electric power system(s), plus the Energy purchased from entities outside the electric
power system(s), minus Energy sold to entities outside the electric power system, with the Demand within the electric power system(s); ii) maintain scheduled interchange with other Control Areas, within the limits of Good Utility Practice; iii) maintain the frequency of the electric power system(s) within reasonable limits in accordance with Good Utility Practice; and iv) provide
sufficient generating capacity to maintain operating reserves in accordance with Good Utility Practice.

Concrete Foundations
A platform made of concrete that provides a solid stable support for large equipment. Concrete foundations or pads are laid for all large equipment, support structures, and control buildings in a substation.

Conductance
The reciprocal of resistance. It is the ratio of current passing through a material to the potential difference at its ends.

Conduction band; Conduction level
Energy level sit which electrons are not bound to (orbiting) a specific atomic nucleus but are free to wander among the atoms. An energy band in which electrons can move freely in a solid, producing a net transport of charge.

Conductivity
The ability of a material to conduct electric current. It is expressed in terms of the current per unit of applied voltage. It is the reciprocal of resistivity.

Conductor
A wire or combination of wires not insulated from one another, suitable

for carrying electric current.

Conduits

Conduits are hollow tubes running from manhole to manhole in an underground transmission or distribution system.

Connection

That part of a circuit that has negligible impedance and that joins components, devices, etc., together.

Connector

A device providing electrical connection/disconnections. It consists of a mating plug and receptacle. Various types of connectors include DIP, card edge, two-piece, hermaphroditic and wire-wrapping configurations. Multiple contact connectors join two or more conductors with others in one mechanical assembly.

Connector Discontinuity

An ohmic change in contact resistance.

Connector Insert

For connectors with metal shells, the insert holds contacts in proper arrangement while electrically insulating them from each other and from the shell.

Connector Shell

The case that encloses the connector insert and contact assembly. Shells of mating connectors can protect projecting contacts and provide proper alignment.

Constant-speed wind turbines

Turbines that operate at a constant rotor revolutions per minute (RPM) and are optimized for energy capture at a given rotor diameter at a particular speed in the wind power curve.

Contact, Female: A contact located in an insert or body in such a manner that the mating contact is inserted into the unit. It is similar in function to a socket contact.

Contact, Male

A contact located in an insert or body in such a manner that the mating portion extends into the female contact. It is similar in function to a pin contact.

Contact Plating

Plated-on metal applied to the base contact metal to provide the required contact resistance and/or wear resistance.

Contact Resistance
Maximum permitted electrical resistance of pin and socket contacts when assembled in a connector under typical service use.

Contact Retainer
A device either on the contact or in the insert to retain the contact.

Contact Size
Defines the largest size wire that can be used with the specific contact. By specification dimensioning, it also defines the diameter of the engagement end of the pin.

Contact resistance
The resistance between metallic contacts and the semiconductor.

Continuity
The state of being whole, unbroken.

Continuous Load
A load where the maximum current is expected to continue for three hours or more. Rating of the branch circuit protection device shall not be less tan 125% of the continuous load.

Control House
The substation control house contains switchboard panels, batteries, battery chargers, supervisory control, power-line carrier, meters, and relays. The control house provides all weather protection and security for the control equipment. It is also called a doghouse.

Control Panels
Control panels contain meters, control switches and recorders located in the control building, also called a doghouse. These are used to control the substation equipment, to send power from one circuit to another or to open or shut down circuits when needed.

Control rods
Devices to absorb neutrons so that the chain reaction in a reactor core may be slowed or stopped by inserting them further, or accelerated by withdrawing them.

Control Room
The area(s) from where power generation and supporting systems are controlled.

Cross-Connect
A wire-termination field that enables administration of telephony, alarm,

or other circuits with jumper wires. *DSX* and *FDI* are examples of cross-connects.

Cross Regulation
For a multiple output converter, the change in voltage on one output (expressed as a percent) caused by a load change on another output.

Control Wires
Control wires are installed connecting the control house control panels to all the equipment in the substation. A typical substation control house contains several thousand feet of conduit and miles of control wire.

Conversion
Chemical process turning U_3O_8 into UF_6 preparatory to enrichment.

Conversion efficiency (cell or module)
The ratio of the electric energy produced by a photovoltaic device (under one-sun conditions) to the energy from sunlight incident upon the cell.

Converter Stations
Converter stations are located at the terminals of a DC transmission line. Converter stations change alternating current into direct current and invert direct current to alternating current.

Coolant
The liquid or gas used to transfer heat from the reactor core to the steam generators or directly to the turbines.

Copper indium diselenide ($CuInSe_2$, or CIS)
A polycrystalline thin-film photovoltaic material (sometimes incorporating gallium (CIGS) and/or sulfur).

Core
The central part of a nuclear reactor containing the fuel elements and control devices.

Cost Shifting
A transfer of costs from one group of customers to another or from one utility to another.

Coulumb
The combined negative electrical charge of 6.24 X 1018 electrons.

Counterflow Heat Exchanger
A heat exchanger in which two fluids flow in opposite directions for transfer heat energy from one to the other.

Coupling Capacitors
Coupling capacitors are used to transmit communication signals to transmission lines. Some are used to measure the voltage in transmission lines.

Cradle
The metal frame that surrounds and protects the generator/engine.

Crest Factor
(Usually refers to current) - the mathematical relationship between RMS current and peak current. A normal resistive load will have a crest factor of 1.4142 which is the normal relationship between peak and RMS current. A typical PC will have a crest factor of 3.

Critical Bus
A critical bus supplies the critical equipment/systems directly through feeders or branch circuits which originate at the bus and terminate at the input terminals of the equipment or control devices such as reduced-voltage motor starters. This definition excludes the use of frequency converters/inverters and transformers that alter the voltage between the bus and the equipment.

Critical Equipment/Systems
Critical equipment/systems include those items of equipment or systems that directly supply power to equipment and systems used to perform the primary mission(s) of the C4ISR site.

Critical Load
That portion of the technical load used to successfully accomplish the site missions and having a requirement for 100 percent continuity in power service, such as from the Uninterruptible Power Supply(UPS) system. These loads also include any equipment which, upon loss of power, will create an unacceptable impact on the mission or mission equipment.Equipment that requires an uninterrupted power input to prevent damage or injury to personnel, facilities, or itself.

Critical mass
The smallest mass of fissile material that will support a self-sustaining chain reaction under specified conditions.

Criticality
Condition of being able to sustain a nuclear chain reaction.

Crude.Oil
Petroleum liquids as they come from the ground, formed from animal and plant material which collected at the bottom of ancient seas.

Crystalline Silicon Photovoltaic Cell

A type of photovoltaic cell made from a single crystal or a polycrystalline slice of silicon. Crystalline silicon cells can be joined together to form a module (or panel).

Cube Law

In reference to wind energy, for any given instant, the power available in the wind is proportional to the cube of the wind velocity; when wind speed doubles, the power availability' increases eight times.

Cubic Feet per Second (CFS)

A measurement of water flow representing one cubic foot of water moving past a given point in one
second.

Current

A flow of electric charge measured in amperes. A flow of electrons in an electrical conductor. The rate of movement of the electricity, measured in amperes. The flow of electricity in a conductor. Current is measured in amperes.Deregulation is the process by which governments removes selected regulations on business in order to (in theory) encourage the efficient operation of markets. The theory is that less regulation will lead to a raised level of competitiveness, therefore higher productivity, more efficiency and lower prices overall. The movement of electrons through a conductor. Measured in amperes and its symbol is "I".

Current,Hold

The largest steady state current that, under specified ambient conditions, can be passed through a PolySwitch device without causing the device to trip. For SiBar devices, the current at which the device resets to a high-impedance state once the surge current dissipates. See also Hold Current.

Current Limiting

Feature that protects the converter (or load) from damage under overload conditions. The maximum converter output current is automatically limited to a predetermined safe value. If the converter is specified for auto restart, normal operatoin is automatically restored when overload condition is removed.

Current at maximum power (Imp)

The current at which maximum power is available from a module. [UL 1703]

Current,Operating Range

The range of normal operating currents in a circuit containing a

PolySwitch device. Typically the hold current of the PolySwitch device should be greater than the top of the operating current range.

Current Rating (Idc)
Is the maximum recommended DC current for the inductor. Expressed in milliamps (mA) or amps (A) maximum. This is limited by the allowable temperature rise.

Current Transformer (CT)
A transformer intended for metering, protective or control purposes, which is designed to have its primary winding connected in series with a circuit carrying the current to be measured or controlled. A current transformer normally steps down current values to safer levels. A CT secondary circuit must never be open circuited while energized. A transformer used in instrumentation to assist in measuring current. It utilizes the strength of the magnetic field around the conductor to form an induced current that can then be applied across a resistance to form a proportional voltage. Usually used in a sensing device, current transformers customarily have a one turn primary. The number of secondary turns is determined by the sensitivity required and is terminated with a resistor. Toroidal in shape, cores of silicon steel, nickel alloy, or ferrite are used. Choice of core material influences cost and accuracy.

Current,Trip
The smallest steady state current that, if passed through a PolySwitch device, will cause the device to trip, under specified conditions.

Curtailment
A temporary, mandatory power load reduction taken when there is a risk that the utility cannot meet its power requirements and retain a prudent reserve margin. A reduction in firm or non-firm transmission service in response to a transmission capacity shortage as a result of system reliability conditions. A reduction in scheduled capacity or energy delivery

Cycle
In one cycle of alternating electric current, the current goes from zero potential or voltage to a maximum in one direction, back to zero, then to a maximum in the other direction and then back again to zero. The number of such complete cycles made each second determines the frequency of the current. (Direct current does not fluctuate from positive to negative and hence cycles or frequency can apply only to alternating current).

Cycle life
Number of discharge-charge cycles that a battery can tolerate under specified conditions before it fails to meet specified criteria as to performance (e.g., capacity decreases to 80-percent of the nominal capacity).

Cyclic Service
The use of a battery with alternate repetition of charging and discharging.

Cycling Losses
The loss of heat as the water circulates through a water heater tank and inlet and outlet pipes.

Cyclone Burner
A furnace/combustion chamber in which finely ground fuel is blown in spirals in the combustion chamber to maximize combustion efficiency.

Czochralski process
A method of growing large size, high quality semiconductor crystal by slowly lifting a seed crystal from a molten bath of the material under careful cooling conditions.

D

Dam
A structure for impeding and controlling the flow of water in a water course, and which increases the water elevation to create the hydraulic head. The reservoir creates, in effect, stored energy

Declared Net Capacity
The maximum power available from generating station on a continuous capability basis less any power
from the network used to run the station.

Degree-Day
A unit measuring the extent to which the outdoor mean (average of maximum and minimum) daily dry-bulb temperature falls below (in the case of heating) or rises above (in the case of cooling) an assumed base. The base is normally taken as 65 degrees Fahrenheit for heating and for cooling unless otherwise designated. One degree-day is counted for each degree of deficiency below (for heating) or excess over (for cooling) the assumed base, for each calendar day on which such deficiency or excess occurs.

Degree Hour
The product of 1 hour, and usually the number of degrees Fahrenheit the

hourly mean temperature is above a base point (usually 65 degrees Fahrenheit); used in roughly estimating or measuring the cooling load in cases where processes heat, heat from building occupants, and humidity are relatively unimportant compared to the dry-bulb temperature.

Demand

The rate at which electric energy is delivered to or by a system, part of a system, or a piece of equipment. It is expressed in kilowatts, kilovoltamperes or other suitable unit at a given instant or averaged over any designated period of time. The primary source of "Demand" is the power-consuming equipment of the customers. The rate at which electricity is delivered to or by a system, part of a system, or piece of equipment expressed in kilowatts, kilovoltamperes, or other suitable unit, at a given instant or averaged over a specified period of time.

Demand Charge

A charge for the maximum rate at which energy is used during peak hours of a billing period. That part of a power provider service charged for on the basis of the possible demand as distinguished from the energy actually consumed.

Demand Costs

Costs that are related to and vary with power demand (i.e., kW), such as fixed production costs, transmission costs, and a portion of distribution costs.

Dcniand(ed) Factor

The ratio of the maximum demand on an electricity generating and distribution system to the total connected load on the system; usually expressed as a percentage.

Demand-Side Management (DSM)

The planning, implementation, and monitoring of utility activities designed to influence customer use of electricity in ways that will produce desired changes in a utility's load shape (i.e., changes in the time pattern and magnitude of a utility's load). Utility programs falling under the umbrella of DSM include: load management, customer generation, and innovative rates. DSM includes only those activities that involve a deliberate intervention by the utility to alter the load shape. These changes must produce benefits to both the utility and its customers.

Demand (Tankless) Water Heater

A type of water heater that has no storage tank thus eliminating storage tank stand-by losses. Cold water travels through a pipe into the unit, and either a gas burner or an electric element heats the water only when needed.

Design Voltage

The nominal voltage for which a conductor or electrical appliance is designed; the reference voltage for identification and not necessarily the precise voltage at which it operates.

Desuperheater

An energy saving device in a heat pump that, during the cooling cycle, recycles some of the waste heat from the house to heat domestic water.

Dimmer

A light control device that allows light levels to be manually adjusted. A dimmer can save energy by reducing the amount of power delivered to the light while consuming very little themselves.

Direct Access

The ability of an electric power consumer to purchase electricity from a supplier of their choice without being physically inhibited by the owner of the electric distribution and transmission system to which the consumer is connected to. (See also Open Access.)

Direct Current (DC)

An electric current that flows in only one direction in a circuit, as from a battery. A type of electricity transmission and distribution by which electricity flows in one direction through the conductor; usually relatively low voltage and high current; typically abbreviated as dc.

Direct-Gain

The process by which sunlight directly enters a building through the windows and is absorbed and stored in massive floors or walls.

Direct Solar Water Heater

These systems use water as the fluid that is circulated through the collector to the storage tank. Also known as "open-loop" systems.

Direct Vent Heater

A type of combustion heating system in which combustion air is drawn directly from outside and the products of combustion are vented directly outside. These features are beneficial in tight, energy-efficient homes because they will not depressurize a home and cause air infiltration, and backdrafting of other combustion appliances.

Direct Water Heater

A type of water heater in which heated water is stored within the tank. Hot water is released from the top of the tank when a hot water faucet is turned. This water is replaced with cold water that flows into the tank and down to just above the bottom plate under which are the burners.

Disordered

Minimizing and lifting of lattice constraints, which provides new degrees of freedom, pennitting the placement of elements in multi-dimensional spaces where they interact in ways not previously available. This allows the use of multi-elements and complex materials where positional, translational, and compositional disorder remove restrictions so new local order environments can be generated controlling the physical, electronic, and chemical properties of the material, thereby permitting the synthesis of new materials with new mechanisms.

Dispatchable Generation

Generation available (contractually or physically) to respond to changes in system demand or to respond to transmission security constraints.

Displaced or Volumetric Pump

A type of water pump that utilizes a piston, cylinder and stop valves to move packets of water.

Displacement Power

A source of power (electricity) that can displace power from another source so that source's power can be transmitted to more distant loads.

Distribution

The act or process of delivering electric energy from convenient points on the transmission or bulk power system to consumers. Also a functional classification relating to that portion of utility plant used for the purpose of delivering electric energy from convenient points on the transmission system to consumers, or to expenses relating to the operation and maintenance of distribution plant.

Distributed Capacitance(CoEv)

In the construction of an inductor, each turn of wire or conductor acts as a capacitor plate. The combined effects of each turn can be presented as a single capacitance known as the distributed capacitance. The capacitance is in parallel with the inductor. This parallel combination will resonate at some frequency, which is called the self-resonant freauencv (SRF). Lower distributed capacitance for a given inductance will result in a higher SRF and vise versa.

Distribution Lines

Wires that bring electricity into your neighbourhood. One or more circuits of a distribution system on the same line or poles or supporting structures' usually operating at a lower voltage relative to the transmission line.

Distribution System

That portion of an electricity supply system used to deliver electricity from points on the transmission system to consumers.

Diversity Factor
The ratio of the sum of the noncoincidental maximum demands of two or more loads to their coincidental maximum demands for the same period.

Donor
In a solar photovoltaic device, an n-type dopant, such as phosphorus, that puts an additional electron into an energy level very near the conduction band; this electron is easily exited into the conduction band where it increases the electrical conductivity over than of an undoped semiconductor.

Dopant
A chemical element (impurity) added in small amounts to an otherwise pure semiconductor material to modify the electrical properties of the material. An n-dopant introduces more electrons. A p-dopant creates electron vacancies (holes).

Doping
The addition of dopants to a semiconductor.

Drainback (Solar) Systems
A closed-loop solar heating system in which the heat transfer fluid in the collector loop drains into a tank or reservoir whenever the booster pump stops to protect the collector loop from freezing.

Draindown (Solar) Systems
An open-loop solar heating system in which the heat transfer fluid from the collector loop and the piping drain into a drain whenever freezing conditions occur.

Dry Steam Geothermal Plants
Conventional turbine generators are used with the dry steam resources. The steam is used directly, eliminating the need for boilers and boiler fuel that characterizes other steam-power-generating technologies. This technology is limited because dry-steam hydrothermal resources are extremely rare. The Geysers, in California, is the nation's only dry steam field.

Dual Duct System
An air conditioning system that has two ducts, one is heated and the other is cooled, so that air of the correct temperature is provided by mixing varying amounts of air from each duct.

Double Glazed Window
Two panes of glass, factory-sealed together with a small air space

between them.

Duty Cycle
The duration and periodicity of the operation of a device.

Duty Rating
The amount of time an inverter (power conditioning unit) can produce at full rated power.

Dynamo
A machine for converting mechanical energy into electrical energy by magneto-electric induction; may be used as a motor.

Dynamometer
An apparatus for measuring force or power, especially the power developed by a motor.

E

ECL
Emitter coupled logic. Extremely high-speed electronic circuitry where changes in binary logic are determined by very fast switching between specific voltage levels, rather than by semiconductor saturation and cutoff.

Earth-Coupled Ground Source (Geothermal) Heat Pump
A type of heat pump that uses sealed horizontal or vertical pipes, buried in the ground, as heat exchangers through which a fluid is circulated to transfer heat.

Earth Ground
A low impedance path to earth for the purpose of discharging lightning, static, and radiated energy, and to maintain the main service entrance at earth potential.

Earthing Device
A means of providing a connection between a conductor and earth being a adequate strength and capability.

Earthling Electrode
A ground electrode, water, pipe, or building steel, or some combination of these, used for establishing a building's earth ground.

Economic Dispatch
The process of determining the desired generation level for each of the generating units in a system in order to meet customer demand at the

lowest possible production cost given the operational constraints on the system.

Economic Efficiency

A term that refers to the optimal production and consumption of goods and services. This generally occurs when prices of products and services reflect their marginal costs.

Economies of Scale

Economies of scale exist where the industry exhibits decreasing average long run costs with size.

Economy Energy

Energy sold on a non-firm basis and subject to recall at the discretion of the selling party.

Eddy Current Losses(CoEv)

Core losses associated with the electrical resistivity of the magnetic material and induced voltages within the material. Eddy currents are inversely proportional to material resistivity and proportional to the rate of change of flux density. Eddy current losses are present in both the magnetic core and windings of an inductor. Eddy currents in the winding, or conductor, contribute to two main types of losses: losses due to proximity effects and skin effects. As for the core losses, an electric field around the flax lines in the magnetic field is generated by alternating magnetic flux. This will result in eddy currents if the magnetic core material has electrical conductivity. Losses result from this phenomenon since the eddy currents flow in a plane that is perpendicular to the magnetic flux lines. Eddy current and hysteresis losses are the two major core loss factors. Eddy current loss becomes dominant in powder cores as the frequency increases.

Edge-defined film-fed growth (EFG)

A method for making sheets of polycrystalline silicon in which molten silicon is drawn upward by capillary action through a mold.

Efficiency

The percentage of input power available for used by the load. The mathematical formula is: Efficiency =

Po/ Pi Where "Po" equals power output, "Pi" equals power input, and power is represented by watts. Relating to heat, a percentage indicating the available Btu input that is converted to useful purposes. It is applied, generally, to combustion equipment.

$E = Btu\ output / Btu\ input$

Elasticity of Demand
The degree to which consumer demand for a product responds to changes in price, availability or other factors.

Elastomer
A material that at room temperature stretches under low stress to at least twice its length and snaps back to original length upon release of stress.

Electric and Magnetic Fields
When energy flows through an energized conductor, two types of fields are created - electric and magnetic. The electric field is created by the voltage impressed on the conductors. The magnetic field is created by current in the conductors. Electric and magnetic fields surround the conductors. Electric and magnetic fields are frequently pictured as "lines of force" emanating in the vicinity of the transmission line. Electric fields are measured in units of volts per meter (v/m) or kilovolts per meter (kV/m). Magnetic fields are measured in units called gauss (G) or tesla (T). One gauss in equal to 10,000 tesla. Transmission line electric and magnetic fields are not constant or "static" fields. The fields created by alternating current (AC) voltages cycle above and below zero at the power frequency. North American AC power lines operate at 60 cycles per second (noted as Hertz or Hz). Voltage, current, and electric and magnetic fields each alternate at this frequency. Fields created by the presence or flow of electricity in an electric conductor or electricity consuming appliance or motor.

Electric Current
A flow of electrically charged particles (electrons) along a conductor, such as wire.

Electric Distribution
The delivery of electric energy to customers on the distribution system. Electric energy is carried at high voltages along transmission lines. For consumers needing lower voltages, it is reduced in voltage at a substation and delivered over primary distribution lines extending throughout the area where the electricity is distributed. For users needing even lower voltages, the voltage is reduced once again by a distribution transformer or a line transformer. At this point it changes from primary to secondary distribution voltage.

Electric Generator
A device that converts another form of energy into electric energy. Common types of electric generators spin an electromagnet on a shaft, which induces electric voltage in coils of wire surrounding the electromagnet. The shaft is driven by an engine attached to it, or by a turbine that is part of the electric generator. A turbine has blades attached

to the shaft, which are turned by the force of steam, hot gasses or wind.

Electric Energy
Available heat in electricity; one kilowatt hour equals 3,412.97 Btu.

Electrical Energy
The energy of moving electrons.

Electrical Charge
A condition that results from an imbalance between the number of protons and the number of electrons in a substance.

Electric Circuit
The path followed by electrons from a generation source, through an electrical system, and returning to the source.

Electric Energy
The amount of work accomplished by electrical power, usually measured in kilowatt-hours (kWh). One kWh is 1,000 Watts and is equal to 3,413 Btu.

Electric Furnace
An air heater in which air is blown over electric resistance heating coils.

Electrical System
All the conductors and electricity using devices that are connected to a source of electromotive force (or generator).

Electrical System Energy Losses
A measure of the amount of energy lost during the generation, transmission, and distribution of electricity.

Electricity Generation
The process of producing electric energy or transforming other forms of energy into electric energy. Also, the amount of electric energy produced or ex pressed in watt-hours (Wh). The process of producing electricity by transforming other forms or sources of energy into electrical energy; measured in kilowatt-hours.

Electricity Grid
A common term referring to an electricity transmission and distribution system.

Electric Plant (Physical)
A facility containing prime movers, electric generators and auxiliary equipment for converting mechanical, chemical and/or fission energy

into electric energy. Also known as Electric Generation Plant and Electric Power Plant.

Electric Power Generation
The large-scale production of electricity in a central plant. A power plant consists of one or more units. Each unit includes an individual turbine generator. Turbine generators (turbines directly connected to electric generators) use steam, wind, hot gas or falling water to generate power.

Electric Power Plant
A station containing prime movers, electric generators, and auxiliary equipment for converting mechanical, chemical, and/or fission energy into electric energy.

Electric Rate
The unit price and quantity to which it applies as specified in a rate schedule or contract.

Electric Rate Schedule
A statement of the electric rate and the terms and conditions governing its application, including attendant contract terms and conditions that have been accepted by a regulatory body with appropriate oversight authority. A statement of the electric rate(s), terms, and conditions for electricity sale or supply.

Electric Power Plant
A facility or piece of equipment that produces electricity.

Electric Power Sector
Those privately or publicly owned establishments that generate, transmit, distribute, or sell electricity.

Electric Power Transmission
The transmission of electricity through power lines.

Electric Reserves
The electric power needed to provide service to customers in the event of generation or transmission system outages, adverse streamflows, delays in the completion of new resources or other factors which may-restrict generating capability or increase loads. Reserves normally are provided from additional resources acquired for that purpose, or from contractual rights to interrupt, curtail or otherwise withdraw portions of the electric power supplied to customers.

Electric Resistance Heating
A type of heating system where heat, resulting when electric current flows through an "element" or conductor, such as Nichrome, which has

a high resistance, is radiated to a room.

Electric Space Heating

Space heating of a dwelling or business establishment or other structure using permanently installed electric heating as the principal source of space heating throughout the entire premises.

Electric System

The generation, transmission, distribution and other facilities operated as an electric utility or a portion thereof. The generation, transmission, distribution and other facilities operated as an electric utility or a portion thereof. The physically connected generation, transmission, and distribution facilities and components operated as a unit.

Electric System Loss(es)

The total amount of electric energy loss in an electric system between the generation source and points of delivery. Amount of electricity lost in system. Losses consist of transmission, transformation and distribution losses between supply sources and delivery points. Loss of electric energy is primarily a result of heating in transmission and distribution elements. Transmission, transformation and distribution losses of electric energy between sources of supply and points of delivery (generally, losses are due to heating of transmission and distribution elements)

Electric Utility

A corporation, person, agency, authority or other legal entity or instrumentality that owns and/or operates facilities within the United States, its territories or Puerto Rico for the generation, transmission, distribution or sale of electric energy primarily for use by the public and files forms listed in the Code of Federal Regulations, Title 18, Part 141. Facilities that qualify as cogenerators or small power producers under the Public Utility Regulatory Policies Act (PURPA) are not considered electric utilities. A corporation, person, agency, authority or other legal entity that owns and/or operates facilities for the generation, transmission, distribution or sale of electricity primarily for use by the public. Also known as a power provider.

Electrical Degrees

One cycle of A.C. power is divided into 360 degrees. This allows mathematical relationships between the various aspects of electricity.

Electrical Energy

The quantity of electricity delivered over a period of time. The commonly used unit of electrical energy is the kilowatt-hour (kWh).

Electrical Power

The rate of delivery of electrical energy and the most frequently used measure of capacity. The basic unit is the kilowatt (kW).

Electric Utility
In a regulated electric market, the entity that owns and/or operates facilities for the generation, transmission, and/or distribution of electricity. In a deregulated market, this entity becomes an electric distribution company responsible for transmission and distribution only.

Electric Vehicles
A battery-powered electrically driven vehicle.

Electrification
The term describing emerging electric technologies such as electric vehicles, industrial process heating, and automation. These technologies have the potential for increasing the productivity, contributing to strategic load growth, or facilitating strategic conservation, peak clipping or load shifting. Examples include robotics and industry automation, microwave heating and drying, and freeze concentration of solutions.

Electromagnet
A soft iron core surrounded by a coil of wire that temporarily becomes a magnet when an electric current flows through the wire.

Electromagnetic
A magnetic field cause by an electric current. Power lines cause electromagnetic fields which can interfere with nearby data cables.

Electro Magnetic Fields (EMF)
Invisible force fields that surround the movement of electricity.

Electromechanical
A mechanical device which is controlled by an electric device. Solenoids and shunt trip circuit breakers are examples of electromechanical devices.

Electron
An elementary particle with a unit negative charge. Electrons surround the positively charged nucleus and determine the chemical properties of the atom.

Electronic Measurement
Measurement of gas flow using electronic equipment that typically records data continuously and may transmit that data to a central operations location.

Electrostatic
A Potential difference (electric charge) measurable between two points which is caused by the distribution if dissimilar static charge along the

points. The voltage level is usually in kilovolts.

Electrostatic Precipitator
A device which extracts particles from combustion gases prior to release from a power plant's stack. An electronic pollution-control device that removes particles of fly ash from a power plant's waste gases.

Electrostatic Shield
A metallic barrier or shield between the primary and secondary windings of a transformer which reduces the capacitive coupling and thereby increases the transformers ability to reduce high frequency noise.

Electron
A particle of an atom with a negative electrical charge.

Electrostatic Precipitator
An air pollution control device that removes particles in a gas stream by giving an electrical charge to the particles for the mechanical collection on an electrode with an opposite charge. Used by coal-fired power stations to remove fly-ash from combustion gases.

Element
Any substance that cannot be separated into different substances by ordinary chemical methods, made up of only one type of atom eg. hydrogen, oxygen and fluorine. Any electric device which has terminals that can be connected to other electric devices (typical limited to a generator, transformer, circuit, circuit breaker or bus section).

Embedded Cost
The historical cost of all facilities in the electric or gas supply system.

Emergency
An abnormal system condition that requires automatic or immediate manual action to limit or prevent loss of transmission facilities or generation supply that might adversely affect the system's reliability

Emergency Energy
Electricity purchased by a member system when an event on that system results in insufficient operating capability to cover its own short-term demand requirements.

Emergency Rating
The rating, as defined by the facility owner, that specifies the level of electrical loading (generally expressed in megawatts or other appropriate units) that a facility can support or withstand for short periods of time.

Emergency Response Rate
Rate of load change a generating unit is capable of achieving under emergency.

Emergency Voltage Limits
The operating voltage range on the interconnected systems, above or below nominal voltage and expressed in kilovolts at the transmission or distribution level and volts at the utilization level, that is acceptable for the time sufficient for system adjustments to be made following a facility outage or system disturbance.

EMF
Electromotive force or voltage.

EMI, RFI
Acronyms for various types of electrical interference: electomagnetic interference, radio frequency interference.

EMS
Energy Management System. The computer system Xcel Energy uses to provide real-time status and remote control of its electrical transmission system. A computer control system used by electric utility dispatchers to monitor the real time performance of the various elements of an electric system and to control Generation and transmission facilities.

Enabling Agreement
An agreement that provides the general terms and conditions for the purchase, sale or exchange of electricity but does not list specific contract details or obligate either party to perform.

Enabling equipment
Equipment such as batteries, inverters and regulators that enable the power generated from the renewable and other sources to be made available for useful purposes.

Enclosed space
A working space, such as a manhole, vault, tunnel, or shaft, that has a limited means of egress or entry, that is designed for periodic employee entry under normal operating conditions, and that under normal conditions does not contain a hazardous atmosphere, but that may contain a hazardous atmosphere under abnormal conditions. Spaces that are enclosed but not designed for employee entry under normal operating conditions are not considered to be enclosed spaces for the purposes of this definition. Similarly, spaces that are enclosed and that are expected to contain a hazardous atmosphere are not considered to be enclosed spaces for the purposes of this definition. Such spaces meet the

definition of permit spaces in 1910.146, and entry into them must be performed in accordance with that standard.

End-User
One who actually consumes energy, as opposed to one who sells or re-sells it.

Energy
The capability of doing work (potential energy) or the conversion of this capability to motion (kinetic energy). Energy has several forms, some of which are easily convertible and can be changed to another form useful for work. Most of the world's convertible energy comes from fossil fuels that are burned to produce heat which is then used as a transfer medium to mechanical or other means in order to accomplish tasks.

Energy Audit
The systematic measuring and recording of energy consumption to identify opportunities for reduce and minimise energy use and cost. A review of the customer's electricity and/or gas usage often including recommendations to alter the customer's electric demand or reduce energy usage. An audit usually includes a visit to the customer's facility.

Energy Charge
This portion of the rates covers the product (energy), based upon kilowatt-hours consumed. That portion of the charge for electric service based upon the electric energy (kWh) consumed or billed. The commodity charge

Energy Efficiency
Relationship between 'Power Out' over 'Power In'. The unattainable objective is 100%, greater than 85% is considered good conversion efficiency. Energy efficiency means conserving energy and increasing the use of renewable sources such as solar, wind, and biomass energy and low-impact hydro-electricity to develop a sustainable energy future.

Energy Efficiency Ratio (EER)
A figure of merit of air conditioning or refrigeration performance. The relative efficiency of an appliance in converting primary energy (e.g., electricity) to useful work (such as for cooling in the case of air conditioners) at the rated condition. EER (Btu/kWh) is the Btu per hour output provided by the unit, divided by the watts of electrical power input. The larger the EER, the more efficient the unit.

Energy Deliveries
Energy generated by one electric utility system and delivered to another system through one or more transmission lines.

Energy Effects
The changes in aggregate electricity use (measured in mWh) for customers that participate in a utility DSM program. Energy Effects should represent changes at the consumer meter (i.e. exclude transmission and distribution effects) and reflect only activities that are undertaken specifically in response to utility-administered programs.

Energy Density
The ration of energy that can be discharged from a battery to the volume of that battery measured in Watt Hours (WH) per cubic inch, or litre.

Energy Efficiency
Using less energy/electricity to perform the same function. Programs designed to use electricity more efficiently - doing the same with less. "Energy conservation" is a term, which has also been used but it has the connotation of doing without in order to save energy rather than using less energy to do the same thing and so is not used as much today. Many people use these terms interchangeably.

Energy Emergency
An energy emergency exists when a system or pool does not have an adequate fuel supply (including water for hydroelectric units) to provide its customers' expected energy requirements over a given period.

Energy Factor (EF)
The measure of overall efficiency for a variety of appliances. For water heaters, the energy factor is based on three factors: 1) the recovery efficiency, or how efficiently the heat from the energy source is transferred to the water; 2) stand-by losses, or the percentage of heat lost per hour from the stored water compared to the content of the water: and 3) cycling losses. For dishwashers, the energy factor is defined as the number of cycles per kWh of input power. For clothes washers, the energy factor is defined as the cubic foot capacity per kWh of input power per cycle. For clothes dryers, the energy factor is defined as the number of pounds of clothes dried per kWh of power consumed.

Energy Imbalance Service
Corrects hourly imbalances between transmission customer's energy scheduled and actually received.

Energy Intensity
The relative extent that energy is required for a process.

Energy isolating device
A physical device that prevents the transmission or release of energy, including, but not limited to, the following: a manually operated electric

circuit breaker, a disconnect switch, a manually operated switch, a slide gate, a slip blind, a line valve, blocks, and any similar device with a visible indication of the position of the device. (Push buttons, selector switches, and other control-circuit-type devices are not energy isolating devices.)

Energy Losses
The general term applied to energy lost in the operation of an electrical system. Losses can be classified as Transformation Losses, Transmission Line Losses or System Losses.

Energy Merchant
An energy merchant buys and sells energy as a commodity. A merchant plant is one that is built with the aim of marketing and selling its output on the open market. This differs from building a plant to meet customer needs and the obligation to serve that a regulated utility has.

Energy payback time
The time required for any energy producing system or device to produce as much useful energy as was consumed in its manufacture and construction.

Energy Receipts
Energy generated by one electric utility system and received by another system through one or more transmission lines.

Energy Source
Raw materials that are converted to electricity through chemical, mechanical or other means. Energy sources include coal, petroleum and petroleum products, gas, water, uranium, wind, sunlight, geothermal and other sources.

Energy Value Chain
The energy value chain links the sources, production, forms, marketing and delivery of energy. Value can be added by analyzing the energy value chain, learning where competitive advantage can be exploited within a firm's value chain and through interrelationships among the value chains that serve different segments, industries or geographic areas.

Enhanced Oil Recovery (EOR)
The introduction of an artificial drive and displacement mechanism, usually steam, into a reservoir to produce oil unrecoverable by primary and secondary recovery methods.

Enriched uranium
Uranium in which the proportion of U-235 (to U-238) has been increased

above the natural 0.7%. Reactor-grade uranium is usually enriched to about 3.5% U-235, weapons-grade uranium is more than 90% U-235.

Enriching
Increasing the heat content of natural gas by mixing it with a gas of higher Btu content (often propane).

Enterprise Resource Planning (ERP)
A collection of software programs that tie together an enterprise's various functions, such as human resources, finance, marketing and sales. The software also enables an analysis of the data to plan production, forecast sales and analyze quality.

Entitlement, Working Interest
A working interest owner's share of production from a well. This amount may not be equal to actual sales due to contractual or market conditions.

Equalisation
An extended charging process over a prescribed period to ensure complete charging of all cells in a battery.

Equipment Capacity
The maximum power capability of piece of equipment. For example, a generating unit might have a rated capacity of 50 megawatts

Equipment Event Log
A record that is kept of equipment problems and activity, to compare against power monitor data to correlate equipment problems with power events.

Error Burst
A large number of errors within a given period of time as compared to preceding and following time periods.

ESCO
Efficiency Service Company. A company that offers to reduce a client's electricity consumption with the cost savings being split with the client.

Essential Facilities
A doctrine developed in anti-trust law which defines certain facilities, found necessary for transporting a product to market, as a potential monopoly and requires such facilities to be made available on a non-discriminatory basis.

ESD
Electrostatic Discharge (static electricity). The effects of static discharge can range from simple skin irritation for an individual to degraded or

destroyed semiconductor junctions for an electronic device.

Ethane (C2H6)
A hydrocarbon molecule consisting of two carbon atoms and six hydrogen atoms, used as petrochemical feedstock in production of chemicals and plastics, and as a solvent in enhanced oil recovery processes.

Ethylene (C2H4)
A hydrocarbon molecule consisting of two carbon atoms and four hydrogen atoms, used as petrochemical feedstock in production of chemicals and plastics, and as a solvent in enhanced oil recovery processes.

Evacuated-Tube Collector
A collector is the mechanism in which fluid (water or diluted antifreeze, for example) is heated by the sun in a solar hot water system. Evacuated-tube collectors are made up of rows of parallel, transparent glass tubes. Each tube consists of a glass outer tube and an inner tube, or absorber. The absorber is covered with a selective coating that absorbs solar energy well but inhibits radiative heat loss. The air is withdrawn ("evacuated") from the space between the tubes to form a vacuum, which eliminates conductive and convective heat loss. Evacuated-tube collectors are used for active solar hot water systems.

Evaporative Cooling
The physical process by which a liquid or solid is transformed into the gaseous state. For this process a mechanical device uses the outside air's heat to evaporate water that is held by pads inside the cooler. The heat is drawn out of the air through this process and the cooled air is blown into the home by the cooler's fan.

Evaporator Coil
The inner coil in a heat pump that, during the cooling mode, absorbs heat from the inside air and boils the liquid refrigerant to a vapor, which cools the house.

Event Summary
A plot of recorded power monitor events over time.

Evergreen Clause
A contract clause that extends the contract beyond the initial term, perhaps on a month-to-month or year-to-year basis, until one of the parties gives a required notice of termination.

EWG
An Exempt Wholesale Generator is an Independent Power Producer (fPP)

whose energy would be purchased based on a price other than the avoided cost of building a new unit.

Exchange
The transfer and return of electricity from one utility to another at different time periods or seasons to achieve a more economic or efficient overall system operation. Such transfers are possible because of differences in electricity demand, generation resource capability or system operating characteristics. Transportation of natural gas by displacement over two pipelines, each of which takes and retains possession of gas contractually allocated to the other.

Exchange Gas
Natural gas that is received from, or delivered to, another party in exchange for natural gas delivered to, or received from, that other party.

Exempt Wholesale Generator (EWG)
A class of generators defined by the Energy Policy Act of 1992 that includes the owners and/or operators of facilities used to generate electricity exclusively for wholesale or that are leased to utilities.

Exercise Price
The price at which an option may be exercised. A decrease in the exercise price has the same effect as an increase in the current price of the underlying asset.

Exercising the Option
The action taken by the owner of a call option if he/she wants to exercise the right to purchase the underlying instrument or to settle in cash, or by the holder of a put option if he/she wants to sell the underlying instrument contract or settle in cash.

Excitation
The power required to energize the magnetic field of a generator.

Existing Contracts ("ETC") or ("E.C.")
The contracts which grant transmission service rights in existence on the ISO Operations Date (including any contracts entered into pursuant to such contracts) as may be amended in accordance with their terms or by agreement between the parties thereto from time to time.

Exit Fee
A fee that is paid by a customer leaving the utility system intended to compensate the utility in whole or part for the loss of fixed cost contribution from the exiting customer.

Expanded Polystyrene
A type of insulation that is molded or expanded to produce coarse, closed cells containing air. The rigid cellular structure provides thermal and acoustical insulation, strength with low weight, and coverage with few heat loss paths. Often used to insulate the interior of masonry basement walls.

Expansion Tank
A tank used in a closed-loop solar heating system that provides space for the expansion of the heat transfer fluid in the pressurized collector loop.

Expansion Valve
The device that reduces the pressure of liquid refrigerant thereby cooling it before it enters the evaporator coil in a heat pump.

External Combustion Engine
An engine in which fuel is burned (or heat is applied) to the outside of a cylinder; a Stirling engine.

Externality
The environmental, social, and economic impacts of producing a good or service that are not directly reflected in the market price of the good or service.

Extraction Loss
The reduction in volume of wet natural gas due to the removal of natural gas liquids, hydrogen sulfide, carbon dioxide, water vapor and other impurities from the natural gas stream. Also called SHRINKAGE.

Extranet
A network that allows a company to share information with specific businesses and other stakeholders, while excluding others. Extranets, which are more private than external Web sites, transmit information over the Internet and require users to have a password to access data on internal company servers.

Extruded Polystyrene
A type of insulation material with fine, closed cells, containing a mixture of air and refrigerant gas. This insulation has a high R-value, good moisture resistance, and high structural strength compared to other rigid insulation materials.

F

Facilities Study
An engineering study conducted by the Transmission Facility Owner to

determine the required modifications to the grid, including the cost and scheduled completion date for such modifications, that will be required to provide the requested transmission service.

Failure Mode

Reason for which a converter either does not meet or stops meeting its specified parameters.

Fan Coil

A heat exchanger coil in which a fluid such as water is circulated and a fan blows air over the coil to distribute heat or cool air to the different rooms.

Fan Velocity Pressure

The pressure corresponding to the outlet velocity of a fan; the kinetic energy per unit volume of flowing air.

Farad

Unit of measurement for capacitance.

Farady Shield

A grounded metallic barrier which can be used for improved isolation between the windings of a transformer. In this application, the shield basically reduces the leakage capacitance between the primary and secondary.

Fast breeder reactor (FBR)

A fast neutron reactor configured to produce more fissile material than it consumes, using fertile material such as depleted uranium in a blanket around the core.

Fast neutron reactor

A reactor with little or no moderator and hence utilizing fast neutrons. It normally burns plutonium while producing fissile isotopes in fertile material such as depleted uranium (or thorium).

Fault Mode Current

Input current drawn by a converter when the output is shorted.

Feather

In a wind energy conversion system, to pitch the turbine blades so as to reduce their lift capacity as a method of shutting down the turbine during high wind speeds.

Feeders

Transmission lines supplying power to a distribution system. A circuit, such as conductors in conduit or a busway run, which carries a large block of power from the service equipment to a sub-feeder panel or a branch circuit panel or to some point at which the block power is broken into smaller circuits.

FERC

Federal Energy Regulatory Commission. (Formerly the Federal Power Commission, or FPC.) FERC is an independent body within the Department of Energy (DOE) regulating interstate transmission, prices of electricity and natural gas. It also licenses hydroelectric projects, interconnections, construction work in progress, rates for wholesale customers, utility accounting practices and procedures.

Ferrite Core

Ferrite is a magnetic material which consists of a mixed oxide of iron and other elements that are made to have a crystalline molecular structure. The crystalline structure is created by firing the ferrite material at a very high temperture for a specified amount of time and temperature profile. The general composition of ferrites is xxFe204 where xx represents one or several metals. The most popular metal combinations are manganese and zinc(MnZn) and nickel and zinc (NiZn). These metals can be easily magnetized. Ferrite is a magnetic material that consists of a mixed oxide of iron and other elements that are made to have a crystalline molecular structure. Firing the ferrite material at a very high temperature for a specified amount of time and temperature profile creates the crystalline structure. The general composition of ferrite is xxFe2O4 where xx represents one or several metals. The most popular metal combinations are manganese and zinc (MnZn) and nickel and zinc (NiZn). These materials can be easily magnetized with little coercive force. Available in a variety of shapes and sizes, these ceramic magnetic cores are composed of ferric oxide and a combination of manganese, zinc, or nickel. The shapes EE, PQ, UU, ETD, and dual-slab are used for high frequency power applications. Telecommunications and low power applications use pot cores, touch tone cores, EP, and RM. Slugs, rods, and beads are used for radio frequency applications.

Ferroresonance

Resonance resulting when the iron core of an inductive component of an LC circuit is saturated, increasing the inductive reactance with respect to the capacitance reactance.

Ferroresonant Transformer

A voltage regulating transformer which depends on core saturation and output capacitance. Transformer in which part of the core is driven in saturation by a resonant tank circuit. The output of the transformer, taken from the saturated protion, is relative immune to variations in input voltage.

Fertile (of an isotope)
Capable of becoming fissile, by capturing neutrons, possibly followed by radioactive decay; e.g., U-238, Pu-240.

Filament
A coil of tungsten wire suspended in a vacuum or inert gas-filled bulb. When heated by electricity the tungsten "filament" glows.

Fill Factor
The ratio of a photovoltaic cell's actual power to its power if both current and voltage were at their maxima. A key characteristic in evaluating cell performance.

Filter (air)
A device that removes contaminants, by mechanical filtration, from the fresh air stream before the air enters the living space. Filters can be installed as part of a heating/cooling system through which air flows for the purpose of removing particulates before or after the air enters the mechanical components.

Filter
A selective network of resistor, inductors, or capacitors which offers comparatively little opposition to certain frequencies or direct current, while blocking or attenuating other frequencies.

Fire Barrier Wall
A wall separating buildings or subdividing a building to prevent the spread of fire and having a fire resistance rating and structural stability.

Fire loading
The amount of combustibles present in a given area, expressed in Btu/ft^2 (kJ/m^2).

Fireplace
A wood or gas burning appliance that is primarily used to provide ambiance to a room. Conventional, masonry fireplaces without energy saving features, often take more heat from a space than they put into it.

Fireplace Insert
A wood or gas burning heating appliance that fits into the opening or protrudes on to the hearth of a conventional fireplace.

Fire point
The lowest temperature at which a liquid in an open container will give

off sufficient vapors to burn once ignited. It generally is slightly above the flash point.

Fire protection rating

The time, in minutes or hours, that materials and assemblies used as opening protection have withstood a fire exposure as established in accordance with test procedures of NFPA 252, Standard Methods of Fire Tests of Door Assemblies, and NFPA 257, Standard on Fire Test for Window and Glass Block assemblies, as applicable.

Fire-Rating

The ability of a building construction assembly (partition, wall, floor, etc.) to resist the passage of fire. The rating is expressed in hours.

Firewall

A wall to prevent the spread of fire; usually made of non-combustible material.

Firm Energy

Energy sales which, although not subject to interruption for economic purposes, may be interrupted for unexpected/uncontrollable events.

Fissionable (of an isotope)

Capable of undergoing fission: If fissile, by slow neutrons; if fertile, by fast neutrons.

Fission

The splitting of a heavy nucleus into two, accompanied by the release of a relatively large amount of energy and usually one or more neutrons. It may be spontaneous but usually is due to a nucleus absorbing a neutron and thus becoming unstable.

Fission products

Daughter nuclei resulting either from the fission of heavy elements such as uranium, or the radioactive decay of those primary daughters. Usually highly radioactive.

Flammable liquid

Any liquid having a flash point below 100°F (37.8°C) and having a vapor pressure not exceeding an absolute pressure of 40 psi (276 kPa) at 100°F (37.8°C).

Flame Spread Classification

A measure of the surface burning characteristics of a material.

Flame Spread Rating

A measure of the relative flame spread, and smoke development, from a material being tested. The flame spread rating is a single number comparing the flame spread of a material with red oak, arbitrarily given the number 100 and asbestos cement board with a flame spread of 0. Building codes require a maximum flame spread of 25 for insulation installed in exposed locations.

Flashing
Metal, usually galvanized sheet metal, used to provide protection against infiltration of precipitation into a roof or exterior wall; usually placed around roof penetrations such as chimneys.

Flashover
Flashing due to high current flowing between two points of different potential. Usually due to insulation breakdown resulting from arcing.

Flashpoint
The minimum temperature at which sufficient vapor is released by a liquid or solid (fuel) to form a flammable vapor-air mixture at atmospheric pressure.

Flat Plate Solar Photovoltaic Module
An arrangement of photovoltaic cells or material mounted on a rigid flat surface with the cells exposed freely to incoming sunlight. An arrangement of photovoltaic cells mounted on a rigid flat surface with the cells exposed freely to incoming sunlight.

Flat-plate Photovoltaic
Refers to a Photovoltaic array or module that consists of non-concentrating elements. Flat-plate arrays and modules use direct and diffuse sunlight, but if the array is fixed in position, some portion of the direct sunlight is lost because of oblique sun-angles in relation to the array.

Flat Roof
A slightly sloped roof, usually with a tar and gravel cover. Most commercial buildings use this kind of roof.

Float charge
Float charge is the voltage required to counteract the self-discharge of the battery at a certain temperature.

Float life
Number of years that a battery can keep its stated capacity when it is kept at float charge (see float charge).

Float-zone process
A method of growing a large-size, high-quality crystal whereby coils

heat a polycrystalline ingot placed atop a single-crystal seed. As the coils are slowly raised the molten interface beneath the coils becomes single crystal. In reference to solar photovoltaic cell manufacture, a method of growing a large-size, high-quality crystal whereby coils heat a polycrystalline ingot placed atop a single-crystal seed. As the coils are slowly raised the molten interface beneath the coils becomes a single crystal.

Float Charge
Process of charging a battery with a current limited constant voltage source, which after initial charge, maintains a steady voltage across the cell sufficient to overcome internal resistance and maintain the battery in a state ready for maximum power delivery.

Float Voltage
The voltage at which a battery continues to charge after the initial charging period.

Flooded Batteries
Batteries that have a free-flowing liquid electrolyte.

Flow
Flow is the volume of water passing through an area in a given time period. It is most often measured in cubic feet per second (cf/s) or gallons per minute (GPM).

Flow Condition
In reference to solar thermal collectors, the condition where the heat transfer fluid is flowing through the collector loop under normal operating conditions.

Flow Restrictor
A water and energy conserving device that limits the amount of water that a faucet or shower head can deliver.

Fluorescent Light
The conversion of electric power to visible light by using an electric charge to excite gaseous atoms in a glass tube. These atoms emit ultraviolet radiation that is absorbed by a phosphor coating on the walls of the lamp tube. The phosphor coating produces visible light.

Flucuation
A surge or sag in voltage amplitude, often caused by load switching or fault clearing.

Flume
Open and closed flumes serve to channel water into a reaction-type water

turbine.

Flux
The lines of force of a magnetic field.

Fly-ash
Fine, solid particles of non-combustible ash.

Flyback
Actually an isolated storage inductor, a flyback transformer is a combination of an isolating transformer, output inductor, and flywheel diode. These use a gapped core and have a power handling capability of 100VA. Storing energy in the gap when the switch is on and delivering energy to the load when the switch is off, they do not perform like standard transformers.

Flyback Converter
Also called a "buck-boost" converter, this topology typically uses a single transistor switch and eliminates the need for an output inductor. Energy is stored in the transformer primary during the first half of the switching period when the transistor switch is on. During the second half or "flyback" period when the transistor is off, this energy is tranferred the transformer secondary and load. Also see Boost Regulator, Buck Regulator, Bridge Converter, Forward Converter, Push-Pull Converter and Resonant Converter.

Flyback Transformer
Transformer used in a flyback power supply. Also called horizontal output transformer.

Foldback Current Limiting
Converter protection technique in which the circuit is protected under overload conditions by reducing the output current as the load approaches short circuit. This minimized internal power dissipation under short circuit conditions.

Forebay
A closed tank at the top end of a hydro power diversion pipeline. It allows the water to settle before entering the penstock. Usually where the primary filter/trash-rack is installed.

Forced Outage
An unplanned component failure (immediate, delayed, postponed, startup failure) or other condition that requires a unit to be removed from service.

Forced Outage Rate

The rate of shutdown of a generating unit, transmission line, or other facility, for emergency reasons or a condition in which the generating equipment is unavailable for load because of unanticipated breakdown.

Forward Converter

Also called a "Buck-Derived" converter, this topology, like the flyback converter, typically uses a single transistor switch. Unlike the flyback converter, energy is tranferred to the transformer secondary while the transistor switch is "on", and stoed in a output inductor. See Boost Regulator, Buck Regulator, Bridge Converter, Flyback Converter, Push Pull Converter and Resonant Converter.

Forward Converter Transformer

A transformer which operates by transferring power to the load during the on time and resetting in the off time. Since this transformer only transfers power during half of an input cycle it is required to be larger than a push-pull transformer for example.

Forward Transfer Impedance

The amount of impedance placed between the source and load with installation of a power conditioner. With no power conditioner, the full utility power is delivered to the load; even a transformer adds some opposition to the transfer of power. On transformer based power conditioners, a high forward transfer impedance limits the amount of inrush current available to the load.

Fossil Fuels

Coal, oil, natural gas and other fuels originating from geologic deposits of ancient plant and animal life. Oil, coal and natural gas that originates from decayed plants and animals. A fuel based on carbon presumed to be originally from living matter, e.g., coal, oil, gas. Burned with oxygen to yield energy, used in a boiler to produce steam for the generation of electrical energy.

FPN

Fine print note. National Electrical Code (NEC) explanatory material.

Francis Turbine

A type of hydropower turbine that contains a runner that has water passages through it formed by curved vanes or blades. As the water passes through the runner and over the curved surfaces, it causes rotation of the runner. The rotational motion is transmitted by a shaft to a generator.

Frequency

On AC circuits, designates number of times per second that the current completes a full cycle in positive and negative directions. See also "alternating current". The number of cycles through which an alternating current passes in a second. The North American standard is 60 cycles per second, known as 60 hertz. The number of cycles occurring in a given interval of time (usually one second) in an electric current. Frequency is commonly expressed in hertz.

Frequency Changers

A frequency changer is a motor-generator set that changes power of an alternating current system from one frequency to one or more different frequencies, with or without a change in the number of phases, or in voltage.

Frequency Deviation

A variation from nominal frequency.

Fresnel lens

An optical device that focuses light like a magnifying glass; concentric rings are faced at slightly different angles so that light falling on any ring is focused to the same point. Fresnel lenses are flat rather than thick in the center and can be stamped out in a mold.

Friction Head

The energy lost from the movement of a fluid in a conduit (pipe) due to the disturbances created by the contact of the moving fluid with the surfaces of the conduit, or the additional pressure that a pump must provide to overcome the resistance to fluid flow created by or in a conduit.

Fuel

Any material that can be burned to make energy.

Fuel assembly

Structured collection of fuel rods or elements, the unit of fuel in a reactor.

Fuel Cell

A device in which fuel and oxygen are combined to produce chemical energy which is then converted directly into electrical energy. A device that generates direct current to electricity by means of an electrochemical process with little or no emission by-product. Static device that converts the chemical energy in natural gas into electricity and hot water through an electrochemical process. A device that converts the energy of a fuel directly to electricity and heat, without combustion. Because there is no combustion, fuel cells give off few emissions; because there are no moving parts, fuel cells are quiet.

Fuel fabrication

Making reactor fuel assemblies, usually from sintered UO_2 pellets which are inserted into zircalloy tubes, comprising the fuel rods or elements.

Fuel Switching

Substituting one fuel for another based on price and availability. Large industries often have the capability of using either oil or natural gas to fuel their operation and of making the switch on short notice.

Full Sun

The amount of power density in sunlight received at the earth's surface at noon on a clear day (about 1,000 Watts/square meter).

Furling

The process of forcing, either manually or automatically, a wind turbine's blades out of the direction of the wind in order to stop the blades from turning. The act of a wind generator Yawing out of the wind either horizontally or vertically to protect itself from high wind speeds.

Furling Tail

A wind generator protection mechanism where the rotor shaft axis is offset horizontally from the yaw axis, and the tail boom is both offset horizontally and hinged diagonally, thus allowing the tail to fold up and in during high winds. This causes the blades to turn out of the wind, protecting the machine

Furnace (Residential)

A combustion heating appliance in which heat is captured from the burning of a fuel for distribution, comprised mainly of a combustion chamber and heat exchanger.

Fuse

A safety device consisting of a short length of relatively fine wire, mounted in a holder or contained in a cartridge and connected as part of an electrical circuit. If the circuit source current exceeds a predetermined value, the fuse wire melts (i.e. the fuse 'blows') breaking the circuit and preventing damage to the circuit protected by the fuse. A short piece of conducting material of low melting point which is inserted in a circuit for the purpose of opening the circuit when the current reaches a certain value. Used to stop too much electricity travelling through a house's wires - it breaks the electricity's pathway.

G

Generator

A machine that converts mechanical energy into electrical energy

Electricity is produced from magnets whirling inside coils of wire in the generator core. A machine which converts mechanical energy into electrical energy through turning a coil of wire within a magnetic field, or visa versa.

Geothermal
Power generated from heat energy derived from hot rock, hot water or steam below the earth's surface.

Geothermal Energy
Energy produced by the internal heat of the earth; geothermal heat sources include: hydrothermal convective systems; pressurized water reservoirs; hot dry rocks; manual gradients; and magma. Geothermal energy can be used directly for heating or to produce electric power. The heat energy available in the subsurface of the Earth.

Geothermal Heat Pump
A type of heat pump that uses the ground, ground water, or ponds as a heat source and heat sink, rather than outside air. Ground or water temperatures are more constant and are warmer in winter and cooler in summer than air temperatures. Geothermal heat pumps operate more efficiently than "conventional" or "air source" heat pumps.

Geothermal Power Station
An electricity generating facility that uses geothermal energy.

GFI (Ground Fault Interrupter)
A device whose function is to interrupt the electric circuit to the load when a fault current to ground exceeds some predetermined value that is less than that required to operate the overcurrent protective device of the supply circuit.

Gigawatt (GW)
1,000,000,000 watts; 1,000,000 kilowatts; 1,000 megawatts.

Gigawatt-Hour (GWh)
1,000 megawatt-hours or 1 billion watt-hours.

Good Utility Practice
Any of the practices, methods and acts engaged in or approved by a significant portion of the electric utility industry during the relevant time period, or any of the practices, Methods and acts which, in the exercise of reasonable judgment in light of the facts known at the time the decision was made, could have been expected to accomplish the desired result of the lowest reasonable cost consistent with good business practices, reliability, safety and expedition. Good Utility Practice is not

intended to be limited to the optimum practice, method or act to the exclusion of all others, but rather to be acceptable practices, methods, or acts generally accepted in the region and consistently adhered to by the Transmission Provider.

Governor

A device that regulates the speed of a rotating shaft, either electrically or mechanically.

Greenhouse Effect

The heating effect of the atmosphere upon the Earth. Light waves from the sun pass through the air and are absorbed by the Earth. The Earth then re-radiates this energy as heat waves that are absorbed by the air, especially by carbon dioxide. This carbon dioxide behaves like the glass in a greenhouse, letting in the light but trapping the heat. It is bélieved that increasing carbon dioxide emissions will increase the global surface temperature. Electricity generation considered to be less intrusive environmentally than traditional generation. Green power sources include wind, water, landfill gas, solar, and others. A general term that describes power that is environmentally friendly. It typically uses a mix of energy sources with renewable energy being at least one of the sources.

Grid

The layout of the electrical transmission system or a synchronized transmission network. A network of electric power lines and connections. The interconnected power lines and generators that supply, transmit and distribute electric power to the customers connected to it. Network of electric transmission lines used to move energy. Under deregulation, the electric transmission grid is operated by a gridco that does not own generation or distribution assets. Network of transmission lines, substations, distribution lines and transformers used by central power systems

Grid-Connected System

Independent power systems that are connected to an electricity transmission and distribution system (referred to as the electricity grid) such that the systems can draw on the grid's reserve capacity in times of need, and feed electricity back into the grid during times of excess production.

Grid-connected distributed photovoltaic power system

System installed on consumers' premises usually on the demand side of the electricity meter. This includes grid-connected domestic photovoltaic power systems and other grid-connected photovoltaic power systems on commercial buildings, motorway sound barriers, etc. These may be used for support of the utility distribution grid.

Grid-connected centralized photovoltaic power system
Power production system performing the function of a centralized power station (also said centralized photovoltaic power plant).

Grid Entry Point
A point at which a generating unit or a CCGT module which connected to the transmission system connects to the NGC transmission system.

Grid Supply Point
A point of supply from the national transmission system to the local System of the distribution network operator.

Ground
A term used in electrical work in referring to the earth as a conductor or as the zero of potential. For safety purposes, circuits are grounded while any work is being done on or near a circuit or piece of equipment in the circuit; this is usually called protective or safety grounding. Connection of one side of a circuit to the earth or a body that serves in place of the earth, through low impedance paths. Sometimes confused with bonding. Grounding should always conform to the National Electrical Code.

Grounded
Connected to earth or to some conducting body that serves in place of the earth.

Ground Fault
Any undesirable current path from a current carrying conductor to ground.

Ground-Fault Circuit Interrupter (GFCI)
A device that instantly breaks the circuit when a short develops. Required for outlets that are used in bathrooms, kitchens, outdoors or wherever electrical equipment might come into contact with water.

Guide Vanes
Used in reaction turbines to change water flow direction by 90 degrees, causing the water to whirl and enter all turbine runner buckets simultaneously, improving turbine efficiency

Guy Anchor
Attaches tower guy wires securely to the earth.

Guy Radius
The distance between a wind turbine tower and the guy anchors.

Guy Wire

Attaches a tower to a Guy Anchor and the ground. Cable use to secure a wind turbine tower to the ground in a safe, stable manner.

H

Heat Content

The amount of heat in a quantity of matter at a specific temperature and pressure.

Heat Engine

A device that produces mechanical energy directly from two heat reservoirs of different temperatures. A machine that converts thermal energy to mechanical energy, such as a steam engine or turbine.

Heat Exchanger

A device used to transfer heat from a fluid (liquid or gas) to another fluid where the two fluids are physically separated.

Heat Gain

The amount of heat introduced to a space from all heat producing sources, such as building occupants, lights, appliances, and from the environment, mainly solar energy.

Heating Capacity (Also specific heat)

The quantity of heat necessary to raise the temperature of a specific mass of a substance by one degree.

Heating Degree Day(s) (HDD)

The number of degrees per day that the daily average temperature (the mean of the maximum and minimum recorded temperatures) is below a base temperature, usually 65 degrees Fahrenheit, unless otherwise specified; used to determine indoor space heating requirements and heating system sizing. Total HDD is the cumulative total for the year/heating season. The higher the HDD for a location, the colder the daily average temperature(s).

Heating Fuels

Any gaseous, liquid, or solid fuel used for indoor space heating.

Heating Fuel Units

Standardized weights or volumes for heating fuels.

Heating Load

The rate of heat flow required to maintain a specific indoor temperature; usually measured in Btu per hour.

Heat Rate

A measure of generating station thermal efficiency, generally expressed in Btu per net kilowatthour. It is computed by dividing the total Btu content of fuel burned for electric generation by the resulting net kilowatthour generation. Natural gas fired plants convert fuel to electricity at different rates that are expressed as .heat rates.. The lower the heat rate, the higher the efficiency of the plant. Put another way, it is the amount of fuel energy required by a power plant to produce one kilowatt-hour of electrical output. It is a measure of generating station thermal efficiency, generally expressed in Btu per net kWh (or alternatively MM Btu per net MWH), computed by dividing the total Btu content of fuel burned for electric generation by the resulting net kWh generation.

Heating Season

The coldest months of the year; months where average daily temperatures fall below 65 degrees Fahrenheit creating demand for indoor space heating.

Heating Value

The amount of heat produced by the complete combustion of a unit quantity of fuel. The gross, or higher, heating value is that which is obtained when all of the products of combustion are cooled to the temperature existing before combustion, the water vapor formed during combustion is condensed, and all the necessary corrections have been made. The net, or lower, heating value is obtained by subtracting the latent heat of vaporization of the water vapor formed by the combustion of the hydrogen in the fuel from the gross, or higher, heating value.

Heat Pipe

A device that transfers heat by the continuous evaporation and condensation of an internal fluid.

Heat Pump

An electricity powered device that extracts available heat from one area (the heat source) and transfers it to another (the heat sink) to either heat or cool an interior space or to extract heat energy from a fluid.

Heat Pump Water Heaters

A water heater that uses electricity to move heat from one place to another instead of generating heat directly.

Heat Rate

The ratio of fuel energy input as heat per unit of net work output; a measure of a power plant thermal efficiency, generally expressed as Btu per net kilowatt-hour.

Heat Recovery Ventilator
A device that captures the heat from the exhaust air from a building and transfers it to the supply/fresh air entering the building to preheat the air and increase overall heating efficiency.

Heat Register
The grilled opening into a room by which the amount of warm air from a furnace can be directed or controlled; may include a damper.

Heat Sink
A structure or media that absorbs heat.

Heat Source
A structure or media from which heat can be absorbed or extracted.

Heat Storage
A device or media that absorbs heat for storage for later use.

Heat Storage Capacity
The amount of heat that a material can absorb and store.

Heat Transfer
The flow of heat from one area to another by conduction, convection, and/or radiation. Heat flows naturally from a warmer to a cooler material or space.

Heat Transfer Fluid
A gas or liquid used to move heat energy from one place to another; a refrigerant.

Heat Transmission Coefficient
Any coefficient used to calculate heat transmission by conduction, convection, or radiation through materials or structures.

Heliochemical Process
The utilization of solar energy through photosynthesis.

Heavy Load Hours
Generally speaking, this refers to the time of day on a system that would be considered peak demand. Actual hours vary by individual power system.

Heavy Oil
The fuel oils remaining after the lighter oils have been distilled off during the refining process.

Hedging

To offset a position with the intent of managing risk. The process of protecting the value of an investment from the risk of loss in case the price fluctuates. Hedging is accomplished by protecting one transaction with another. A long position in an underlying instrument can be hedged or protected with an offsetting short position in a related underlying instrument.

Helium (HE)

A light, colorless, nonflammable gaseous element found especially in conjunction with natural gas and used mainly in cryogenic applications, medical technology, military uses and welding.

Helium, Contained

The helium constituent in crude helium.

Helium, Crude

The mixture of elemental helium and other constituents of natural gas, principally nitrogen, extracted from natural gas by helium extraction plants. Crude helium is typically 60-80% contained helium.

Helium, Refined

Helium that is of a high level of purity after the processing of crude helium.

Henry

Unit of measurement for inductance.

Hertz (HZ)

Unit of frequency, one hertz (Hz) equals one cycle per second.The term denoting frequency, equivalent to cycles per second. The unit of frequency for alternating current. Formerly called cycles per second. The standard frequency for power supply in North America is 60 Hz. A measure of the "frequency" of an electric current, or the number of times an alternating current (AC) "alternates" direction each second. Frequency is measured as "cycles per second." One hertz equals one cycle per second. The standard frequency in the U.S. is 60 Hz, or 60 cycles per second.

High-Pressure Sodium Lamp

A type of High-Intensity Discharge (HID) lamp that uses sodium under high pressure as the primary light-producing element. These high efficiency lights produce a golden white color and are used for interior industrial applications, such as in warehouses and manufacturing, and for security, street, and area lighting.

Highwall

The unexcavated face of exposed overburden and coal of a surface mine or the exposed face or bank of a hill on the uphill side of a contour mine excavation site.

HV(High Voltage)
A voltage exceeding 650 volts. It is the rated voltage above lkV and medium voltage and is commonly
used for distribution systems, with rated voltages above lkV and generally applied up to and including
52kV.

Hold-UpTime
The time after loss of input mains power, during which the output of a power supply continues to provide normal regulated, output voltage and current.

Hopper Cars
Open freight cars with a floor sloping to one or more hinged doors for discharging bulk materials such as coal.

Horse Power
A British unit of the measure for the rate at which energy is produced or used. 1 Hp = 746 watts. A unit of rate of operation. Electrical hp: a measure of time rate of mechanical energy output; usually applied to electric motors as the maximum output; 1 electrical hp is equal to 0.746 kilowatts or 2,545 Btu per hour. Shaft hp: a measure of the actual mechanical energy per unit time delivered to a turning shaft; 1 shaft Hp is equal to 1 electrical Hp or 550 foot pounds per second. Boiler Hp: a measure to the maximum rate to heat output of a steam generator; 1 boiler Hp is equal to 33,480 Btu per hour steam output.

Horsepower Hour (hph)
One horsepower provided over one hour; equal to 0.745 kilowatt-hour or 2,545 Btu.

Host Control Area
The control area within the metered boundaries a unit not owned by the host or a unit jointly owned by the host and another entity is physically located.

Hot Air Furnace
A heating unit where heat is distributed by means of convection or fans.

Hot Dry Rock
A geothermal energy resource that consists of high temperature rocks above 300 F (150 C) that may be fractured and have little or no water. To extract the heat, the rock must first be fractured, then water is injected

into the rock and pumped out to extract the heat. In the western United States, as much as 95,000 square miles (246,050 square km) have hot dry rock potential.

Hot Transfer
See Closed Transition Transfer

Hourly Peak
The maximum demand for energy from a transmission or distribution system in any hourly period of time.

Hourly Value
Data measured on a clock-hour basis.

Hub
An interchange where multiple pipelines or electric transmission lines interconnect and form a market center.

HX(Heat Exchanger)
It is used in remote terminal cabinets to dissipate equipment heat to the outside environment without
mixing outside air with cabinet air.

Hybrid
A device which is composite of differing technologies to create a better functionality.

Hybrid System
A renewable energy system that includes two different types of technologies that produce the same type of energy; for e.g., a wind turbine and a solar photovoltaic array combined to meet a power demand.

Hybrid power system
A power system making use of more than one power resource to generate electricity. A diesel-solar, diesel-wind or a diesel-solar-wind power system are examples of hybrid systems.

Hydrocarbons
A vast family of compounds containing carbon and hydrogen in various combinations, found particularly in fossil fuels. Organic compound made up of carbon and hydrogen atoms. Heavier fossil fuels, such as coal, have a large ratio of carbon to hydrogen, while natural gas (methane) is the lightest hydrocarbon, with one atom of carbon and four atoms of hydrogen (CH_4). Natural gas liquids are heavier than methane but lighter than crude oil. Crude oil is a complex of many hydrocarbons.

Hydroelectric Plant
A plant in which the turbine generators are driven by falling water. A plant which uses natural water flows to turn turbines. A power plant that produces electricity by the force of water falling through a hydro turbine that spins a generator.

Hydroelectric Pumped Storage
A plant generating electricity during peak loads by using water previously pumped into an elevated storage reservoir during off-peak periods when excess generating capacity is available to do so.

Hydroelectricity
The production of electric energy by a water-powered turbine generator.

Hydro energy
Hydro energy is produced by harnessing the movement of water from rivers and lakes. Dams or weirs enable water to be stored and used as power source to generate electricity. A hydroelectric generator consists of a water turbine to convert the energy of flowing water into mechanical energy, and an electric generator to convert mechanical energy into electrical energy.

Hydronic Heating Systems
A type of heating system where water is heated in a boiler and either moves by natural convection or is pumped to heat exchangers or radiators in rooms; radiant floor systems have a grid of tubing laid out in the floor for distributing heat. The temperature in each room is controlled by regulating the flow of hot water through the radiators or tubing.

Hydrothermal fluids
These fluids can be either water or steam trapped in fractured or porous rocks; they are found from several hundred feet to several miles below the Earth's surface. The temperatures vary from about 90 F to 680 F (32 C to 360 C) but roughly 2/3 range in temperature from 150 F to 250 F (65.5 C to 121.1 C). The latter are the easiest to access and, therefore, the only forms being used commercially.

I

I2R
The expression of power resulting from the flow of current through a resistance: P = I2R.

IEEE
Institution of Electrical and Electronic Engineers.

IER
Incremental Energy Rate.

IHR
Incremental Heat Rate.

Imbalance, Electric
Occurs when the generation and interchange schedules do not match demand.

Imbalance, Gas
A discrepancy between a transporter's receipts and deliveries of natural gas for a shipper. Most pipelines require that a shipper's deliveries to the pipeline and receipts from the pipeline remain in balance over a given period of time or the pipeline may assess charges until the imbalance is cured.

Imbalance Penalties
Penalties implemented by a pipeline to provide an incentive for shippers to maintain actual receipts and deliveries at nominated and confirmed levels.

Impairment or Asset Impairment
Impairment or asset impairment occurs when, due to changed circumstances, the previously allowed recovery of costs of a regulatory asset through rates is eliminated or removed by action of a regulatory body.

Impedance
The opposition in an electrical circuit to the flow of alternating current (AC). The ratio of electromotive force to the effective currenl.The ratio of voltage-variation vs current-variation when an AC signal flows in an electrical circuit of unknown resistance and reactance. With regard to batteries this is the change of battery terminal voltage as a function of current flow either into or out-of the battery. Forces which resist current flow in A.C. circuits, i.e. resistance, inductive reactance, capacitive reactance.

Impulse Turbine
A turbine that is driven by high velocity jets of water or steam from a nozzle directed to vanes or buckets attached to a wheel. (A pelton wheel is an impulse hydro turbine).
Impulse turbines produce power when a jet of water from an enclosed diversion pipeline 'shoots' through a small nozzle directly onto the

turbine runner. Impulse turbines are best for 'high head' sites (with 20 feet of head or more), but they do not require vey high flow rates. Pelton and Turgo turbines are two of the most common impulse turbine families.

Imprudence
In the context of FERC rate methodology, a determination that certain of a pipeline's costs have not been prudently incurred, with the result that the pipeline is prohibited from placing such costs in its rates. See PRUDENT INVESTMENT.

Impulse
See TRANSIENT

Imputed
In the context of FERC rate methodology, an arbitrarily attributed, rather than actual value.

Inadvertent Energy Balancing
A control area's accounting of its inadvertent interchange. Adjacent control areas must agree on these values daily. The difference is repaid usually with energy, not money.

Inadvertent Interchange
The accumulated difference between the control area's net actual interchange and net scheduled interchange.

Incandescent
These lights use an electrically heated filament to produce light in a vacuum or inert gas-filled bulb.

Incentive Rates
Rates which permit increased profits as a reward for increases in cost savings and efficiencies.

Incoming Breaker
The customer-owned breaker which connects Xcel Energy source of power to the Customer's bus.

Independent System Operator (ISO)
An organization that operates an electric-transmission system that it does not own. Usually, the transmission system it operates includes transmission lines owned by more than one electric utility. An ISO's responsibilities include insuring that there is enough generation available at all times so that if one generating plant fails, others will pick up the load immediately without interrupting service to customers.Electric transmission systems do not have valves that can control the flow of

electricity over the transmission lines. Therefore, an ISO operates the transmission system by controlling the amount of electricity that is generated at each point in the transmission system so that the transmission lines do not become over loaded. The abbreviation ISO sometimes refers to any ISO, and sometimes to refers to the California Independent System Operator.

Independent Power Producer
A company or individual that is not directly regulated as a power provider. These entities produce power for their own use and/or sell it to regulated power providers.

Indirect Solar Gain System
A passive solar heating system in which the sun warms a heat storage element, and the heat is distributed to the interior space by convection, conduction, and radiation.

Indirect Solar Water Heater
These systems circulate fluids other than water (such as diluted antifreeze) through the collector. The collected heat is transferred to the household water supply using a heat exchanger. Also known as "closed-loop" systems.

Inductance
The ability of a coil to store energy and oppose changes in current flowing through it. A function of the cross sectional area, number of turns of coil, length of coil and core material.

Induction
The production of an electric current in a conductor by the variation of a magnetic field in its vicinity.

Induction Generator
A device that converts the mechanical energy of rotation into electricity based on electromagnetic induction. An electric voltage (electromotive force) is induced in a conducting loop (or coil) when there is a change in the number of magnetic field lines (or magnetic flux) passing through the loop. When the loop is closed by connecting the ends through an external load, the induced voltage will cause an electric current to flow through the loop and load. Thus rotational energy is converted into electrical energy.

Induction Motor
A motor in which a three phase (or any multiphase) alternating current (i.e. the working current) is supplied to iron-cored coils (or windings) within the stator. As a result, a rotating magnetic field is set up, which

induces a magnetizing current in the rotor coils (or windings). Interaction of the magnetic field produced in this manner with the rotating field causes rotational motion to occur.

Industrial Process Heat
The thermal energy used in an industrial process.

Inductor
(Also called "choke") - A coiled conductor which tends to oppose any change in the flow of current. Usually has coils wrapped around ferrous core.

Inert Gas
A gas that does not react with other substances; e.g. argon or krypton; sealed between two sheets of glazing to decrease the U-value (increase the R-Value) of windows.

In-Lieu Energy
Energy exchanged between a reservoir owner and the owner of a downstream project. The agreement allows reservoir owners to retain water above a reservoir's energy content curve; however, owners of downstream projects may request release of such water. Upstream project owners must then release the water or provide an amount of energy in lieu of the release equal to the amount of energy which could have been generated downstream had the release been made.

Inrush Current
The initial surge current demand before the load resistance or impedance increases to its normal operating value.

Insolation
The amount of energy in sunlight reaching an area. Usually expressed in watts per square meter (W/m^2), but also expressed on a daily basis as watts per square meter per day (W/m^2/day). Incident solar radiation (irradiation),or the level of intensity of energy from the sun that strikes the earth. Usually given as watts per square metre (W/m^2). A common peak level in Australia in summer is about $1000W/m^2$.

Installed Capacity
The total capacity of generation units installed at a power station.

Installed power
Power delivered by a photovoltaic module or a photovoltaic array, under standard test conditions (irradiance of 1 000 W/m^2, cell junction temperature of 25°C, AM1,5 solar spectrum). Also said STC output power. Unit: W.

Insulation
Any material that provides high resistance to the flow of heat, sound or electricity from on surface or area to another.

Intake
The point at which water is diverted from a river or stream to the turbine via a diversion. A trash rack/filter and settling tank are often installed at the intake point to prevent debris and sand or silt from reaching the turbine.

Integrated Resource Plan (IRP)
A plan developed by an electric power provider, sometimes as required by a public regulatory commission or agency, that defines the short and long term capacity additions (supply side) and demand side management programs that it will undertake to meet projected energy demands.

Interconnector
A connection or link between power systems that enables them to draw on each other's reserve capacity in time of need.

Interconnection Agreement
An agreement made between the system operator and an externally interconnected system operator and/or an interconnector user relating to an external interconnection and/or an agreement under which an interconnector user can use an external interconnection.

Intermittent Generators
Power plants, whose output depends on a factor(s) that cannot be controlled by the power generator because they utilize intermittent resources such as solar energy or the wind.

Internal Combustion Electric Power Plant
The generation of electric power by a heat engine which converts part of the heat generated by combustion of the fuel into mechanical motion to operate an electric generator.

Internal Gain
The heat produced by sources of heat in a building (occupants, appliances, lighting, etc).

Internal Mass
Materials with high thermal energy storage capacity contained in or part of a building's walls, floors, or freestanding elements.

Internal Rate of Return
A widely used rate of return for performing economic analysis. This

method solves for the interest rate that equates the equivalent worth of an alternative's cash receipts or savings to the equivalent worth of cash expenditures, including investments. The resultant interest rate is termed the internal rate of return (IRR).

Interruptible Load
Energy loads that can be shut off or disconnected at the supplier's discretion or as determined by a contractual agreement between the supplier and the customer.

Intertie
A transmission line that links two or more regional electric power systems.

Intert ripping
The tripping of circuit-breakers by commands initiated from protection at a remote location independent of the state of the local protection.

Inter-zonal
Between different zones.

Inch of Mercury
A pressure unit representing the pressure required to support a column of mercury one inch high; 2.036 inches of mercury is equal to one pound per square inch at sea level.

Inch of Water
A pressure unit representing the pressure required to support a column of water one inch high. Usually reported as inches W.C. (water column); 27.68 inches of water is equal to one pound per square inch.

Incremental Cost
The change in total costs when output is increased or decreased by an increment or block of output for which costs can be accurately determined, usually calculated as the change in cost divided by the change in volume (for example as cents per Mcf); marginal cost.

Incremental Energy Cost
Cost incurred by producing or purchasing next available unit of energy (gas, electricity, oil, coal, etc.).

Incremental Heat Rate
Efficiency of a plant in producing the next increment of additional output. Expressed in Btu/kWh.

Indefinite Price Escalator
Contract provision that allows for future price adjustments that cannot

be determined when the contract is executed; e.g., area rate clause, most favored nations clause.

Independent Power Producer
A non-utility power generating entity, defined by the 1978 Public Utility Regulatory Policies Act, that typically sells the power it generates to electric utilities at wholesale prices.

Independent System Operator - ISO
The independent system operator (ISO) has been granted the authority by multiple utilities to operate in a non-discriminatory manner all the transmission assets of a fixed geographic area.

Index
A measure of relative value attached to a specific commodity or group of commodities or stocks. An index option is an option contract based on an index instead of an individual stock or commodity. A measure of market trends.

Indexing
Tying the commodity price of gas in a contract to published prices.

Industrial Bypass
A situation in which large industrial customers buy power directly from a non-utility generator, bypassing the local utility system. Deregulation of generation and transmission in some instances has opened up the opportunity for large electricity users to purchase services from a supplier other than the local retail utility.

Industrial Customer
The industrial customer is generally defined as manufacturing, construction, mining, agriculture, fishing and forestry establishments, Standard Industrial Classification (SIC) codes 01-39. The utility may classify industrial service using the SIC codes, or based on demand or annual usage exceeding some specified limit. The limit may be set by the utility based on the rate schedule of the utility.

Infill Drilling
Drilling between existing well locations for the purpose of increasing reserves or productive capacity.

Injected Gas
Natural gas placed in underground storage or returned to the producing reservoir to maintain pressure.

Input Rating
The designed rate of fuel acceptance by a burner.

Input/Output Test
The periodic testing that generating units undergo to establish their efficiency (heat rate) at various loadings or operating outputs.

Installed Capacity
The measure of a power station's electric generating capacity at full production, usually measured in megawatts (MW).

Instantaneous Demand
Rate of energy use at any given instant.

Instantaneous Service
The ability to change deliveries on a pipeline simultaneously with a change in nominations on the same business day.

Integrated Demand
Average of instantaneous demands over a time interval.

Integrated Gas Company
A company that obtains significant portions of its natural gas revenues from the operations of both a retail natural gas distribution system and a natural gas transmission system.

Integrated Resource Planning (IRP)
A public planning process and framework within which the costs and benefits of both demand and supply side resources are evaluated to develop the least total cost mix of utility resource options. In many states, IRP includes a means for considering environmental damages caused by electricity supply/transmission and identifying cost effective energy efficiency and renewable energy alternatives. IRP has become a formal process prescribed by law in some states and under some provisions of the Clean Air Act Amendments of 1992.

Interchange (or transfer)
The net of all power flows across the tie lines of a given control area or the net of all power flows between two adjacent control areas.

Interchange Arrangement
The process of finding a seller and buyer for an interchange transaction, plus reserving transmission and Interconnected Operations Services.

Interchange Energy Agreements
Interchange energy agreements assure all parties an equal ability to serve their firm loads. If a party cannot meet its load in a given month, that party has the right to request interchange energy from another that has a surplus. The party with excess is obligated to meet the request. The price

of interchange energy is set by parties to the agreement.

Interchange Schedule
The planned energy interchange between control areas. It is the algebraic sum of all interchange transactions between two control Areas

Interchange Transaction
An agreement, arranged by purchasing-selling entities' merchant function, to transfer energy from a point of receipt to a point of delivery.

Interconnected Operations Services (IOS)
Services offered on a voluntary basis by transmission providers to transmission customers in addition to ancillary services.

Interconnected System
A system which has two or more power systems normally operating in synchronism and having connecting tie lines.

Interconnection
When this term is capitalized (Interconnection), any one of the four synchronized bulk electric system networks in North American Electric Reliability Council: Eastern, Western, ERCOT and Quebec, which are only connected through DC ties. When this term is not capitalized (interconnection), the facilities that connect two systems or control areas.

Interface
The direct interconnections between two areas or between two areas comprising one or more electrical systems.

Intermediary Control Area
A control area with connecting facilities in the scheduling path between the sending and receiving control areas and operating agreements that establish the conditions for the use of such facilities.

Intermediate Capacity
Capacity designed to operate less hours than baseload but more than peaking capacity (typically 20% -60%).

Intermediate Load (Electric System)
The range from base load to a point between base load and peak. This point may be the midpoint, a percent of the peakload or the load over a specified time period.

Intermediate load plant
Intermediate-load generating units meet system requirements that are greater than base load but less than peak load. Intermediate-load

generating units are used during the transition between baseload and peak load requirements.

Internal Combustion Plant

A plant in which the prime mover is an internal combustion engine. An internal combustion engine has one or more cylinders in which the process of combustion takes place, converting energy released from the rapid burning of a fuel-air mixture into mechanical energy. Diesel or gas-fired engines arc the principal types used in electric plants. The plant is usually operated during emergencies or periods of exceptionally high demand for electricity.

Interruptible Demand (Customer)

The magnitude of customer demand that, in accordance with contractual arrangements, can be interrupted by direct control of the system operator, remote tripping or by action of the customer at the direct request of the system operator.

Interruptible Gas

Gas sold to customers with a provision that permits curtailment or cessation of service at the discretion of the supplier under certain circumstances, as specified in the sendee contract.

Interruptible Load

Demand that can be interrupted by direct action of the supplying system's system operator in accordance with contractual provisions at times of seasonal peak load. It usually involves commercial and industrial consumers. In some instances, the load reduction may be affected by direct action of the system operator (remote tripping) after notice to the consumer in accordance with contractual provisions. For example, loads that can be interrupted to fulfill planning or operation reserve requirements should be reported as Interruptible Load. Interruptible Load as defined here includes Direct Load Control and Other Load Management.

Intertie

A transmission line that links two or more regional electric power systems.

Intrastate Market

The market for natural gas consumed in the same state as it is produced, without the natural gas having been transported by an interstate pipeline.

Intrastate Pipeline

A natural gas pipeline company that is engaged in the transportation of natural gas not subject to the FERC jurisdiction under the NGA.

Intra-zonal
Within the same zone.

Inverted Block Rate (Graduated Rate)
A rate structure that prices successive blocks of power use at increasingly higher per-unit prices. The more energy a customer uses, the greater the average price.

Inverter
A device, usually electronic, to change direct current to alternating current. A device used to change DC into AC power. An electronic device that converts DC power into AC power at standard mains voltage (240 V) and frequency (50 Hz). There are different basic types of inverters, including sine wave and modified square-wave inverters. Some inverters incorporate added facilities for automatic operation of diesel system and monitoring.

Investor-Owned Utility (IOU)
A utility organized under state law as a publicly traded corporation for the purpose of providing electric power service and earning a profit for its stockholders. Those electric utilities organized as tax-paying businesses usually financed by the sale of securities in the free market, and whose properties are managed by representatives regularly elected by their shareholders. Investor-owned electric utilities, which may be owned by an individual proprietor or a small group of people, are usually corporations owned by the general public.

Interconnected System
A system consisting of two or more individual power systems connected together by tie lines.

Interconnection
The physical system of electrical transmission between the Customer's generation and the utility.

Interruptible Load
Refers to a contractual arrangement in which a customer's energy load can be interrupted at times of seasonal peak load by direct control of the utility system operator, or by action of the customer at the direct request of the system operator. This usually involves commercial and industrial customers.

Interrupting Capacity
The amount of current a switch, fuse, or circuit breaker can safely interrupt.

Interruption
A temporary discontinuance of the supply of electric power.

Intertie (Interutility Tieline)
Transmission circuit used to tie or inter-connect two load areas of two utility systems.

Investor Owned Utility (IOU)
A utility organized under state law as a publicly traded corporation for the purposes of providing power service and earning a profit for its stakeholders.

Inverted Block Rate
A rate structure that prices successive blocks of power use at increasingly higher per-unit prices. The more electricity a customer uses, the greater the average price.

Inverter
A device that converts direct current electricity (from for example a solar photovoltaic module or array) to alternating current for use directly to operate appliances or to supply power to a electricity grid.

Ionizer
A device that removes airborne particles from breathable air. Negative ions are produced and give up their negative charge to the particles. These new negative particles are then attracted to the positive particles surrounding them. This accumulation process continues until the particles become heavy enough to fall to the ground.

IPP
Independent Power Producer. An organization, which is not a utility, that operates a power plant, produces energy and then sells it to a utility.

Irregular Bill
A bill covering service for a period less than or in excess of the regular billing cycle.

Island
A part of an interconnected system may be isolated during a system disturbance and start operating as a subsystem with its own generation, transmission and distribution capability. Then the subsystem becomes an island of the main interconnected system without a tie. In such a case, the islanded system and the main interconnected system will operate at different frequencies and voltages. A part of one or more power systems electrically separated from the main grid as a result of the tripping of transmission system elements.

ISO

Independent System Operator. ISOs operate, but do not own, transmission systems. On an hour-by-hour basis, the ISO plays traffic cop for buyers and sellers using energy transmission systems. Because power takes the route of least resistance and pays no attention to company boundaries, all providers transmitting energy affect each other when energy flows over transmission lines. Several large transactions taking place simultaneously can cause reliability problems for companies in the middle. An independent organization with jurisdictional control is supposed to avoid bottlenecks or other problems – and ensure some measure of reliability.

Isolation

The disconnection of HV apparatus from the remainder of the system in which that HV apparatus is situated.

Isolation Transformer

A multiple winding transformer with primary and secondary windings physically separated and designed to permit magnetic coupling between isolated circuits while minimizing electrostatic coupling. See also "electrostatic shield".

Itemized Service

Charges for electric service broken down into its basic components, including generation, transmission, distribution, billing and metering services

J K L

Jacket

The enclosure on a water heater, furnace, or boiler

Joule

s A watt/second. A measurement of work in time. 1 joule equals 0.0002778 watt/hours. 1 kilowatt hour is equivalent to 3,600,000 joules.

Kaplan Turbine

A type of turbine that has two blades whose pitch is adjustable. The turbine may have gates to control the angle of the fluid flow into the blades

Kerosene

A type of heating fuel derived by refining crude oil that has a boiling range at atmospheric pressure from 400 degrees to 550 degrees F. A unit of apparent power, equal to 1,000 volt-amperes; the mathematical product of the volts and amperes in an electrical circuit.

Kilovolt (kV)
One thousand volts.

Kilovolt-Ampere (kVA)
One thousand volt amperes. See the definition for Apparent Power.

Kilowatt (kW)
An electric unit of power which equals 1,000 watts. A unit of power, usually used for electric power (equal to 1000 watts), or the consumption of energy (at a rate of 1000 joules per second). A standard unit of electrical power equal to one thousand watts, or to the energy consumption at a rate of 1000 Joules per second.

Kilowatthour (kWh)
One thousand watts of power supplied for one hour. A basic unit of electric energy equal to the use of 1 kilowatt for a period of one hour. The amount or work or energy delivered during the steady consumption of 1 kilowatt of power for a period of one hour. A household that uses an average of one kWh for every hour over an average month would be billed by the utility for 730 kWh for that average month. A unit or measure of electricity supply or consumption of 1,000 Watts over the period of one hour; equivalent to 3,412 Btu.

Kilowatt-year (kW-Y)
A unit of electrical capacity demanded for 8760 hours.

Kinetic Energy
Energy available as a result of motion that varies directly in proportion to an object's mass and the square
of its velocity.

Kneewall
A wall usually about 3 to 4 feet high located that is placed in the attic of a home, anchored with plates between the attic floor joists and the roof joist. Sheathing can be attached to these walls to enclose an attic space.

Lagging Load
An inductive load with current lagging voltage. Since inductors tend to resist changes in current, the current flow through an inductive circuit will lag behind the voltage. The number of electrical degrees between voltage and current is known as the "phase angle". The cosine of this angle is equal to the power factor (linear loads only).

Lagging Power Factor
Occurs when reactive power flows in the same direction as real power.

Lamp
A light source composed of a metal base, a glass tube filled with an inert gas or a vapor, and base pins to attach to a fixture.

Leading Power Factor
Occurs when reactive power flows in the opposite direction of real power.

Lambda (I)
The measure of the rate at which fuel is consumed relative to electric output, expressed in Btu's per kWh.

Lateral
A pipe that branches away from the central and primary part of the system.

LC Circuit
An electrical network containing both inductive and capacitive elements.

Lead Acid Battery
An electrochemical battery that uses lead and lead oxide for electrodes and sulfuric acid for the electrolyte.

Leading Edge
In reference to a wind energy conversion system, the area of a turbine blade surface that first comes into contact with the wind. The edge of a blade that faces toward the direction of rotation.

Leading Load
A capacitive load with current leading voltage. Since capacitors resist changes in voltage, the current flow in a capacitive circuit will lead the voltage.

Leaking Electricity
Related to stand-by power, leaking electricity is the power needed for electrical equipment to remain ready for use while in a dormant mode or operation. Electricity is still used by many electrical devices, such as TVs, stereos, and computers, even when you think they are turned "off."

Lease
Any instrument that gives a producer the right to drill for, produce and dispose of oil and natural gas in, under and from the lands described therein.

Least Cost Alternatives
The lowest cost option for providing for incremental demands. In least cost planning to serve electric demands, the least cost alternatives are

often construed broadly to include demand-side management as well as various generation and purchased power options.

Leeward
Away from the direction from which the wind blows. *See also: Airfoil, Windward*

Levelized Life-Cycle Cost
The present value of the cost of a resource, including capital, financing and operating costs, converted into a stream of equal annual payments.

Leverage Ratio
The ratio of total debt to total assets: i.e. a measure that indicates the financial ability to meet debt service requirements.

Liability
An amount payable in dollars or by future services to be rendered.

Life Line Rates
A charge for a specified basic block of residential electricity followed by a higher rate for use beyond that block. Such rates are to assure that certain categories of customers have enough electricity for basic uses.

Lift
The force exerted by moving air on asymmetrically-shaped wind generator blades at right angles to the direction of relative movement. Ideally, wind generator blades should produce high Lift and low Drag

Light-Handed Regulation
Regulatory approval of rate levels resulting from arm's length negotiations, rather than calculated on a cost of service basis, and subject to challenge only under a complaint proceeding.

Light Load Hours
Generally speaking, the term for that time of day on a system that could be considered off peak. Actual hours will vary with each power system.

Light Oil
Lighter fuel oils distilled off during the refining process. Virtually all petroleum used in internal combustion and turbine engines is light oil.

Lignite
Low-rank, brown coals which are distinctly brown and woody or claylike in appearance, and which contain relatively high moisture contents of between 30 and 70 percent of the fuel by weight. Sulfur may range from low to high and heating value may range from 3,500 to 7,000 Btu/lb.

Limit
In a futures trading session, the maximum advance or decline in a futures price.

Limit Order
A contingent order in futures trading specifying a maximum or minimum price.

Limiting Element
The device in a system that has the lowest energy rating, thereby setting the maximum amount of energy that can be transferred.

Linear Load
A load in which the current relationship to voltage is constant based on a relatively constant load impedance.

Line Conditioner
An electrical device designed to reduce electrical noise and provide constant output voltage.

Line Loss
The reduction in the quantity of natural gas flowing through a pipeline that results from leaks, venting and other physical and operational circumstances on a pipeline system. Electrical energy converted to heat in the resistance of all transmission and/or distribution lines and other electrical equipment.

Line Pack and Draft
Packing the line increases the amount of gas in the system by adding gas and/or increasing pressure and drafting the line decreases the amount of gas in the system by decreasing gas and/or decreasing pressure.

Line Imbalance
Unequal loads on the phase lines of a multiphase feeder.

Liquid-Based Solar Heating System
A solar heating system that uses a liquid as the heat transfer fluid.

Liquid-To-Air Heat Exchanger
A heat exchanger that transfers the heat contained in a liquid heat transfer fluid to air.

Liquid-To-Liquid Heat Exchanger
A heat exchanger that transfers heat contained in a liquid heat transfer fluid to another liquid.

Liquidation
The closing of futures positions.

Liquefied Natural Gas (LNG)
Natural gas which has been changed into a liquid by cooling to approximately -160°C.

Liquefied Petroleum Gas (LPG)
Principally propane and butane, it is a gas which turns to a liquid at normal room temperature and moderate pressure.

Liquidity
A high level of trading activity.

Liquids, Natural Gas
Those liquid hydrocarbon mixtures that are gases at reservoir temperatures and pressures, but can be recovered by condensation or absorption. Natural gasoline and liquefied petroleum gases fall in this category.

Lithium-Sulfur Battery
A battery that uses lithium in the negative electrode and a metal sulfide in the positive electrode, and the electrolyte is molten salt; can store large amounts of energy per unit weight.

Load
The amount of electric power delivered or required at any specific point or points on a system. The requirement originates at the energy-consuming equipment of the consumer.The driven device that uses the power supplied from the source. A term that is sometimes used to refer to the cumulative electric demand of a geographic area, such as a city or an electric utility. It is measured in megawatts. The total amount of electricity required to meet customer demand at any moment. The load equation fluctuates depending on electricity use throughout any given day. The amount of electric power delivered or required at any specific point or points on a system. The requirement originates at the energy-consuming equipment of the consumers. The load of an electric utility system is affected by many factors and changes on a daily, seasonal and annual basis, typically following a pattern. Electric System load is usually measured in megawatts (MW). Also, to "load" a governor is to set the governor to maintain a given pressure as the rate of gas flow through the governor varies. Compare DEMAND. The power and energy requirements of users on the electric power system in a designated area. Any electrical device that uses power supplied by the source.

Load Analysis
Assessing and quantifying the discrete components that comprise a load.

This analysis often includes time of day or season as a variable.

Load Balancing
Switching the various loads on a multi-phase feeder to equalize the current in each line.

Load Building
Refers to programs that are aimed at increasing the usage of existing electric equipment or the addition of electric equipment.

Load Centers
A geographical area where large amounts of power are drawn by end-users.

Load Curve
A curve of power versus time showing the level of a load for each time period covered.

Load Cycle
Time period spanning one peak load.

Load Density
The concentration of natural gas load for a given area expressed as an amount of natural gas per unit of time and per unit of area.

Load Duration Curve
A curve of loads, plotted in descending order of magnitude, against time intervals for a specified period. The curve indicates the period of time load was above certain magnitude. Load duration curves are profiles of system demand that can be drawn for specified periods of time (e.g., daily, monthly, yearly). The coordinates may be absolute quantities or percentages. A curve that displays load values on the horizontal axis in descending order of magnitude against the percent of time (on the vertical axis) that the load values are exceeded.

Load Factor
The ratio of the average load during a designated period to the peak or maximum load in that same period. Usually expressed in per cent. The ratio of average load to peak load during a specific period of time, expressed as a percent. The load factor indicates to what degree energy has been consumed compared to maximum demand or the utilization of units relative to total system capability. An electric system's load factor shows the variability in all customers' demands.The ratio of the average load in kilowatts supplied during a designated period to the peak or maximum load in kilowatts occurring in that period. Load factor, in percent, also may be derived by multiplying the kilowatthours in the

period by 100 and dividing by the product of the maximum demand in kilowatts and the number of hours in the period.

Load Fault
A malfunction that causes the load to demand abnormally high amounts of current from the source.

Load Following
An electric system's or plant's ability to regulate its generation to follow the instantaneous changes in its customers' demand. Planning by utilities to ensure that electric generators operate as scheduled, based upon load forecasts (also, operating a generator to balance short-term load fluctuations)

Load Forecast
The anticipated amount of electricity required by customers in the future.

Load Leveling
The deferment of certain loads to limit electrical power demand, or the production of energy during off-peak periods for storage and use during peak demand periods.

Load Management
The management of load patterns in order to better utilize the facilities of the system. Generally, load management attempts to shift load from peak-use periods to other periods of the day or year. To influence the demand on a power source.

Load pocket
A concentration of load (i.e. demand) isolated from the balance of the electrical system by transmission constraints (i.e. congestion). Load pockets typically produce higher prices.

Load Profile or Shape
A curve on a chart showing power (kW) supplied (on the horizontal axis) plotted against time of occurrence (on the vertical axis) to illustrate the variance in a load in a specified time period.

Load Regulation
A term used to describe the effects of low forward transfer impedance. A power conditioner with "load regulation" may not have voltage regulation. Removing the power conditioner altogether will improve load regulation.

Load Response
Reducing electricity use from the grid during peak periods to increase reliability and moderate the energy-clearing price during system-wide

peak demand; reducing electric load or using qualifying emergency generators on the customer side of the meter

Load serving agreements
Arrangement to meet the energy demands within a control area on a real-time basis. Fulfilling this requirement mandates the procurement of energy supply on a 24-hour, 7-daya-week basis to follow or match the load or energy demand. Also referred to as load following.

Load Shape
The variation in the magnitude of the power load over a daily, weekly or annual period.

Load Shedding
Removal of pre-selected customer demand from a power system, as a result of the occurrence of an abnormal condition, in a effort to maintain the integrity of the system and minimize overall customer outages. Turning off or disconnecting loads to limit peak demand.

Load Shifting
A load management objective that moves loads from on-peak periods to off-peak periods.DSM programs designed to shift load from on-peak times of the day to off-peak times.

Load Switching
Transferring the load from one source to another.

Load Unbalance
Unequal loads on the phase lines of a multi phase system.

Load Valley
A period of reduced load, as contrasted with peak load.

Local Distribution Company (LDC)
A company that obtains the major portion of its revenues from the operations of a retail distribution system for the delivery of electricity or gas for ultimate consumption.

Long (or long position)
The position of a party who has bought and is holding futures or options contracts or owns a commodity that has not been settled by sale or delivery.

Long Position
A position of a futures contract buyer which requires the buyer to accept a delivery unless the contract is liquidated with an offsetting sale.

Long Run Marginal Costs
All costs associated with the lowest cost incremental unit including variable production costs, fixed O&M
and capital costs.

Longwall Miner
A deep mining machine that uses a steel plow or rotating drum, which is pulled mechanically back-and-forth across a long face of coal. The loosened coal falls onto a conveyor for removal from the mine.

Longwall Mining
An underground mining process in which a panel or block of coal is completely extracted.

Lookback Option
An option that allows the buyer the right, retroactively to buy (sell) the underlying commodity or security at its minimum (maximum) price within the lookback period.

Loop
An electrical circuit that provides two sources of power to a load or substation so that if one source is deenergized the remaining source continues to provide power

Loop Flow
The tendency of electricity to flow along the path of least resistance, which may not necessarily be the same as that intended in the contract between the two transmitting entities. If power sold along a contractual path utilizes a different physical path, the power-flow may interfere with control of the systems which were unaware of the contractual power transfer.

Looping
Laying additional pipeline beside and connected to an existing pipeline in order to increase the capacity of the system.

Loss of Load Probability (LOLP)
A measure of expectation that system demand will exceed capacity during a given period, often expressed as the expected number of days per year (e.g., one day in ten years).

Loss Supply
An ancillary service where the wheeling utility provides supplemental power to compensate for losses incurred in the power system during transmission.

Lot
The standard unit of futures trading specifying a definite quantity of the commodity of uniform grade.

Low-Pressure Sodium Lamp
A type of lamp that produces light from sodium gas contained in a bulb operating at a partial pressure of 0.13 to 1.3 Pascal. The yellow light and large size make them applicable to lighting streets and parking lots.

Low Voltage
In relation to alternating current, a voltage exceeding 50 volts measured between phase conductors (or between phase conductors and earth), but not exceeding 1000 volts measured between phase conductors (or 600 volts if measured between phase conductors and earth).

LP Gas-Air Mixture
Mixture of liquefied petroleum gas and air to obtain a desired Btu value, capable of being distributed through a distribution system; also used for standby and peak shaving by natural gas utilities.

LVD
Low Voltage Disconnect - A module usually intended for the disconnection of a battery from its load under conditions of extended discharge, to prevent irreparable damage to the battery.

M

Magnetic Field
A field of force around a magnet's poles or around a wire carrying an electric current.

Magnetic Synthesizer
A three-phase ferroresonant based system with zigzag output windings to allow the Ferro to handle unbalanced loads.

Main Protection
Protection equipment or system expected to have priority in initiating either a fault clearance or an action to terminate an abnormal condition in a power system.

Main Service Entrance
The enclosure containing connection panels and switchgear, located at the point where the utility power lines enter a building.

Make-Before-Break
Operational sequence of a switch or relay where the new connection is made prior to disconnecting the existing connection.

MAPP

Mid-Continent Area Power Pool: a NERC (North American Electric Reliability Council) region. An organization of power suppliers in the Upper Midwest that plans for power availability by coordinating power exchanges between members. MAPP's current 41 members include investor-owned companies such as Xcel Energy, municipal systems, rural cooperatives and the federal Missouri Basin hydroelectric system.

Margin

The difference between net capacity (a system's total capacity resources) and net internal demand, that is generally expressed in MW for operating reserves and as a percentage of cither system load or installed generating capacity for planning reserves

Marginal Cost

The cost of providing additional electricity; "The competitive price of a MWh of electricity is equal to the additional amount it would cost to generate an additional MWh, once all current demand is met. This additional cost is commonly referred to as the marginal cost. The marginal cost of generating electricity rises as more electricity is produced, because different generators use different types and amounts of fuel... .under competition, the rising marginal cost of electricity leads to high prices when demand is high and low prices during low-demand periods."

Mechanical Drive

Mechanical Drive refers to those applications requiring variable speed power equipment to drive gas compressors, gas/oil re-injectors, etc.

MEGA(M)

A metric prefix meaning 1,000,000 or 106.

Megawatt (MW)

A unit of electrical power equal to 1000 kilowatts or one million watts. One million watts. Standard measure of generating plant capacity equal to one thousand kilowatts, or one million watts. Medium to large power stations have capacity typically in the range of 500 MW to 2,000 MW.

Megawatt-Hour (MWh)

One thousand kilowatt-hours.

Mercury Vapor Lamp

A high-intensity discharge lamp that uses mercury as the primary light-producing element. Includes clear, phosphor coated, and self-ballasted lamps.

Metal Halide Lamp

A high-intensity discharge lamp type that uses mercury and several halide additives as light-producing elements. These lights have the best Color Rendition Index (CRI) of the High-Intensity Discharge lamps. They can be used for commercial interior lighting or for stadium lights.

Metal Oxide Varistor (MOV)
A MOV is a voltage sensitive breakdown device which is commonly used to limit overvoltage conditions (electrical surges) on power and data lines. When the applied voltage exceeds the breakdown point, the resistance of the MOV decreases from a very high level (thousands of ohms) to a very low level (a few ohms). The actual resistance of the device is a function of the rate of applied voltage and current.

Meter
Used at your home or other buildings to measure and record the amount of electricity used at that site.

Methane
A colourless, odourless, flammable gas and the main constituent of natural gas. It has been identified as a greenhouse gas.

MIL
A unit of length equal to one-thousandth, 10-3 of an inch.

Micro (U)
A metric prefix meaning one millionth of a unit or 10-6.

Micro **Hydro**
Hydro power systems with a power output of less than lOOkW.

Micron
A metric term meaning one millionth of a meter.

Milli (M)
A metric prefix meaning one thousandth of a unit or 10-3.

Mimic Board
A switchgear or control panel, or an assembly consisting of a single-line diagram of the main connections of a system constructed on the face, with instruments, switches, or status lights mounted in appropriate locations

Modem
A modem is a contraction of modulator-demodulator. The device is used to connect data equipment to a communication line. Modems are commonly used to connect computer equipment to telephone lines.

Molecule
Atoms combined to form the smallest natural unit of an element or compound.

Momentary Parallel
See Closed Transition Transfer

Motor
A machine which converts electrical energy into mechanical energy or which does work.

Mounting structure
With the rapid growth of grid-connected distributed systems, a wide range of products have been developed for installing PV modules on buildings. These include mounting structures for PV facades, roof profiles, flat roofs and even 'PV tiles' that can be used to replace conventional roof tiles. New products are addressing the need for ease of integration into the building envelope and aesthetic appeal.

MPPT
Maximum Power Point Tracker - An electronic device that enables the most efficient use of the power generated through solar arrays.

MTBF
(Mean Time Between Failure) the probable length of time that a component taken from a particular batch will survive if operated under the same conditions as a sample from the same batch.

MTTR
Mean Time To Repair.

Municipal Solid Waste (MSW)
Waste material that is collected from homes and businesses. Waste materials from industrial processes that are not considered safe to place into landfills are not allowed to become MSW, and recycled materials are not included in MSW. MSW is referred to in common parlance as garbage.

N

Nacelle
The protective covering over a generator or motor

Naked in the Option
The owner of the option has no position in the underlying security or commodity.

Nameplate Capacity (or Installed Capacity)
The full-load continuous rating of a generator, prime mover or other electric power production equipment under specific conditions as designated by the manufacturer. Installed generator nameplate rating is usually indicated on a nameplate physically attached to the generator.

Nameplate Rating
The initial capability of a piece of electrical equipment as stated on the attached nameplate. Actual capability can vary from the nameplate rating due to age, wear, maintenance or ambient conditions.

Native Load
The requirements of a wholesale utility's local retail market.

Natural Cooling
Space cooling achieved by shading, natural (unassisted, as opposed to forced) ventilation, conduction control, radiation, and evaporation; also called passive cooling.

Natural Gas
A naturally occurring mixture of hydrocarbon and non-hydrocarbon gases found in porous geological formations beneath the earth's surface, often in association with petroleum. The principal constituent is methane, CH_4.

Natural Gasoline
Those liquid hydrocarbon mixtures containing substantial quantities of pentane and heavier hydrocarbons which have been extracted from natural gas.

Natural Monopoly
A situation where one firm can produce a given level of output at a lower total cost than can any combination of multiple firms. Natural monopolies occur in industries, which exhibit decreasing average long run costs due to size (economies of scale). According to economic theory, a public monopoly governed by regulation is justified when an industry exhibits natural monopoly characteristics.

Natural Ventilation
Ventilation that is created by the differences in the distribution of air pressures around a building. Air moves from areas of high pressure to areas of low pressure with gravity and wind pressure affecting the airflow. The placement and control of doors and windows alters natural ventilation patterns.

Need Study
An engineering study conducted by the Electric System Operator to

determine the required modifications to the grid, including the cost, that will be required to meet the need of customers on the transmission system.

Neighboring System
See ADJACENT SYSTEM.

Net Actual Generation (MWh)
Actual number of electrical megawatt-hours generated by the unit during the period being considered less any generation (MWh) utilized for that unit's station service or auxiliaries.

Net Availability Capacity
Gas Available Capacity less the unit capacity utilized for that unit's station service or auxiliaries.

Net-Back Price
The effective wellhead price to the producer of natural gas, based on the downstream market price for the natural gas less the charges for delivering the natural gas to market.

Net Benefit Test
In the context of ratemaking, an analysis to determine whether rolled-in or incremental rates for new construction benefit existing customers on a pipeline.

Net Capability
The maximum load-carrying ability of a power plant, exclusive of station use, under specified conditions
for a given time interval, independent of the characteristics of the load. Capability is determined by design
characteristics, physical conditions, adequacy of prime mover, energy supply and operating limitations such
as cooling and circulating water supply and temperature, headwater and tailwater elevations and electrical
use.

Net Capacity
Total Owned Capacity + Contractor Capacity Available from Independent Power Producers + Net of Total
Capacity Purchases and Sales - Sum of Inoperable Capacity and Planned Outage = Net Capacity.

Net Dependable Capacity
Maximum capacity sustained by a unit in a specified period modified for seasonal limitations and reduced by the capacity required for station service or auxiliaries.

Net Energy for Load (Control Area)
Net system generation plus Interchange received minus Interchange delivered.

Net Internal Demand
Metered Net Outputs of all Generators within a System + Metered Line Flows into the System - Metered
Line Flows out of the System - Direct Control Load Management - Interruptible Demand = Net Internal
Demand.

Net-metering
A form of buy-back agreement in which the grid-supplied house electricity meter turns or measures in the utility's favour when grid electric power is consumed by the house, and in the house owner's favour when the house's own generation exceeds its needs and electricity flows into the grid. At the end of the payment period, when the meter is read, the system owner pays the utility the difference between what the house consumed and what was supplied to the grid.

Net Position
In futures trading, the difference between the open long contracts and open short contracts relating to any one commodity.

Net
Maximum Capacity-Gross Maximum Capacity less the unit capacity utilized for that unit's station service or auxiliaries.

Net Settlement
A condition of a swap agreement that simplifies the settlement process by having the counterparty that
owes the larger amount pay the net of the larger and smaller gross obligations.

Net Summer Capability
The steady hourly output which generating equipment is expected to supply to system load exclusive of auxiliary power, as demonstrated by tests at the time of summer peak demand.

Net Winter Capability
The steady hourly output which generating equipment is expected to supply to system load exclusive of auxiliary power, as demonstrated by tests at the time of winter peak demand.

Netting Agreement
A provision in a swap contract that allows for the offset of settlement

payments and receipts on all contracts between the same two counterparties. Although not fully established, this provision is intended to limit default exposure to a counterparty.

Network

An interconnected system of electrical transmission lines, transformers, switches and other equipment connected together in such a way as to provide reliable transmission of electrical power from multiple generators to multiple load centers. A network implies redundancy provided through the use of multiple parallel flow paths.

Neutron

An unchanged elementary particle that has a mass nearly equal to that of a proton. Present in the nuclei of all known atoms except hydrogen.

Newton

The force required to change the velocity of a one-kilogram mass one metre per second in a period of one second. Corresponds approximately to 4.4 pounds offeree.

No-Bump Rule

Rule which protects a shipper with flowing gas from losing capacity (being bumped) by a higher priority shipper in the interruptible queue deciding to increase its gas volumes.

Nominal Voltage

The voltage standards recommended by manufacturers of electrical equipment and the electric utilities in the United States to assure that electrical equipment will be designed for the voltage range that will be encountered in actual use so that satisfactory operation of equipment will be obtained. The Nominal Standard Distribution Voltages are established by each company for service supplied to residential and commercial customers.

Nomination

A request for service under a service agreement.

Non-coincident Demand (NCD) or Non-coincident Peak Load

A customer's maximum energy demand during any stated period. Customers who use large quantities of electricity may pay a monthly demand charge based on their maximum electric demand during each month. This maximum demand in the electric industry can also be called a customer's monthly non-coincident demand.

Non-firm Electricity Transaction

These transactions are typically for short periods and subject to curtailment or cessation of delivery by the supplier or purchaser in accordance with prior agreements or under specified conditions. Non-firm sales are sometimes called economy or interruptible sales.

Non-firm Energy
Energy that is not guaranteed to be continuously available. Non-firm energy is available in varying amounts depending upon season and weather conditions.

Non-jurisdictional Sales
A direct sale by an interstate pipeline to an end-user over which the FERC has no jurisdiction, as contrasted with a pipeline's sale for resale in interstate commerce which is jurisdictional.

Non-operator
A working interest owner in a well or facility that is not the party designated to operate it.

No-notice Service
A pipeline delivery service which allows customers to receive gas on demand without making prior nominations to meet peak service needs and without paying daily balancing and scheduling penalties.

Non-performance
A contractual breach, such as contracted gas that is not delivered.

Non-recallable Available Transfer Capability (NATC)
Transmission Capability - Transmission Reliability Margin - Non-recallable Reserved Transmission Service = Non-recallable Available Transfer Capability.

Non-Renewable Resources
Energy resources which are depletable, for example, fossil fuels.

Non-Spinning Reserve
All unloaded generating capability not meeting the Spinning Reserve criteria that can be made fully effective in 10 minutes. This may include generation that shall be made available within 10 minutes by interrupting or curtailing loads or changing schedules. Generating units that are not connected to the system but are capable of coming on line within a specified time, or interruptible load that can be removed from the system in a specified time.

Non-utility Generator (NUG)
Facility for generating electricity that is not exclusively or primarily owned by an electric utility and which operates connected to an electric

utility system. Any entity not regulated by the government as a public utility that owns or operates a generating facility and offers electric power for sale to utilities or the public (also known as Independent Power Producer).

Non-utility Power Producer
A corporation, person, agency, authority or other legal entity or instrumentality that owns electric generating capacity and is not an electric utility. Non-utility power producers include qualifying cogenerators, qualifying small power producers and other non-utility generators (including independent power producers) without a designated franchised service area, and which do not file forms listed in the Code of Federal Regulations, Title 18, Part 141.

NOPR
Notice of Proposed Rule Making. A draft generic policy change promulgated by regulatory agencies.

Normal (Pre-Contingency) Operating Procedures
Operating procedures that are normal activities of a system operator to alleviate potential facility overloads or other potential system problems.

Normal Rating
The ratings as defined by the facility owner that specify the level of electrical loading (generally expressed in megawatts or other appropriate units) that a facility can support or withstand through the daily demand cycles without loss of equipment life of the facility or equipment involved.

Normal Recovery Capacity
A characteristic applied to domestic water heaters that is the amount of gallons raised 100 degrees Fahrenheit per hour (or minute) under a specified thermal efficiency.

Normal Voltage Limits
The operating voltage range on the interconnected systems, above or below nominal voltage and generally expressed in kilovolts, that is acceptable on a sustained basis.

Nuclear Fuel
Fissionable materials that have been enriched to such a composition that, when placed in a nuclear reactor, will support a self-sustaining fission chain reaction, producing heat in a controlled manner for process use.

Nuclear Power
Power released in exothermic (a reaction which gives off heat) nuclear

reactions which can be converted to electric power by means of heat transformation equipment and a turbine-generator unit.

Nuclear Power Plant
A facility in which heat produced in a reactor by the fissioning of nuclear fuel is used to drive a steam turbine.

Nuclear Reactor
A device in which a fission chain reaction can be initiated, maintained and controlled. Nuclear reactors are used in the power industry to produce steam for electricity.

Nucleus
The central part of an atom where most of the mass and all of the positive charge is concentrated.

O

OASIS (Open Access Same-time Information System)
An internet based system designed to allow all participants in the power market to obtain information concerning the capability and use of the transmission system in a non discriminatory manner. The new name of the Real-Time Information Network rule or "RINS." Required by FERC to be the only source of information on electric transmission capacity availability. For both affiliated transactions and outside entities.

Obligation to Serve
The obligation of a utility to provide electric service to any customer who seeks that service, and is willing to pay the rates set for that service. Traditionally, utilities have assumed the obligation to serve in return for an exclusive monopoly franchise.

Off-grid domestic photovoltaic power system
System installed in households and villages that are not connected to the utility grid. Usually, a means to store electricity is used (most commonly lead-acid battery). Also said "stand-alone photovoltaic power system".

Off-grid non-domestic photovoltaic power system
System used for a variety of applications such as water pumping, remote communications, telecommunication relays, safety and protection devices, etc. which are not connected to the utility grid. Usually a means to store electricity is used. Also said "stand-alone photovoltaic power system".

Off-Grid Power

Power or electricity generated outside the major supply distribution areas of a region or Territory. Diesel generators are the most common means of off-grid power generation in the Territory. In the Northern Territory the Power and Water Corporation supplies power through two separate power grids, one around Darwin and another around Alice Springs. Power and Water also provides electricity and other essential services to other major towns and over 80 remote and isolated communities in the Territory.

Off-Peak

Energy supplied during periods of relatively low demand. A period of time when there is a low demand for electricity on a utility's generation system. Period of low energy demand (load), as opposed to maximum or peak demand.

Off-Peak Gas

Natural gas supplied during periods of relatively low system demands.

Offset

The liquidation or closing out of an open contract position.

Offshore

Any area in the United States federal offshore, i.e. three miles or more offshore, except ten miles or more offshore Texas. A well may be located completely under state waters miles from land and still be classified as an onshore well.

Off-Site Power Mode

The mode of operation in which off-site power exclusively is used for facility operations.

Off-Site/On-Site Power Mode

The mode of operation allowing paralleling of off-site and on-site power supplies to permit transition of the system load from one to the other without power interruption or unacceptable perturbation

Off-System Sale

Sale by a pipeline to a customer other than one of its own traditional firm sales customers.

Off-System Supply

Natural gas supply purchased from other than the delivering pipeline or local distribution company. See SYSTEM SUPPLY.

Ohm

The practical unit of electrical impedance equal to the resistance of a circuit in which a potential difference of 1 volt produces a current of 1 ampere. The unit of measure of electrical resistance. One volt will force a current of one ampere through a resistance of one ohm. The unit of measurement for electrical resistance or opposition to current flow.

OHM'S Law
The relationship between voltage (pressure), current (electron flow), and resistance. The current in an electrical circuit is directly proportional to the voltage and inversely proportional to the resistance. E=IR, or I=E/R, or R=E/I. Where E=voltage, I=current, and R=resistance.

Oil, Heavy
Heavy, thick and viscous oils, particularly those found naturally in certain reservoirs in and around Kern County, California, and refinery residuals commonly specified as grades 5 and 6.

One Hundred Percent Load Factor
The circumstance in which a customer actually takes all of the service to which it is entitled during a specific period of time.

One-Line Diagram
A diagram in which several conductors are represented by a single line and in which various devices or pieces of equipment are denoted by simplified symbols. The purpose of such a diagram is to present an electrical circuit or circuits in a simple way so that their function can be readily grasped.

On-line -
A generating plant that is operating. When an operational plant is not on-line, it is "down."

ON-PEAK
A period of time when there is a high demand for electricity on a utility's generation system.

On-Peak Energy
Electricity supplied during a period of high system demands as specified by the supplier.

On-Site Power Mode
The mode of operation in which all power is generated by the on-site power supply system, and operational steps are taken to isolate the C4ISR power system from the outside operational environmentand the commercial power source.

Open Access
Non-discriminatory, fully equal access to transportation or transmission

services offered by a pipeline or electric utility. Ability to send or wheel electric power to a customer over a transmission and distribution system that is not owned by the generator of the power

Open-Circuit Voltage

The maximum possible voltage across a photovoltaic cell; the voltage across the cell in sunlight when no current is flowing. The voltage across a photovoltaic cell or module in sunlight when no current is flowing; the maximum possible voltage. Unit: V.

Open Contract, Interest or Commitment

Future(s) contracts during a given period of time which have not been satisfied by an offsetting sale or purchase or actual delivery.

Open-Loop Geothermal Heat Pump System

Open-loop (also known as "direct") systems circulate water drawn from a ground or surface water source. Once the heat has been transferred into or out of the water, the water is returned to a well or surface discharge (instead of being recirculated through the system). This option is practical where there is an adequate supply of relatively clean water, and all local codes and regulations regarding groundwater discharge are met.

Open Order

An order that is good until cancelled.

Open Outcry

Public auction with verbal bids in the trading pits.

Open Season

A period of time in which potential customers can bid for pipeline services, and during which such customers are treated equally regarding priority in the queue for service.

Open Transition Transfer

In this scheme, a customer's source of power is transferred from Source 1 to Source 2 and vice-versa without momentarily connecting the two sources together. Here, the Customer's load is interrupted momentarily during the transfer process through a mechanical or electrical interlock.

Operated by Others

A property in which a producer has an interest but of which it is not the operator.

Operable Nuclear Unit

A nuclear unit is "operable" after it completes low-power testing and is granted authorization to operate at Ml power. This occurs when it receives its full power amendment to its operating license from the Nuclear Regulatory Commission.

Operating Code
The portion of the grid code which is identified as the operating code.

Operating Cycle
The processes that a work input/output system undergoes and in which the initial and final states are identical.

Operating Head
The vertical distance that water drops to the tailrace to generate hydroelectric power, measured in feet.

Operating Procedures (contingency)
A set of written step-by-step practices or procedures that may be automatically implemented, or manually implemented by the system operator within a specified time frame, to maintain the operational integrity of the interconnected electric systems when specific anticipated contingencies occur. These actions or system adjustments may be implemented in anticipation of or following a system contingency (facility outage) or system disturbance, and include, among others, opening or closing switches (or circuit breakers) to change the system configuration, the redispatch of generation, and the implementation of Direct Control Load Management or Interruptible Demand programs.

Operating Reserve
The sum of Spinning and NonSpinning Reserve. The reserve generating capacity necessary to allow an electric system to recover from generation failures and provide for load following and frequency regulation. It consists of spinning and non-spinning reserves. The generating capability (spinning and non-spinning reserve) above firm system demand needed to provide for regulation, load forecasting errors, scheduled and unplanned equipment outages and local area protection.

Operating Security
The ability of a power system to withstand or limit the adverse effects of any credible contingency to the system including overloads beyond emergency ratings, excessive or inadequate voltage, loss of stability or abnormal frequency deviations.

Operating Security Limit
The value of a system operating parameter (e.g. total power transfer across an interface) that satisfies the most limiting of prescribed pre- and post-contingency operating criteria as determined by equipment loading capability and acceptable stability and voltage conditions.

Operational Balancing Agreements (OBAs)
Agreements between pipelines and parties at delivery or receipt points, whereby the parties agree to specified procedures for balancing discrepancies between the nominated levels of service and the actual quantities. The agreements specify gas custody transfer procedures for confirmation of scheduled quantities at specific points.

Operational Flow Orders (OFOs)
Orders which are issued by a pipeline to protect the operational integrity of the line. The orders may either restrict service or require affirmative action by shippers, such as line pack or draft.

Operator
The party in control of the physical operation and maintenance of a well or other facility.

Option
The right but not the obligation to buy or sell something at a specified price for a specified time period. The seller of an options contract receives a premium from the buyer of the option and has the obligation to deliver if the contract is exercised by the buyer. Options are also referred to as Caps, Floors or Ceilings. See also PUT OPTION and CALL OPTION.

Orderly Shutdown
The sequenced shutdown of units comprising a computer system to prevent damage to the system and subsequent corruption or loss of data.

Oscillator
An electric circuit that produces an alternating electric current, which repeatedly changes direction.

Oscillation
The variation, usually with time, of the magnitude of quantity with respect to a specified reference when the magnitude is alternately greater and smaller than the reference.

Output
The amount of power delivered from a generating station during a specified period.

Outage
See blackout. Periods, both planned and unexpected, during which power system facilities (generating unit, transmission line or other facilities) cease to provide generation, transmission or the distribution of power. A planned or unplanned operational interruption of part of a power system (e.g. generating unit, transmission or distribution lines).

Outside Coil
The heat-transfer (exchanger) component of a heat pump, located outdoors, from which heat is collected in the heating mode, or expelled in the cooling mode

Over-the-Counter Market
A general name for any transaction that does not take place on an exchange. There is no central exchange facility for an over-the-counter market which operates through "middlemen", or dealers. The dealer stands ready to buy or sell a given security on request. The dealer provides the service of allowing the buyer or seller of an asset to make the exchange when he or she desires, rather than waiting to locate a party who wants to do business. An over-the-counter option is a call or a put whose strike price, expiration and premium are negotiated between two parties.

Overburden
Earth and rock layers covering coal seam.

Over speed
The speed of the turbine runner when, under design conditions, all external loads are removed.

Overvoltage
A voltage greater than the rating of a device or component. Normally overvoltage refers to long term events (several AC cycles and longer). The term can also apply to transients and surges.

Ovshinsky Effect
The effect by which a specific glassy thin film switches from a nonconductor to a semiconductor upon application of a minimum voltage.

P

Panelboard
A single panel or group of panel units designed for assembly in the form of a single panel; including buses, overcurrent protection devices (with or without switches) for the control of power circuits.

Parallel Operation
The connection of the outputs of two or more power conditioners for use as one unit. Paralleling for capacity means that the units are paralleled for the sum of their individual ratings, i.e. two 125 KVA systems paralleled for use as a single 250 KVA system. Paralleling for redundancy means using one or more additional units to maintain power even when

one unit fails. The operation of a customer-owned generator while connected to the utility's grid: Parallel operation may be required solely for the Customer's operating convenience or for the purpose of delivering power to the utility's grid.

Parallel Path Flow
The difference between scheduled and real power flows on a transmission path, assuming zero inadvertent interchange (also called loop flow, unscheduled power flow, or circulating power flow)

Parity Error
An unintentional change in the bit structure of a data word due to the presence of a spurious pulse or transient.

Passive Solar Heater
A solar water or space-heating system in which solar energy is collected, and/or moved by natural convection without using pumps or fans. Passive systems are typically integral collector/storage (ICS; or batch collectors) or thermosyphon systems. The major advantage of these systems is that they do not use controls, pumps, sensors, or other mechanical parts, so little or no maintenance is required over the lifetime of the system.

Peak capacity
Peak capacity refers to the maximum power a system like solar or wind generator can generate under the standard or prescribed operating conditions. An 80-watt solar panel, for example, can produce a maximum of 80 watts when insolation is lOOOwatts/square meter. Peak capacity for a hybrid system would mean the maximum kW for the total system over a 30-minute period.

Peak Demand/Load
The maximum energy demand or load in a specified time period. The maximum energy load during a specified time period.

Peaking Capacity
Power generation equipment or system capacity to meet peak power demands.

Peaking Hydropower
A hydropower plant that is operated at maximum allowable capacity for part of the day and is either shut down for the remainder of the time or operated at minimal capacity level.

Peak Power
Power generated that operates at a very low capacity factor; generally

used to meet short-lived and variable high demand periods. PV modules are rated by their total power output. The peak power is the amount of power output a PV modules produces at Standard test conditions (STC) of a module operating temperature of 25 degrees Celsius in full sunshine (irradiance) of 1 000 watts per square meter. This is a clear summer day with sun approximately overhead and the cells faced directly towards the sun. Unit: Watt (W), also wirtten Wp by professionals in the field.

Peak Line Current
Maximum instantaneous current during a cycle.

Peak Day Demand
The maximum daily quantity of gas used during a specified period, such as a year.

Peak Demand
The maximum load during a specified period of time.

Peak Load
The maximum electric load consumed or produced in a stated period of time. Peak Load The maximum demand for electric energy from all of the customers of a utility or over a geographic area. It usually refers to the largest demand experienced during a calendar year, though it can be the largest demand for a month, or other specified period. The maximum amount of power delivered during a stated period of time.The maximum load consumed or produced by a unit or group of units in a stated period of time.

Peak Load Plant or Peaker Unit
A plant usually housing low-efficiency, quick response steam units, gas turbines, diesels or pumped-storage hydroelectric equipment normally used during the maximum load periods. Peakers are characterized by quick start times and generally high operating costs, but low capital costs.

Peak/Energy Exchange
Exchange of peaking capacity for off-peak energy between two or more systems.

Peak Responsibility
The load of a customer, a group of customers or part of a system at the time of occurrence of the system peak load.

Peak Shaving
Methods to reduce the peak demand for gas or electricity.Generator operation which results in reducing customer's peak load or demand.

Closed-transition peak shaving is the condition where the generator is in a parallel operation with Xcel Energy's system. Open-transition peak shaving is the condition where the generator is not connected in parallel with the Xcel Energy System.

Peak Shifting

The process of moving existing loads to off-peak periods.

Peak Sun Hours

The equivalent number of hours per day when solar irradiance averages 1 kW/m^2. For example, six peak sun hours means that the energy received during total daylight hours equals the energy that would have been received had the irradiance for six hours been 1 kW/m One PSH = lkWh/square meter. PSH indicate approximate solar energy availability at a location in a day. This can be calculated from a solar radiation plot by assuming the insolation to be constant at 1000 watts/sq. meter for a time (hours) during the day where the total solar energy received is still the same. For example, if PSH= 6 the total incoming ration in a day would be 6 kWh. And hence if a solar array is rated at 1500 watts, then the maximum output from the array for the location is calculated at 1500 watts x 6 PSH = 9 kWh. Remember, though, the actual output will be influenced by efficiency corrections depending on the number and type of equipment in the system.

Peak Watt

A unit used to rate the performance of a solar photovoltaic (PV) cells, modules, or arrays; the maximum nominal output of a PV device, in Watts (Wp) under standardized test conditions, usually 1000 Watts per square meter of sunlight with other conditions, such as temperature specified.

Peak Wind Speed

The maximum instantaneous wind speed (or velocity) that occurs within a specific period of time or interval.

Peaking Capacity

Capacity of generating equipment normally reserved for operation during the hours of highest daily, weekly or seasonal loads. Some generating equipment may be operated at certain times as peaking capacity and at other times to serve loads on an around-the-clock basis.

Peaking Supply

A supply of natural gas that is available to meet peak demand. Peaking supply is generally associated with seasonal demand, i.e., colder than normal days. Peaking supply may be provided out of storage facilities, from LNG facilities, from Btu enhancement through the injection of propane or other high-Btu substances, or other means.

Peaking Supply Service
A service that entitles a buyer to a certain quantity of natural gas delivered at the buyer's request during peak periods.

Pelton Turbine
A type of impulse hydropower turbine where water passes through nozzles and strikes cups arranged on the periphery of a runner, or wheel, which causes the runner to rotate, producing mechanical energy. The runner is fixed on a shaft, and the rotational motion of the turbine is transmitted by the shaft to a generator. Generally used for high head, low flow applications.

Penstock
A component of a hydropower plant; a pipe that delivers water to the turbine.

Perfluorocarbon Tracer Gas Technique (PFT)
An air infiltration measurement technique developed by the Brookhaven National Laboratory to measure changes over lime (one week to five months) when determining a building's air infiltration rate. This test cannot locate exact points of infiltration, but it does reveal long-term infiltration problems.

Performance Ratings
Solar collector thermal performance ratings based on collector efficiencies, usually expressed in Btu per hour for solar collectors under standard test or operating conditions for solar radiation intensity, inlet working fluid temperatures, and ambient temperatures.

Performance ratio
Ratio of the final annual (monthly, daily) yield to the reference annual (monthly, daily) yield, where the reference annual (monthly, daily) yield is the theoretically annual (monthly, daily) available energy per kilowatt of installed power.

Perimeter Heating
A term applied to warm-air heating systems that deliver heated air to rooms by means of registers or baseboards located along exterior walls.

Period Hours
Number of hours a unit was in the active state. A unit generally enters the active state on its service date.

Permeance
A unit of measurement for the ability of a material to retard the diffusion of water vapor at 73.4 F (23 C). A perm, short for permeance, is the number

of grains of water vapor that pass through a square foot of material per hour at a differential vapor pressure equal to one inch of mercury.

Petroleum Coke

A final product, often called a "waste product," of the petroleum refining process, which is the output of the refinery after all of the higher distillates and oils have been distilled from crude oil, leaving a product that has the appearance of coal, and can be found in various types of petroleum coke, depending on the size of the output product, including "sponge," "shot," and "fluid" coke. Petroleum coke may be calcined for specialty uses, including anode production or it may be burned as fuel in various processes, ranging from power plants to cement kilns, which is currently the largest single use of petroleum coke. The fuel product is typically high in sulfur (although there are exceptions), low in volatile matter, low in ash and low in moisture. Heating value is typically 14,200 Btu/lb.

Phantom Load

Any appliance that consumes power even when it is turned off. Examples of phantom loads include appliances with electronic clocks or timers, appliances with remote controls, and appliances with wall cubes (a small box that plugs into an AC outlet to power appliances).

Phase

Alternating current is carried by conductors and a ground to residential, commercial, or industrial consumers. The waveform of the phase power appears as a single continuous sine wave at the system frequency whose amplitude is the rated voltage of the power.

Phase Change

The process of changing from one physical state (solid, liquid, or gas) to another, with a necessary or coincidental input or release of energy.

Phase-Change Material

A material that can be used to store thermal energy as latent heat. Various types of materials have been and are being investigated such as inorganic salts, eutectic compounds, and paraffins, for a variety of applications, including solar energy storage (solar energy heats and melts the material during the day and at night it releases the stored heat and reverts to a solid state).

Photobiological Hydrogen Production

A hydrogen production process that process uses algae. Under certain conditions, the pigments in certain types of algae absorb solar energy. An enzyme in the cell acts as a catalyst to split water molecules. Some of the bacteria produces hydrogen after they grow on a substrate.

Photocurrent

An electric current induced by radiant energy.

Photoelectric Cell

A device for measuring light intensity that works by converting light falling on, or reach it, to electricity, and then measuring the current; used in photometers.

Photoelectrochemical Cell

A type of photovoltaic device in which the electricity induced in the cell is used immediately within the cell to produce a chemical, such as hydrogen, which can then be withdrawn for use.

Photoelectrolysis Hydrogen Production

The production of hydrogen using a photoelectrochemical cell.

Photogalvanic Processes

The production of electrical current from light.

Photon

A particle of light that acts as an individual unit of energy.

Photovoltaic (Conversion) Efficiency

The ratio of the electric power produced by a photovoltaic device to the power of the sunlight incident on the device.

Photovoltaic (PV; Solar) Array

A group of solar photovoltaic modules connected together. A mechanically integrated assembly of modules and panels together with support structure to form a d.c. power producing unit.

Photovoltaic cell

A basic photovoltaic device, which generates electricity when, exposed to a light such as the solar radiation. All photovoltaic cells produce direct current (d.c). Treated semiconductor material that converts solar irradiance to electricity.

Photovoltaic Device

A solid-state electrical device that converts light directly into direct current electricity of voltage-current characteristics that are a function of the characteristics of the light source and the materials in and design of the device. Solar photovoltaic devices are made of various semi-conductor materials including silicon, cadmium sulfide, cadmium telluride, and gallium arsenide, and in single crystalline, multi-crystalline, or amorphous forms.

Photovoltaic (Solar) Module or Panel

A solar photovoltaic product that generally consists of groups of PV cells electrically connected together to produce a specified power output under standard test conditions, mounted on a substrate, sealed with an encapsulant, and covered with a protective glazing. Maybe further mounted on an aluminum frame. A junction box, on the back or underside of the module is used to allow for connecting the module circuit conductors to external conductors. PV or solar panels use solar cells to convert solar energy to electricity. Solar panels are used as part of the power generating equipment in renewable energy power systems in remote locations or as standalone power supply systems. The smallest complete environmentally protected assembly of interconnected photovoltaic cells. For crystalline silicon cells, after testing and sorting to match the current and voltage, the cells are interconnected and encapsulated between a transparent front, usually glass, and a backing material. This 'module' is then typically mounted in an aluminium frame. Modules are normally rated between 50 and 200 W, although several manufacturers now offer modules above 200 W.

Photovoltaic panel

A group of modules fastened together, pre-assembled and wired, designed to serve as an installable unit in a photovoltaic array.

Photovoltaic Peak Watt

see Peak Watt.

Photovoltaic power system

Set of interconnected elements such as photovoltaic modules, inverters that convert d.c. current of the modules into a.c. current, storage batteries and all installation and control components with a photovoltaic power capacity of 40 W or more. The typology is different according to application: see off-grid and grid-connected photovoltaic power systems.

Photovoltaics

The process that produces electricity from sunlight. "Photo" refers to light and "voltaic" to voltage.

Photovoltaic (Solar) System

A complete PV power system composed of the module (or array), and balance-of-system (BOS) components including the array supports, electrical conductors/wiring, fuses, safety disconnects, and grounds, charge controllers, inverters, battery storage, etc.

Photovoltaic-Thermal (PV/T) Systems

A solar energy system that produces electricity with a PV module, and collects thermal energy from the module for heating. There are no commercially available systems available (as of 11/97).

Physical Vapor Deposition
A method of depositing thin semiconductor photovoltaic) films. With this method, physical processes, such as thermal evaporation or bombardment of ions, are used to deposit elemental semiconductor material on a substrate.

Pitch Control
A method of controlling a wind turbine's speed by varying the orientation, or pitch, of the blades, and thereby altering its aerodynamics and efficiency.

P-I-N
A semiconductor (photovoltaic) device structure that layers an intrinsic semiconductor between a p-type semiconductor and an n-type semiconductor; this structure is most often used with amorphous silicon PV devices.

P/N
A semiconductor (photovoltaic) device structure in which the junction is formed between a p-type layer and an n-type layer.

Plenum
The space between a hanging ceiling and the floor above or roof; usually contains HVAC ducts, electrical wiring, fire suppression system piping, etc.

Plug Flow Digester
A type of anaerobic digester that has a horizontal tank in which a constant volume of material is added and forces material in the tank to move through the tank and be digested.

Point-Contact Cell
A high efficiency silicon photovoltaic concentrator cell that employs light trapping techniques and point-diffused contacts on the rear surface for current collection.

Polycrystalline
A semiconductor (photovoltaic) material composed of variously oriented, small, individual crystals.

Polyethylene
A registered trademark for plastic sheeting material that can be used as a vapor retarder. This plastic is used to make grocery bags. It is a long chain of carbon atoms with 2 hydrogen atoms attached to each carbon atom.

Porous Media
A solid that contains pores; normally, it refers to intercomiected pores that can transmit the flow of fluids. (The term refers to the aquifer geology when discussing sites for CAES.)

Portfolio Standard
The requirement that an electric power provider generate or purchase a specified percentage of the power it supplies/sells from renewable energy resources, and thereby guarantee a market for electricity generated from renewable energy resources.

Potable Water
Water that is suitable for drinking, as defined by local health officials.

Potential Energy
Energy available due to position.

Pound of Steam
One pound of water in vapor phase; is NOT steam pressure, which is expressed as pounds per square inch (psi).

Pound Per Square Inch Absolute (psia)
A unit of pressure [hydraulic (liquid) or pneumatic (gas)] that does not include atmospheric pressure.

Power
Energy that is capable or available for doing work; the time rate at which work is performed, measured in horsepower, Watts, or Btu per hour. Electric power is the product of electric current and electromotive force.

Power Coefficient
The ratio of power produced by a wind energy conversion device to the power in a reference area of the free windstream.

Power Conditioning
The process of modifying the characteristics of electrical power (for e.g., inverting dc to ac).

Power (Output) Curve
A plot of a wind energy conversion device's power output versus wind speed.

Power Density
The amount of power per unit area of a free windstream.

Power Factor (PF)
The ratio of actual power being used in a circuit, expressed in watts or

kilowatts, to the power that is apparently being drawn from a power source, expressed in volt-amperes or kilovolt-amperes.

Power Generation Mix
The proportion of electricity distributed by a power provider that is generated from available sources such as coal, natural gas, petroleum, nuclear, hydropower, wind, or geothermal.

Power Provider
A company or other organizational unit that sells and distributes electrical power (e.g., private or public electrical utility), either to other distribution and wholesale businesses or to end-users. Sometimes power providers also generate the power they sell.

Power (Solar) Tower
A term used to describe solar thermal, central receiver, power systems, where an array of reflectors focus sunlight onto a central receiver and absorber mounted on a tower.

Power Transmission Line
An electrical conductor/cable that carries electricity from a generator to other locations for distribution.

Preheater (Solar)
A solar heating system that preheats water or air that is then heated more by another heating appliance.

Present Value
The amount of money required to secure a specified cash flow at a future date at a specified return.

Pressure Drop
The loss in static pressure of a fluid (liquid or gas) in a system due to friction from obstructions in pipes, from valves, fittings, regulators, burners, etc, or by a breech or rupture of the system.

Pressurization Testing
A technique used by energy auditors, using a blower door, to locate areas of air infiltration by exaggerating the defects in the building shell. This test only measures air infiltration at the time of the test. It does not take into account changes in atmospheric pressure, weather, wind velocity, or any activities the occupants conduct that may affect air infiltration rates over a period of time.

Primary Air
The air that is supplied to the combustion chamber of a furnace.

Prime Mover
Any machine capable of producing power to do work.

Process Heat
Thermal energy that is used in agricultural and industrial operations.

Products of Combustion
The elements and compounds that result from the combustion of a fuel.

Producer Gas
Low or medium Btu content gas, composed mainly of carbon monoxide, nitrogen(2), and hydrogen(2) made by the gasification of wood or coal.

Programmable Thermostat
A type of thermostat that allows the user to program into the devices' memory a pre-set schedule of times (when certain temperatures occur) to turn on HVAC equipment.

Projected Area
The net south-facing glazing area projected on a vertical plane. Also, the solid area covered at any instant by a wind turbine's blades from the perspective of the direction of the windstream (as opposed to the swept area).

Propane
A hydrocarbon gas, C3H8, occurring in crude oil, natural gas, and refinery cracking gas. It is used as a fuel, a solvent, and a refrigerant. Propane liquefies under pressure and is the major component of liquefied petroleum gas (LPG).

Propeller (Hydro) Turbine
A turbine that has a runner with attached blades similar to a propeller used to drive a ship. As water passes over the curved propeller blades, it causes rotation of the shaft.

Proximate Analysis
A commonly used analysis for reporting fuel properties; may be on a dry (moisture free) basis, as "fired", or on an ash and moisture free basis. Fractions usually reported include: volatile matter, fixed carbon, moisture, ash, and heating value (higher heating value).

PV
Abbreviation of photovoltaic (adjective) or photovoltaics (noun).

PVPS
Abbreviation of photovoltaic power system(s).

Peripheral
Any device used to process data for entry into or extraction from a computer.

Phase Compensation
Switching capacitors into or out of a power distribution network to compensate for load power factor variations.

Photovoltaic Cell
A device which produces an electric current from solar radiation. Materials which can be used in the production of photovoltaic cells include silicon and cadmium sulfide.

Pico (P)
A metric prefix meaning one million millionth or 10-12.

Plant
A facility at which are located prime movers, electric generators and auxiliary equipment for converting mechanical, chemical and/or nuclear energy into electric energy. A plant may contain more than one type of prime mover. Electric utility plants exclude facilities that satisfy the definition of a qualifying facility under the Public Utility Regulatory Policies Act of 1978. A station.

Plant Factor
The ratio of the average generation and capacity of a plant during a specified period of time, expressed as a percentage. Sometimes called capacity factor.

Plant Load Factor
A measure of how intensely each type of plant is used. It is calculated as the average hourly quantity of electricity supplied during the year, expressed as a percentage of the average output capability at the beginning and the end of the year.

Plant Margin
The amount by which the total installed generating plant capacity exceeds the peak demand, expressed as a percentage of the net amount of the weather corrected peak demand less the total imports from external utilities.

Plant Thermal Reduction (PTR)
The Btu equivalent of the liquid products extracted from natural gas by a processing plant, plus the natural gas used as plant fuel to extract those liquids, plant flare and other losses. When expressed as a volume (in Mcf), plant thermal reduction is referred to as Plant Volume Reduction (PVR).

Plant-Use Electricity
The electric energy used in the operation of a plant. This energy total is subtracted from the gross energy production of the plant; for reporting purposes the plant energy production is then reported as a net figure. The energy required for pumping-storage plants is, by definition, subtracted, and the energy production for these plants is then reported as a net figure.

Point of Delivery (POD)
Point on the transmission provider's transmission system where the transmission grid connects to a receiving party for the delivery of electricity.

Point of Energy Exchange
The point in the delivery system where one party takes delivery of the energy from the other party. This point is defined in the contract between Xcel Energy and the Customer. It is often the point where facility ownership changes. This point may also be called the Point of Interchange when dealing with a bidirectional energy exchange or the Point of Delivery if the energy flows in one direction.

oint of Interconnection
The point where the Customer's conductors meet Xcel Energy's (point of ownership change).

Point of Metering
The point where metering equipment (meters, transducers, current transformers, potential transformers, etc.) is or will be installed to measure the power flow and energy exchange between Xcel Energy and the Customer. **Actual, Active or Real Power.** The time rate of transferring or transforming energy or the power that accomplishes work. Measured in Watts. The rate at which work is done or energy expended. It is measured in units of energy per unit of time, such as calories per second. Electrical energy measured according to voltage and current (normally watts). Power in watts equals volts times amperes for DC circuits. For single phase AC circuits, watts equal volts times amperes times power factor.

Point of Receipt (POR)
Point on the transmission provider's transmission system where the grid connects to a generator for the loading of electricity on to the transmission system.

Point of Unbundling
The farthest point upstream on a pipeline's system (usually in or contiguous to the production area) when transportation is unbundled from the sale and the point at which title to the gas passes.

Point or Tick
The smallest monetary unit of change in a futures price.

Point-to-Point Service
(Similar to the concept of contract path) point-to-point service provides a customer the ability to use only that portion of a transmission owner's integrated facility to input power at a specified point and take out the power at a specified point regardless of actual flow.

Poolco
The term for a form of partial deregulation of the electric utility industry where certain generation remains centrally dispatched and sold by multiple utilities. There is some limited opportunity for non-utility entities to supply additional generation to the power system.

Poolco
Poolco refers to a specialized, centrally dispatched spot market power pool that functions as a short term market. It establishes the short term market clearing price and provides a system of long term transmission compensation contracts. It is regulated to provide open access, comparable service and cost recovery. A Poolco would make ancillary generation services, including load following, spinning reserve, backup power and reactive power, available to all market participants on comparable terms. In addition, the Poolco provides settlement mechanisms when differences in contracted volumes exist between buyers and sellers of energy and capacity.

Pooling Point
The point (either physical or theoretical) at which gas is aggregated from many receipt points in order to serve several contracts without tying a specific receipt point to a specific contract. "Paper pooling" refers to aggregation as a matter of accounting, as opposed to physical pooling in a supply basin.

Polyphase
An alternating current supply with two or more hot conductors. Voltage is measurable between the conductors and the voltage waveforms for each conductor are usually displaced 120 degrees. When a neutral is present, the voltage from each hot conductor to neutral is equal.

Power Conditioner
Any device whose main function is to provide acceptable electrical power to the load it is protecting.

Power Factor
Watts divided by voltamps, KW divided by KVA. Power factor: leading and lagging of voltage versus current caused by inductive or capacitive

loads, and 2) harmonic power factor: from nonlinear current. The ratio of actual power (kW) to apparent power (kVA). The phase relationship between actual current flowing in an impedance containing resistance and capacitance or inductance; and the current that would flow in a purely resistive impedance of the same value, due to the application of a voltage of equal frequency and amplitude. Equipment designers usually strive for a Power Factor of Unity or Cos(0°). The fraction of power actually used by a customer's electrical equipment compared to the total apparent power supplied, usually expressed as a percentage. Power factors apply only to alternating current circuits; direct current circuits always exhibit a power factor of 100 percent. A power factor indicates how far a customer's electrical equipment causes the electric current delivered at the customer's site to be out of phase with the voltage.

Power Factor Adjustment

A calculation or charge on industrial or commercial customers' bills reflecting an adjustment in billing demand based on customer's actual metered power factor. If the power factor stays within a specified range, there is no adjustment.

Power Flow

One-way power flow is the condition where the flow of power is entirely into the Customer's facility.Two way power flow is the condition where the net flow of power may be either into or out of the Customer's facility depending on the operation of the generator and other customer load.

Power Grid

A network of electrical power lines and associated equipment used to transmit and distribute electricity.

Power Pool

The entity (either independent or the owner of transmission) that coordinates operations to maintain electric system stability and achieve least-cost dispatch by providing backup, short-term excess sales, reactive power support and spinning reserve; a power pool may also arrange transactions among generators and enforce rules of conduct for market activity .Two or more interconnected electric systems planned and operated to supply power in the most reliable and economical manner for their combined load requirements and maintenance programs. Two or more interconnected electric systems that seek to obtain greater reliability of service and efficiency of operation by coordinating the development and operation of their electric generation and transmission facilities.

Pacific Northwest Coordination Agreement

An agreement between federal and non-federal owners of hydroelectric generation on the Columbia River system, which resulted from the 1964 Columbia River Treaty. The PNCA governs the release of stored water to obtain the maximum usable energy and directs operations of the major generating facilities as if they belonged to a single owner.

Paper Hearing
A process used by FERC to expedite decisions on the basis of a written record submitted directly to the Commission, instead of an oral hearing before an Administrative Law Judge.

Parallel Path Flow
The flow of electric power on an electric system's transmission facilities resulting from scheduled electric power transfers between two other electric systems.

Participating Collar
Unlike a standard collar, which requires the hedger to give up the benefit of favorable prices on one side of the band, a participating collar allows the hedger to participate in a portion of the price decline below the lower level of the band.

Participating Swap
A swap which is structured to hedge floating rate exposure while allowing the hedger to retain some benefit from a favorable move in rates.

PCBs
Synthetic chemicals (polychlorinated biphenyls), manufactured from 1929 to 1977, found in electrical equipment, such as voltage regulators and switches and used to cool electrical capacitors and transformers. The manufacture of PCBs was banned in 1979.

Peak Day Demand
The maximum daily quantity of gas used during a specified period, such as a year.

Peak Demand
The maximum load during a specified period of time.

Peak Load
The maximum load consumed or produced by a unit or group of units in a stated period of time.

Peak Load Plant or Peaker Unit
A plant usually housing low-efficiency, quick response steam units, gas turbines, diesels or pumped-storage hydroelectric equipment normally used during the maximum load periods. Peakers are characterized by

quick start times and generally high operating costs, but low capital costs.

Peak/Energy Exchange
Exchange of peaking capacity for off-peak energy between two or more systems.

Peak Responsibility
The load of a customer, a group of customers or part of a system at the time of occurrence of the system peak load.

Peak Shaving
Methods to reduce the peak demand for gas or electricity.

Peaking Capacity
Capacity of generating equipment normally reserved for operation during the hours of highest daily, weekly or seasonal loads. Some generating equipment may be operated at certain times as peaking capacity and at other times to serve loads on an around-the-clock basis.

Peaking Supply
A supply of natural gas that is available to meet peak demand. Peaking supply is generally associated with seasonal demand, i.e., colder than normal days. Peaking supply may be provided out of storage facilities, from LNG facilities, from Btu enhancement through the injection of propane or other high-Btu substances, or other means.

Peaking Supply Service
A service that entitles a buyer to a certain quantity of natural gas delivered at the buyer's request during peak periods.

Period Hours
Number of hours a unit was in the active state. A unit generally enters the active state on its service date.

Performance Based Rate
A method of establishing rates which departs from the cost-of-service standard in setting just and reasonable utility rates. Performance Based Rates generally afford utilities the opportunity to increase profits by exceeding targets for efficiency and cost savings. This type of methodology purports to streamline regulatory process by replacing rate hearings with annual, accounting-type reviews. Cost of service studies might not be required at all, once initial rates are fixed.

Permeability
A measure of the ease with which a fluid flows through rock in response

to pressure differences (measured in darcys). Permeability implies that there is some degree of porosity in the rock.

Petroleum
A complex mixture of various hydrocarbons existing in the liquid state found in natural underground
reservoirs, often associated with gas. Petroleum includes fuel oil No. 2, No. 4, No. 5, No. 6; topped crude; kerosene: and jet fuel.

Petroleum Coke
A final product, often called a "waste product," of the petroleum refining process, which is the output of the refinery after all of the higher distillates and oils have been distilled from crude oil, leaving a product that has the appearance of coal, and can be found in various types of petroleum coke, depending on the size of the output product, including "sponge," "shot," and "fluid" coke. Petroleum coke may be calcined for specialty uses, including anode production or it may be burned as fuel in various processes, ranging from power plants to cement kilns, which is currently the largest single use of petroleum coke. The fuel product is typically high in sulfur (although there are exceptions), low in volatile matter, low in ash and low in moisture. Heating value is typically 14,200 Btu/lb.

Petroleum Industry Data Exchange
API's Subcommittee serving as an action group for the oil and gas industry.

Photovoltaic Conversion
The process of converting the sun's light energy directly into electric energy, through the use of photovoltaic cells.

Photovoltaic power
Photovoltaic power comes from harnessing solar energy with non-mechanical semiconductors that convert sunlight to direct current energy.

Pipeline
An entity engaged in the transportation of natural gas in interstate or intrastate commerce. Also, the actual facility itself.

Pipeline Day
An arbitrary 24-hour period of time established by a pipeline for the operation of its system, often beginning at seven or eight o'clock in the morning.

Pipeline Interconnection
A point at which facilities of two or more pipelines interconnect.

Pipeline Quality Gas
See GAS, MARKETABLE.

Pipeline System
A collection of pipeline facilities used to transport natural gas from source of supply to burner tip, including gathering, transmission or distribution lines, treating or processing plants, compressor stations and related facilities.

Plain Vanilla
A term used to describe the most basic form of a single- currency, constant-notional-principal interest rate swap in which fixed-rate cash flows are exchanged for floating-rate payments.

Planned Derating
Advance reduction in capacity required by scheduled removal of a component for repairs with a predetermined duration.

Planned Outage
The removal of a unit from service to perform work on specific components that is scheduled well in advance and has a predetermined duration (e.g., annual overhaul, inspections, testing).

Plant
A facility at which are located prime movers, electric generators and auxiliary equipment for converting mechanical, chemical and/ or nuclear energy into electric energy. A plant may contain more than one type of prime mover. Electric utility plants exclude facilities that satisfy the definition of a qualifying facility under the Public Utility Regulatory Policies Act of 1978. A station.

Plant Factor
The ratio of the average generation and capacity of a plant during a specified period of time, expressed as a percentage. Sometimes called capacity factor.

Plant Thermal Reduction (PTR)
The Btu equivalent of the liquid products extracted from natural gas by a processing plant, plus the natural gas used as plant fuel to extract those liquids, plant flare and other losses. When expressed as a volume (in Mcf), plant thermal reduction is referred to as Plant Volume Reduction (PVR).

Plant-Use Electricity
The electric energy used in the operation of a plant. This energy total is subtracted from the gross energy production of the plant; for reporting

purposes the plant energy production is then reported as a net figure. The energy required for pumping-storage plants is, by definition, subtracted, and the energy production for these plants is then reported as a net figure.

Point of Unbundling
The farthest point upstream on a pipeline's system (usually in or contiguous to the production area) when transportation is unbundled from the sale and the point at which title to the gas passes.

Point or Tick
The smallest monetary unit of change in a futures price.

Point-to-Point Service
(Similar to the concept of contract path) point-to-point service provides a customer the ability to use only that portion of a transmission owner's integrated facility to input power at a specified point and take out the power at a specified point regardless of actual flow.

Poolco
The term for a form of partial deregulation of the electric utility industry where certain generation remains centrally dispatched and sold by multiple utilities. There is some limited opportunity for non-utility entities to supply additional generation to the power system.

Poolco
Poolco refers to a specialized, centrally dispatched spot market power pool that functions as a short term market. It establishes the short term market clearing price and provides a system of long term transmission compensation contracts. It is regulated to provide open access, comparable service and cost recovery. A Poolco would make ancillary generation services, including load following, spinning reserve, backup power and reactive power, available to all market participants on comparable terms. In addition, the Poolco provides settlement mechanisms when differences in contracted volumes exist between buyers and sellers of energy and capacity.

Pooling Point
The point (either physical or theoretical) at which gas is aggregated from many receipt points in order to serve several contracts without tying a specific receipt point to a specific contract. "Paper pooling" refers to aggregation as a matter of accounting, as opposed to physical pooling in a supply basin.

Porosity
The presence of spaces (pores) between the grains of sand making up a

rock formation. Porosity is measured by dividing pore volume by total rock volume.

Portal
Any entrance to a mine.

Portal
An internal or external Web site that functions as an informational hub, aggregating links that connect the portal's users to various information sources. Portals are typically positioned as starting points for users.

Position
In futures trading, one's status as long or short.

Post-Contingency Operating Procedures
Operating procedures that are invoked by the system operator to mitigate or alleviate system problems after a contingency has occurred.

Power
A term usually meant to imply both capacity and energy. The rate at which energy is transferred. Electrical energy is usually measured in watts.

Power Authorities
Quasi governmental agencies that perform all or some of the functions of a public utility.

Power Factor
The fraction of power actually used by a customer's electrical equipment compared to the total apparent power supplied, usually expressed as a percentage. Power factors apply only to alternating current circuits; direct current circuits always exhibit a power factor of 100 percent. A power factor indicates how far a customer's electrical equipment causes the electric current delivered at the customer's site to be out of phase with the voltage.

Power Factor Adjustment
A calculation or charge on industrial or commercial customers' bills reflecting an adjustment in billing demand based on customer's actual metered power factor. If the power factor stays within a specified range, there is no adjustment.

Power Marketing Administrations
Congress established five federal power marketing administrations (PMAs) to sell hydroelectric power generated by federal dams and power plants. These PMAs and their headquarters are:

- Bonneville Power Administration (BPA) - Portland, Oregon
- Western Area Power Administration (WAPA) - Golden, Colorado
- Southwestern Power Administration (SWPA) - Tulsa, Oklahoma
- Southeastern Power Administration (SEPA) - Elberton, Georgia
- Alaska Power Administration (APA) - Juneau, Alaska

The Tennessee Valley Authority (TVA) is a separately constituted federal power agency which serves similar functions and customers. Its headquarters is in Chattanooga, Tennessee.

Power Plant
An industrial facility that has the production of kilowatt hours of power as its primary product. The power is produced from a raw material such as oil, coal or nuclear. A plant that converts mechanical energy to electric energy.

Power Pool
An entity established to coordinate short-term operations to maintain system stability and achieve least cost dispatch. The dispatch provides backup supplies, short-term excess sales, reactive power support and spinning reserve. Historically, some of these services were provided on an unpriced basis as part of the members' utility franchise obligations. Coordinating short-term operations includes the aggregation and firming of power from various generators, arranging exchanges between generators and establishing (or enforcing) the rules of conduct for wholesale transactions. The pool may own, manage and/or operate the transmission lines ("wires") or be an independent entity that manages the transactions between entities. Often, the power pool is not meant to provide transmission access and pricing, or settlement mechanisms if differences between contracted volumes among buyers and sellers exist.

Power Station
A factory that makes electricity through the use of a generator.

Power Surge
A sudden change in an electrical system's voltage that is capable of damaging electrical equipment. The most severe surges are caused by lightning.

Power System
The interconnected facilities of an electrical utility. A power system includes the generation, transmission, distribution, transformation, and protective components necessary to provide service.

Power System Stabiliser
Equipment controlling the exciter output via the voltage regulator in

such a way that power oscillations of the synchronous machines are dampened. Input variables may be speed, frequency or power (or a combination of these.)

Primary Electricity
Electricity obtained from Nuclear, Hydro and Non-Thermal renewables, i.e. not from fossil fuels.

Primary Fuels
Fuels obtained from natural sources directly, for example coal, oil and natural gas.

Primary Recovery
The recovery of oil and/or natural gas by any method (natural flow or artificial lift) that may be employed to produce them through a single well bore; the fluid enters the well bore by the action of native reservoir energy or gravity.

Prime Mover
The engine, turbine, water wheel or similar machine that drives an electric generator; or, for reporting purposes, a device that converts energy to electricity directly (e.g., photovoltaic solar and fuel cells).

Processing Plant
A facility in which raw natural gas from the wellhead is made to meet pipeline quality specifications and prepared for sale to consumers by reducing or removing undesirable impurities and extracting commercially desirable non-methane hydrocarbons from the gas stream.

Propagation
The travel of an electrical waveform along a medium. In other words, a surge passing along a power cord to a system.

Propeller Turbine
A type of reaction turbine with a propeller-style runner. Water passes through the runner and drives the propeller blades. Propeller turbines can be used from 2 to 300 feet of head, and can be as large as 100 megawatts

Protector
A protector is another name for an arrester or diverter.

Protection
All of the relays and other equipment which are used to open the necessary circuit breakers to clear lines or equipment when trouble develops. The provisions for detecting abnormal conditions on a system and initiating

fault clearance or actuating signals or indications.

Protection Apparatus

A group of one or more protection relays and/or logic elements designated to perform a specified protection function.

Proton

An elementary particle found in the nucleus of all atoms. It carries a positive charge equal to the negative charge of the electron.

Psi

Pounds of pressure per square inch.

Psia

Pounds/force per square inch absolute.

Psig

Pounds/force per square inch gauge.

Psychrometer

An instrument for measuring relative humidity by means of wet and dry-bulb temperatures.

Psychrometrics

The analysis of atmospheric conditions, particularly moisture in the air.

Psophometric

A variety of filter used for the band limiting of noise to certain frequencies so that its effects can be determined on various electronic system components used for transmission of signals.

Pulse-Width-Modulated (PWM) Wave Inverter A type of power inverter that produce a high quality (nearly sinusoidal) voltage, at minimum current harmonics.

Pumped Storage Facility

A type of power generating facility that pumps water to a storage reservoir during off-peak periods, and uses the stored water (by allowing it to fall through a hydro turbine) to generate power during peak periods. The pumping energy is typically supplied by lower cost base power capacity, and the peaking power capacity is of greater value, even though there is a net loss of power in the process.

Pumped-Storage Hydroelectric Plant

A plant that generates electric energy by using water pumped by reversible pump-turbines during off-peak periods into an elevated storage reservoir. At peak periods, when additional generating capacity is needed, the water is released from the elevated storage reservoir down to the turbine generators in the plant at a lower elevation. A plant that generates electric energy by using water pumped during off-peak periods into an elevated storage reservoir. At peak periods, when additional generating capacity is needed, the water is released from the elevated storage reservoir to turbine generators in a power plant at a lower elevation. A hydroelectric power plant that uses both pumped water and natural stream flow to produce electricity is a Combined Pumped-Storage Hydroelectric Plant.

Pumping Hours
The total number of hours a turbine/generator unit was operated as a pump/motor set (for hydro and pumped storage units only).

Pure Pumped-Storage Hydroelectric Plant
A plant that produces power only from water that has previously been pumped to an upper reservoir.

Pyranometer
A device used to measure total incident solar radiation (direct beam, diffuse, and reflected radiation) per unit time per unit area.

Pyrheliometer
A device that measures the intensity of direct beam solar radiation.

Pyrolysis
The transformation on a compound or material into one or more substances by heat alone (without oxidation). Often called destructive distillation. Pyrolysis of biomass is the thermal degradation of the material in the absence of reacting gases, and occurs prior to or simultaneously with gasification reactions in a gasifier. Pyrolysis products consist of gases, liquids, and char generally. The liquid fraction of pyrolisized biomass consists of an insoluble viscous tar, and pyroligneous acids (acetic acid, methanol, acetone, esters, aldehydes, and furfural). The distribution of pyrolysis products varies depending on the feedstock composition, heating rate, temperature, and pressure.

Q

Qualifying Facilities (QFs)
A designation created by the Public Utility Regulatory Policies Act of 1978 (PURPA), for non-utility power producers that meet certain operating, efficiency and fuel use standards set by the Federal Energy Regulatory Commission. To receive status as a qualifying facility (QF) under PURPA, the facility must produce electric energy and "another

form of useful thermal energy through the sequential use of energy," and meet certain ownership, operating and efficiency criteria established by the Federal Energy Regulatory Commission (FERC). (See the Code of Federal Regulations, Title 18, Part 292.) QFs may rely on renewable energy sources or cogeneration.

R

R-Value

In thermal insulation, the thermal resistance of insulation materials or constructions.

Radial

A transmission or distribution system that is not networked and does not provide multiple parallel flow paths.

Radial Array

A group of earthing electrodes or conductors of equal length and ampacity, connected at a central point and extending outward at equal angles, spoke fashion, to provide a low earth impedance reference.

Railroad and Railway Services

Railroad and railway services include electricity supplied and services rendered to railroads and interurban and street railways, for general railroad use, including the propulsion of cars or locomotives, where such electricity is supplied under separate and distinct rate schedules.

RAPS

Remote Area Power Supply Systems. A power generation system which can provide electricity to remote and rural homes, usually incorporating power generated from renewable sources such as solar panels and wind generators, as well as non-renewable sources such as diesel or petrol powered generators.

Ratchet or Ratcheted Demand Charge

The Demand Charge level that a customer pays each month regardless of actual consumption. The demand charge is based on the peak consumption rate during a rolling period of time (usually 12 months.)

Rate

The unit charge or charges made by an energy company or utility to customers for energy. Rate structures include:

- Block - A rate that provides different unit charges for consumption falling within various blocks of demand or consumption.

- Flat - A rate that provides for a specified charge irrespective of the quantity used or the contract demand
- Lifeline - A rate structure applicable for residential customers that includes a specified block of energy use priced below the allocated cost of service. The block of energy may be priced at a flat amount for the entire block or on a per unit basis.
- Mileage-Based - A rate determined by the length of the haul (e.g. 4>/100 miles.)
- One-Part - A commodity charge (per-unit rate) with no component charging for reservation, demand, etc.
- Postage-Stamp - Transportation rate which applies for a given zone or area rather than the distance of actual transportation.
- Seasonal - A rate that varies based on the season during which the service is received.
- Step - A rate based on a tiered, or "stepped" price structure. The rate or price depends on the particular step within which the last consumed unit falls.
- Straight-Line - A charge per unit that is constant regardless of the level of service; i.e., the price does not change with an increase or decrease in the number of units used.
- Three-Part - A rate that provides three components for determining the total bill, (1) customer charge, (2) demand charge and (3) commodity charge.
- the total bill, (1) demand charge and (2) commodity charge.
- Volumetric - A rate or charge for a commodity or service that is calculated and charged on the basis of the amount or volume actually received by the purchaser.
- Zone - Rate charged for service in a particular zone, where each zone through which energy moves bears a different rate.

Rate Base

The value of property upon which a utility is given the opportunity to earn a specified rate of return as established by a regulatory authority. The rate base generally represents the value of property used by the utility in providing service and may be calculated by any one or a combination of the following accounting methods: fair value, prudent investment, reproduction cost or original cost. The rate base may include a working capital allowance covering such elements as cash, working capital, materials and supplies, prepayments, minimum bank balances and tax offsets. The rate base may be adjusted by deductions for accumulated provision for depreciation, contributions in aid of construction, accumulated deferred income taxes and accumulated deferred investment tax credits. The value established by a regulatory authority, upon which a utility is permitted to earn a specified rate of return. Generally, this represents the amount of property used and useful in public service and may be based on the following values or combinations thereof; fair value, prudent investment, reproduction cost, or original cost; and may provide for the inclusion of cash working capital, Construction Work in Progress, Materials and Supplies, and deductions for: Accumulated Provision for Depreciation, Customer Advances for Construction, and Accumulated Deferred Income Taxes and Accumulated Deferred Investment Tax Credits.

Rate Class
A group of customers identified as a class and subject to a rate different from the rates of other groups. See also Classes of Electric Service.

Rate Design
The development of electricity prices for various customer classes to meet revenue requirements dictated by operating needs and costs within current regulatory and legislative policy goals.

Rate of Return
The profit a regulated utility is given the opportunity to earn. The allowed rate of return is the percentage determined by the jurisdictional state or federal commission based on standards including the cost of capital in other sectors with comparable risk. The achieved rate of return is the actual result the utility obtained over any given period. In the utility industry, rate of return usually refers to the rate of return on rate base.

Rate Schedule
The rates, charges and provisions under which service is supplied to a designated class of customers. Also referred to as a Service Classification.

Rated Power Output
Used by wind generator manufacturers to provide a baseline for measuring performance. Rated output may vary by manufacturer. For example, one manufacturer's 1500 watt turbine mayproduce that amount of power at a 30 mph windspeed, while another brand of 1500 watt turbine may not make 1500 Watts until it gets a 40 mph windspeed! So read manufacturer's ratings statements very carefully.

Reactance
Opposition to the flow of alternating current. Capacitive reactance is the opposition offered by capacitor, and inductive reactance is the opposition offered by a coil or other inductance.

Recloser
The automatic closing of a circuit-interrupting device following automatic tripping.

Rectifier
An electrical device used to change AC power into DC power. A battery charger is a rectifier.

Re-Regulating Reservoir
A reservoir located downstream from a hydroelectric peaking plant which stores the widely fluctuating discharges from the upstream plant in order to release them downstream in a relatively uniform manner.

Reaction Turbine
Reaction turbines produce power from the pressure of water 'falling' on the runners after flowing through the guide vanes. Reaction turbines can operate with head as low as two feet, but require much higher flow rates than impulse turbines.

Reactive Power
The power that oscillates back and forth between inductive and capacitive circuit elements without ever being used. The function of reactive power is to establish and sustain the electric and magnetic fields required to perform useful work. Reactive power is utilized to control voltage on the transmission network, particularly, the portion of the electrical power flow incapable of performing real work or energy transfer (see REAL POWER). Reactive power is that portion of electricity that establishes and sustains the electric and magnetic fields of alternating current equipment. It must be supplied to most types of magnetic equipment, such as motors and transformers. It also must supply the reactive losses on transmission facilities. Reactive power is provided by generators, synchronous condensers or electrostatic equipment, such as capacitors, and directly influences electric system voltage. It is measured in megavars. The product of voltage and current and the sine of the phase angle between them measured in units of voltamperes reactive and standard multiples thereof, ie: 1000 VAr = 1 kVAr 1000 kVAr = lMvar

Reactive Power Generation
The production of electric current that leads or lags the phase of the electric voltage. Reactive power supplies the charging power for electromagnetic loads and the reactive needs of the transmission system.

Real Power
Watts. The portion of the electrical power flow capable of performing real work or energy transfer. Real power is utilized to supply customer load on the transmission network and is expressed in megawatts.

Real Power Loss Service
Compensates for losses measured in KWh incurred by the Host Control Area(s) as a result of the interchange transaction for a transmission customer.

Real-Time Market
The competitive generation market controlled and coordinated by the ISO for maintaining system balance by increasing or decreasing energy supply as needed.

Real-Time Pricing
Time of day pricing whereby the customer receives frequent signals on the cost of consuming electricity at that time.

Recallable Available Transmission Capability (RATC)
Transmission Capability - Transmission Reliability Margin - Contracted Recallable Transmission Service -Non-Recallable Transmission Service = Recallable Available Transmission Capability

Recall Rights
The provision for a wholesale seller of power to cease to perform, generally in order to use such power to serve its indigenous retail loads.

Receipt Point
The point on a pipeline's system at which it receives natural gas into its system.

Received Energy
Energy received by Xcel Energy from the Customer.

Receiving Control Area
The control area within whose metered boundaries a schedule of capacity and/or energy is consumed. Absent other offsetting simultaneous interchange schedules, the Receiving Control Area will accept a net import schedule of capacity and/or energy, in lieu of, or in addition to, its own generation to meet Control Area load requirements.

Reciprocity
Requires those that own, control or operate transmission facilities and request open-access service to, in turn, provide open access service to the transmitting utility.

Recirculation Systems
A type of solar heating system that circulate warm water from storage through the collectors and exposed piping whenever freezing conditions occur; obviously a not very efficient system when operating in this mode.

Reclose
To return a circuit breaker to its closed position after it has opened by relay action.

Recoverable Gas Reserves
The quantity of natural gas determined to be economically recoverable and available for delivery from a well or wells at a given price over a specific period of time.

Recycle
To process waste materials in order to regain new material for human use.

Redelivery
Delivery of natural gas by a pipeline back to a shipper or to a shipper's account that the pipeline had received from the shipper.

Redundancy
The inclusion of additional assemblies and circuits (as within a UPS) with provision for automatic switchover from a failing assembly or circuit to its backup counterpart.

Refill
The annual process of filling a reservoir; also refers to the point at which the hydroelectric system is considered "full" from the seasonal snowmelt runoff.

Refined Helium
See HELIUM, REFINED.

Reflection
The return wave generated when a traveling wave reaches a load, a source, or a junction where there is a change in line impedance.

Reforming
A chemical process that uses heat in presence of a catalyst to break down a substance into desired components; e.g., natural gas or light oils may be reformed into lower Btu fuel gas. Also used to describe the process of refining gasoline designed to burn with fewer emissions.

Regenerative Cooling
A type of cooling system that uses a charging and discharging cycle with a thermal or latent heat storage subsystem.

Regenerative Heating
The process of using heat that is rejected in one part of a cycle for another function or in another part of the cycle.

Registered Capacity
Full load capability of a generating unit as declared by the generator,

less the energy consumed through the unit transformer.

Regulator
A device used to control the current and voltage from power generating sources such as solar arrays and wind generators to allow charging of batteries.

Relamping
The replacement of a non-functional or ineffective lamp with a new, more efficient lamp.

Reliability
The ability of the electric system to adequately supply customers at all times, taking into account scheduled and unscheduled outages of system facilities. It is also the ability of the electric system to withstand sudden disturbances, such as electric short circuits or unanticipated loss of system facilities.

Renewable Energy
Electricity produced by sources that are capable of being replaced naturally and do not involve the burning of fossil fuels or the use of nuclear energy. Renewable energy is considered less harmful to the environment because it results in lower air pollution, emissions and waste than electricity from traditional sources. Some examples of renewable energy sources are solar, wind and geothermal (heat from the earth) sources and from the burning of biomass (agricultural or other wastes). Energy derived from resources that are regenerative. This includes solar power, wind, wave and tide and hydroelectricity. Wood, straw and waste are often called solid renewable energy, while landfill gas and sewage gas can be described as gaseous renewable.

RFI
Radio Frequency Interference.

Regulation
The governmental function of controlling or directing economic entities through the process of rulemaking and adjudication.

Regulating Reserve
The amount of spinning reserve responsive to automatic generation control, which is sufficient to provide normal regulating margin.

Regulatory Out Clause
A contractual provision whereby a party is excused from performance due to the actions of a jurisdictional regulatory agency.

Ridethrough
The ability of a power conditioner to supply output power when input power is lost.

Relative Strength Index
A principal momentum indicator or price oscillator used with natural gas futures. RSI values fluctuate between 0 and 100; 70+ indicates an overbought market and 30 or less indicates an oversold market.

Relay
A device that is operative by a variation in the condition of one electric circuit to affect the operation of another device in the same or in another electric circuit.

Releasing Shipper
A shipper who is the original capacity holder of firm space on a pipeline for which reservation fees are paid, and who desires to sell this capacity under the capacity release program.

Reliability
The statistical probability of trouble-free operation of a given component or assembly. Used principally as a function of MTBF and MTTR. The degree to which the performance of the elements of a system results in power being delivered to consumers within accepted standards and in the amount desired. The degree of reliability may be measured by the frequency, duration and magnitude of adverse effects on consumer service. The guarantee of system performance at all times and under all reasonable conditions to assure constancy, quality, adequacy and economy of electricity. It is also the assurance of a continuous supply of electricity for customers at the proper voltage and frequency.

Remote Terminal Unit (RTU)
A remotely controlled unit which gathers accumulated and instantaneous data to be telemetered to a specified control center which displays the current status of the generation facility. Inputs can be used for economic dispatch.

Removal Permit
A permit for the removal (export) of gas from a given Canadian province issued by the appropriate government body.

Renewable Energy
Any source of energy that is continually available or that can be renewed or replaced. Examples include wind, solar, geothermal, hydro, photovoltaic, wood and waste. Nonrenewable energy sources include coal, oil, and gas which all exist in finite amounts. Energy that is generated

from replaceable or non-depletable sources. These sources include sunlight or solar energy and other sources like wind, biomass and hydro energy. Tidal energy, wave energy and geothermal energy are also considered as renewable.

Renewable Resources
Energy resources that, when used, are not depleted eg. wind energy and solar energy A power source that is continuously or cyclically renewed by nature, i.e. solar, wind, hydroelectric, geothermal, biomass or similar sources of energy..

Replacement Shipper
A shipper who acquires firm transportation capacity after release by another shipper under the capacity release program. (Also known as "acquiring shipper.")

Repowering
The partial or complete replacement of the existing steam supply system with a new (and usually technologically different) steam supply system. Most other systems and components, including the steam-turbine generator, are refurbished and reused. Repowering generally increases the output of the plant and reduces its heat rate, thus improving overall efficiency.

Repressuring
Forcing natural gas or water, under pressure, into the oil reservoir in an attempt to increase the recovery of crude oil.

Requirements, Full
A sale by a supplier to a purchaser in which the seller pledges to meet all of the purchaser's requirements, or the purchaser pledges to buy all of its requirements from the seller, or both.

Requirements, Partial
A sale by a supplier to a purchaser in which the seller pledges to meet a part of the purchaser's energy requirements.

Relating
Change in a generator's capability as a result of changes in conditions such as age, auxiliary equipment, cooling, etc.

Reregulation
The design and implementation of regulatory practices to be applied to the remaining regulated entities after restructuring of the vertically integrated electric utility. The remaining regulated entities would be those that continue to exhibit characteristics of a natural monopoly, where

imperfections in the market prevent the realization of more competitive results, and where, in light of other policy considerations, competitive results are unsatisfactory in one or more respects. Reregulation could employ the same or different regulatory practices as those used before restructuring.

Reservation Fee

A set unit charge payable at the outset by the recipient of a service based on total entitlement. Similar to an "option" charge or "demand" charge. Currently used by natural gas transmission pipelines for firm transportation service.

RESERVE

The availability of additional generation.

Installed reserve is the amount of existing generation that is higher than needed to meet a forecasted peak load.

Operating reserve is the amount of generation that may be used to offset a loss of supply to maintain a power system.

Reserve Capacity

Capacity in excess of that required to carry peak load, available to meet unanticipated demands for power or to generate power in the event of loss of generation.

Reserve Generating Capacity

The extra generating capacity required on any power system over and above the expected peak load. Such a reserve is required mainly for two reasons: (i) in case of an unexpected breakdown of generating equipment; (ii) in case the actual peak load is higher than forecast.

Reserve Margin

The difference between the peak load and the portion of electric resources that are expected to be able to operate during the peak load of a utility or geographic area. Reserve margin is expressed in megawatts or the percentage by which the available portion of the resources exceeds the peak load.The amount of unused available capability that can be applied to the system within 10 minutes at peakload for a utility system, expressed as a percentage of total capability.

Reserve Shutdown

A state in which the unit was available for service but not electrically connected to the transmission system for economic reasons.

Reserves

Natural gas in natural underground formation in wells, fields or pools.

Reserves to Production Ratio (R/P)
An estimate used to project the productive life of a field based upon the size of the field compared to the annual production capacity.

Reservoir
Man-made: a structure which stores water for later use in the production of electricity. Natural: a rock stratum that forms a trap in which oil and natural gas may accumulate.

Residential
The residential sector is defined as private household establishments which consume energy primarily for space heating, water heating, air conditioning, lighting, refrigeration, cooking and clothes drying. The classification of an individual consumer's account, where the use is both residential and commercial, is based on principal use.

Residential with Electric Space Heating
A subdivision of the residential classification that includes those customers who use electricity as the principal source of space heating throughout the entire premises from permanently installed electric heating equipment.

Residual Fuel Oil
The topped crude of refinery operation after the removal of valuable distillates like gasoline; includes No. 5 and No. 6 fuel oils. Residual fuel oil is used for the production of electric power, space heating, vessel bunkering and various industrial purposes. Imports of residual fuel oil include imported crude oil burned as fuel.

Resistance
The inherent characteristic of a material to inhibit the transfer of energy. In electrical conductors, electrical resistance results in the generation of heat. Electrical resistance is measured in Ohms. The heat transfer resistance properties of insulation products are quantified as the R-value.

Resistance Heating
A type of heating system that provides heat from the resistance of an electrical current flowing through a conductor.

Resistive Voltage Drop
The voltage developed across a cell by the current flow through the resistance of the cell.

Resource Efficiency
The use of smaller amounts of physical resources to produce the same product or service. Resource efficiency involves a concern for the use of

all physical resources and materials used in the production and use cycle, not just the energy input.

Resource Recovery
The process of converting municipal solid waste to energy and/or recovering materials for recycling.

Resources
A term that refers to the cumulative capacity of a set of electric power plants. The set of power plants may be in a defined geographic area, such as the Bay Area; power plants owned by a single party such as an electric utility; or all of the power plants available to meet the load of a utility or ISO, regardless of their location on the transmission system or ownership of the power plants.

Resting Order
In futures trading, an order away from the market waiting to be executed.

Restoration Service
Source of power which enables a host control area to restore its system and a transmission customer to start its generating units or restore service to its customers when local power is not available.

Restructuring
The unbundling of pipeline transportation, storage, gathering and sales services and associated realignment of service obligations resulting from Order No.636.

Retail
Sales covering electrical energy supplied for residential, commercial and industrial end-use purposes. Other
small classes, such as agriculture and street lighting, also are included in this category.

Retail Competition
A system under which more than one electric provider can sell to retail customers, and retail customers are allowed to buy from more than one provider. See also DIRECT ACCESS.

Retail Wheeling
The sale of electricity by a utility or other supplier to a customer in another utility's retail service territory. Refers to the use of the local utility's transmission and distribution lines to deliver the power from a wholesale supplier to a retail customer by a third parry. A term for the process of transmitting electricity over transmission lines not owned by the supplier of the electricity to a retail customer of the supplier. With retail wheeling,

an electricity consumer can secure their own supply of electricity from a broker or directly from the generating source. The power is then wheeled at a fixed rate, or at a regulated "non-discriminatory" rate set by a utility commission.

Retroactive Ratemaking
A practice prohibited under the Natural Gas Act which bars increasing gas rates on a retroactive basis.

Return Duct
The central heating or cooling system contains a fan that gets its air supply through these ducts, which ideally should be installed in every room of the house. The air from a room will move towards the lower pressure of the return duct.

Return on Capital Employed (ROCE)
A measure of the effectiveness of a business in using its sources of capital to generate earnings. It is a measure of EBIT divided by capital employed. Capital employed represents the total debt and equity components of the balance sheet.

Return on Equity
Compensation for the investment of capital; i.e., earnings. Regulated public utilities statutorily entitled to charge rates that permit them to earn a fair return on their equity invested.

Return on Invested Capital (ROIC)
A fundamental measure of the earning power of a company. It is equal to earnings before interest and taxes times one minus the tax rate, all divided by total assets minus current liabilities.

Revenue
The total amount of money received by a firm from sales of its products and/or services, gains from the sales or exchange of assets, interest and dividends earned on investments and other increases in the owner's equity except those arising from capital adjustments.

Revenue Requirement
The amount of funds (revenue) a utility must take in to cover the sum of its estimated operation and
maintenance expenses, debt service, taxes and allowed rate of return. Revenue requirement is often defined as: Revenue requirement + expenses + depreciation + taxes + (rate of return x rate base) or:

$RR=E + D + T+(rxRB)$

- E = Operating expenses (including taxes other than income taxes)
- D = Depreciation expense

- T = Income taxes
- r = Rate of return (percentage authorized to the utility)
- RB = Rate base (net investment in facilities serving customers)

Reverse Thermosiphoning
When heat seeks to flow from a warm area (e.g., heated space) to a cooler area, such as a solar air collector at night without a reverse flow damper.

Reversing Valve
A component of a heat pump that reverses the refrigerant's direction of flow, allowing the heat pump to switch from cooling to heating or heating to cooling.

Ribbon (Photovoltaic) Cells
A type of solar photovoltaic device made in a continuous process of pulling material from a molten bath of photovoltaic material, such as silicon, to form a thin sheet of material.

RIN
Real-time Information Network. Method proposed by the FERC to have information available via an Electronic Bulletin Board about transmission availability, scheduling, economic dispatch, service interruptions and system reliability. See also OASIS.

Right of First Refusal
Process which allows any long-term firm gas transportation customer, including formerly bundled city-gate sales customers, to continue receiving firm gas transportation service by paying up to the maximum rate and matching the length of a term offered by another customer who is seeking service.

Risk Management
Risk management is the reducing of the prospect of losses which will interfere with the execution of a company's business strategy. It allows managers to focus directly on shareholder value as an objective in decision making. A risk management program frequently involves five steps:

- identify the source of exposure
- quantify the exposure
- clarify the impact of the exposure on the company's overall business strategy
- assess the capability for managing the exposure internally
- select the appropriate risk management products.

RMS

(Root mean square) used for AC voltage and current values. It is the square root of the average of the squares of all the instantaneous amplitudes occurring during one cycle. RMS is called the effective value of AC because it is the value of AC voltage or current that will cause the same amount of head to be produced in a circuit containing only resistance that would be caused by a DC voltage or current of the same value. In a pure sine wave the RMS value is equivalent to .707 times the peak value and the peak value is 1.414 times the RMS value. The normal home wall outlet which supplies 120 volts RMS has a peak voltage of 169.7 volts.

Rolling blackouts

Rolling blackouts are controlled power outages designed to lessen the threat of an overload or crashing of major transmission systems brought on by short supply and high demand for power. Rolling blackouts are scheduled for predetermined sectors of the transmission grid at timed intervals. This spreads the burden of power shortages across the entire region for short, manageable time periods (usually no more than a few hours) rather than allowing unplanned blackouts to hit and jeopardize public safety and sensitive equipment.

Rolled-in Pricing

A pricing method which establishes rates on a weighted average of all costs, as opposed to allocating specific costs to specific customers.

Rollover Clause

In natural gas contracts, a contract clause that permits a contract to extend beyond the initial term. In
futures contracts, a straddle trading procedure involving the shift of one month of a straddle into a future month, while maintaining the other contract month of the original spread.

Root

The area of a blade nearest to the hub. Generally the thickest and widest part of the blade. Root Mean Square (RMS)
The square root of the average square of the instantaneous values of an AC output. For a sine wave the RMS value is 0.707 times the peak value. The equivalent value of AC current, I, that will produce the same heating in a conductor with resistence, R, as a DC current of value I.the corrosion of the protected structure.

Rotating Field

The electrical field that develops in a multiphase generator. The varying currents of through pairs of stator winding cause the magnetic field to vary as if it was a single rotating field.

Rotating Outage

Also known as rolling blackouts, these are controlled events to turn off electricity to selected areas to keep the electricity supply and load in balance. To make sure that no one neighborhood or region bears the entire burden of energy shortages, outages are rotated through multiple areas of a utility's service area. During an emergency, a system operator sequentially rotates portions of its system that will be without power so that the total system load remains under its maximum load level and no one customer is without power for the entire emergency.

Rotor

An electric generator consists of an armature and a field structure. The armature carries the wire loop, coil, or other windings in which the voltage is induced, whereas the field structure produces the magnetic field. In small generators, the armature is usually the rotating component (rotor) surrounded by the stationary field structure (stator). In large generators in commercial electric power plants the situation is reversed. In a wind energy conversion device, the blades and rotating components.

Roundturn

The completion of a purchase and a sale of a futures contract.

Royalty

With respect to oil and gas properties, a share of production, which may or may not bear a share of expenses of production, depending upon the terms of the specific lease.

Royalty Owner

A person who owns a royalty interest in production.

RTG

Regional Transmission Group.

Rules of Conduct

Rules set in advance to delineate acceptable activities by participants, particularly participants with significant market power.

Run-of-River Plant

A hydroelectric plant which depends chiefly on the flow of a stream as it occurs for generation, as opposed to a storage project, which has space available to store water from one season to another. Some run-of-river projects have a limited storage capacity (pondage) which permits them to regulate streamflow on a daily or weekly basis.

Running and Quick-Start Capability

In general, quick-start capability refers to generating units that can be available for load within a 3-minute period.

Runner
The part of a micro hydro turbine that actually attaches to the alternator drive shaft. The *buckets' on the runner are what the water pushes against to turn the runner and generate electricity.

R-Value
A measure of the capacity of a material to resist heat transfer. The R-Value is the reciprocal of the conductivity of a material (U-Value). The larger the R-Value of a material, the greater its insulating properties.

S

Saccrificial Anode
A piece of metal buried near a structure that is to be protected from corrosion. The metal of the scrificial anod is intended to corrode and reduce the corrosion of the protected structure.

Safety Disconnect
An electronic (automatic or manual) switch that disconnects one circuit from another circuit. These are used to isolate power generation or storage equipment from conditions such as voltage spikes or surges, thus avoiding potential damage to equipment.

Safety Ground
An alternate path of return current, during a fault condition, for the purpose of tripping a circuit breaker. Also, the means of establishing a load at earth level.

Safety Switch (Residual Current Device)
An electrical safety device specifically designed to immediately switch the electricity off when electricity leaking to earth is detected as a level harmful to you. These devices offer a high level of personal protection from electric shock.

SAG
A short duration low voltage condition .A period of lower than normal voltage, causing motor heating and disk drive problems.

Sales
The amount of kilowatt-hours sold in a given period of time, usually grouped by classes of service, such as residential, commercial, industrial and other. Other sales include public street and highway lighting, other sales to public authorities and railways, and interdepartmental sales.

Sand

Sand or porous sandstone in underground strata that contains natural gas.

Saturation, Appliance or Customer

The number of appliances or customers divided by the basic units or total potential of the market. The term should not be used alone, but should be related to customers, families, households, population or other qualifying terms indicating the relevant market.

SCADA

Supervisory Control and Data Acquisition - A system of remote control and telemetry used to monitor and control a transmission system.

Schedule

An agreed-upon transaction size (measured in MW), start and end times, start and end ramp times and rates required for delivery and receipt of power and energy between contracting parties and the control areas involved in the transaction

Scheduled Interchange

Electric power schedules to flow between control areas. Typically, this is the net of all sales, purchases and wheeling transactions between those areas at a given time.

Scheduled Outage

The shutdown of a generating unit, transmission line or other facility, for inspection or maintenance, in accordance with an advance schedule.

Scheduling

Operating a power system to balance generation and loads; managing the accounting, billing and information reporting for such operations.

Scheduling Area

A scheduling area is similar to a control area, in that a utility schedules energy and provides capacity for a defined area. The utility will run a 24 hour control center and is recognized as a MAPP Scheduling Area. Unlike a control area, a scheduling area does not have generators that can follow the load in their area, and are completely captured within one or more control areas. They must contract for load following services. Within MAPP, a scheduling area must identify a Host Control Area.

Scheduling Penalty

A penalty assessed for differences between the amount of gas scheduled and the amount of gas tendered for delivery.

SCR

(Semiconductor, or silicon, controlled rectifier) an electronic DC switch which can be triggered into conduction by a pulse to a gate electrode, but can only be cut off by reducing the main current below a predetermined level (usually zero).

Scroll Case

An enclosure used by some reaction water turbines to channel the water into the turbine guide vanes as the optimal angle to maximize the turbine's efficiency.

Seasonal Rate

See RATE, SEASONAL.

Seasonal Service

Service sold only during certain periods of the year. Seasonal service may be sold either on a firm or on an interruptible basis.

Secondary Fuels

Fuels obtained from primary sources for example, electricity generated from burning coal, gas or oil.

Secondary Recovery

All methods of oil and natural gas extraction in which energy sources extrinsic to the reservoir other than pumps or pumping units are used.

Sectors

The retail power market is commonly divided into several sectors for energy planning. These can include residential, commercial, industrial, agricultural, public agency and street lighting.

Securitize

The aggregation of contracts for the purchase of the power output from various energy projects into one pool which then offers shares for sale in the investment market. This strategy diversifies project risks from what they would be if each project were financed individually, thereby reducing the cost of financing.

Security

The ability of the bulk electric power system to withstand sudden disturbances and remain in operation.

Security Coordinator

The entity that provides the security assessment and emergency operations coordination for a group of control areas. Security Coordinators must not participate in the wholesale or retail merchant functions.

Seasonal Energy Efficiency Ratio (SEER)
Standard measurement of the overall efficiency of a heat pump or air conditioner during the cooling season. It is the total season heat removed (Btu) divided by the total electrical energy input (watthours) during the same period. The larger the SEER, the more efficient the unit.

Selectable Load
Any device, such as lights, televisions, and power tools, which is plugged into your central power source and used only intermittently.

Selective Absorber
A solar absorber surface that has high absorbence at wavelengths corresponding to that of the solar spectrum and low emittance in the infrared range.

Self-Excited
An electric machine in which the field current is secured from its own armature current.

Self-Generation
A generation facility dedicated to serving a particular retail customer, usually located on the customer's premises. The facility may either be owned directly by the retail customer or owned by a third party with a contractual arrangement to provide electricity to meet some or all of the customer's load. On-site production and use of electricity by an industrial facility or other energy customer.

Self-Service Generators
Generators operated in parallel with the Xcel Energy System only for the purpose of reducing the Customer's peak load. These generators are not normally dispatchable by Xcel Energy.

Seller (Writer) of Option
The seller of an option is obligated to make or take delivery according to the terms of the contract if the buyer chooses to exercise the option. The seller is paid a premium by the buyer for assuming this risk. The seller is also known as the option grantor.

Semiconductor
A semiconductor is an electronic conductor (ex., silicon, selenium or germanium) with a resistivity between metals and insulators. Current flows through the semiconductor normally via holes or electrons.

Sending Control Area
The Control Area within whose metered boundaries a schedule of capacity and/or energy originates. When there are no offsetting

simultaneous interchange schedules, the Sending Control Area will increase generation, or use generation not needed for load requirements to effectuate a net export schedule of capacity and/or energy.

Sendout
The total natural gas produced or purchased (including exchange gas receipts), or the net natural gas withdrawn from underground storage within a specified time interval, measured at the point of production, purchase or withdrawal, adjusted for changes in local storage quantity. Gas send-out is comprised of natural gas sales, exchanges, deliveries, natural gas used by the company and unaccounted-for gas.

Sensible Cooling Effect
The difference between the total cooling effect and the dehumidifying effect.

Sensible Cooling Load
The interior heat gain due to heat conduction, convection, and radiation from the exterior into the interior, and from occupants and appliances.

Sensible Heat
The heat absorbed or released when a substance undergoes a change in temperature.

Sensible Heat Storage
A heat storage system that uses a heat storage medium, and where the additional or removal of heat results in a change in temperature.

Separately Excited
Use of an exciter for sending current through the field windings of an electric machine in place of taking the field current from its own armature current.

Series
A configuration of an electrical circuit in which the positive lead is connected to the negative lead of another energy producing, conducting, or consuming device. The voltages of each device are additive, whereas the current is not.

Series Connection
A way of joining photovoltaic cells by connecting positive leads to negative leads; such a configuration increases the voltage.

Series Resistance
Parasitic resistance to current flow in a cell due to mechanisms such as resistance from the bulk of the semiconductor material, metallic contacts, and interconnections.

Setting Angle

The angle between the blade Chord and the plane of the blade's rotation. Also called Pitch or blade angle. A blade carved with a Twist has a different setting angle at the Tip than at the Root.

Service Area

The territory in which a utility system is required or has the right to supply service to ultimate customers. The geographical territory served by an electric company.

Service Classification

See RATE SCHEDULE.

Service Connection (Service Pipe)

The pipe that carries natural gas from a main to a customer's meter.

Service Drop

The overhead conductors between the electric supply, such as the last pole, and the building or structure being served.

Service Entrance

The equipment installed between the utility's service drop, or lateral, and the customer's conductors. Typically consists of the meter used for billing, switches and/or circuit breakers and/or fuses, and a metal housing.

Service Factor

(Of a motor) a measurement of the motor's ability to operate under abnormal conditions. A 1.15 times its rated load continuously when operated at its rated voltage, frequency, temperature, etc. Therefore, a 125 horsepower motor could be operated as a 143.75 h.p. motor under normal conditions.

Service Obligation

The obligation of a natural gas company to perform the services required by law or certificate regardless of whether the company has contractual duties.

Service Voltage

The voltage level at which a customer is connected to the electric transmission and distribution system.

SG: Specific Gravity

The ratio of the mass of a given volume of any substance to that of the same volume of another substance used as a standard (usually water for solids and liquids).

Shaft
The rotating part in the center of a wind generator or motor that transfers power.

Shaft Horsepower
Energy created through rotational or motive force through a coupling.

Shallow Discharge
Removal of Ampere-Hours from a battery such that more than 50% of capacity remains at the end of the discharge process.

Shaping
The scheduling and operation of generating resources to meet changing load levels. Load shaping on a hydroelectric system usually involves the adjustment of water releases from reservoirs so that generation and load are continuously in balance.

Shaving
See PEAK SHAVING.

Shielding
Imposing a metallic barrier to reduce the coupling of undesirable signals.

Shipper
One who contracts with a pipeline for transportation of natural gas and who retains title to all natural gas while it is being transported by the pipeline.

Short (or short position)
A short position is the trading position of a person who has sold securities or commodities that they do not own with the hope of buying at a later date at a lower price. A short sale is a contract for the sale of something, such as a commodity or futures contract, that the seller does not own. It is a method of profiting from the expected fall in price of the commodity but risky because if the commodity goes up, the owner of the short will have to purchase the underlying commodity at whatever price it reaches to cover the short sale.

Short Circuit Current
The current flowing freely through an external circuit that has no load or resistance; the maximum current possible. The current flowing freely from a photovoltaic cell or module through an external circuit that has no load or resistance; the maximum current possible. Unit: Ampere (A).

Short Run Avoided Cost (SRAC)
A calculation of the costs that are not or would not be incurred by a

utility because it takes power from a of over a modest, specified (e.g., one month) period.

Short Run Marginal Cost
All variable production costs.

Short-term Parallel
See Closed Transition Transfer

Shrinkage
The reduction in volume of wet natural gas due to the removal of natural gas liquids, hydrogen sulfide, carbon dioxide, water vapor and other impurities from the natural gas

Shunt Load
An electrical load used to safely use excess generated power when not needed for its primary uses. A shunt load in a residential photovoltaic system might be domestic water heating, such that when power is not needed for typical building loads, such as operating lights or running HVAC system fans and pumps, it still provides value and is used in a constructive, safe manner.

Sine Wave
A graph, with the x axis for amplitude and the y axis for time, depicting AC voltage or current. The center line of the x axis is zero and divides polarity (direction).

Single-Package System
A year 'round heating and air conditioning system that has all the components completely encased in one unit outside the home. Proper matching of components can mean more energy-efficient operation compared to components purchased separately.

Single-Phase
A generator with a single armature coil, which may have many turns and the alternating current output consists of a succession of cycles. (With a three phase source) one or tow phase conductors. (Single phase source) A single output which may be center tapped for dual voltage levels.

Single Phase Condition
An unusual condition where one phase of a three-phase system is lost. It is characterized by unusual effects on lighting and other loads.

Sinudoidal Waveform
A waveform that can be expressed mathematically by using the sine function.

Sizing
The process of designing a solar system to meet a specified load given the solar resource and the nominal or rated energy output of the solar energy collection or conversion device.

Slamming
The practice of switching a customer's energy supply service without the customer's authorization. This practice is illegal.

Soft-Start Circuit
Circuitry that limits the initial power demand when a UPS has been operating in emergency mode and commercial power is restored. Also, it controls the rate at which UPS output increases to normal.

Solar Collectors
A device designed to capture light or heat energy from the sun. Solar thermal collectors are used in solar hot water systems (often found in homes) and photovoltaic collectors are used in solar electric systems

Solar Energy
Radiation energy from the sun falling upon the Earth's surface. Solar energy refers to energy generated directly from sunlight. The two main processes are conversion to electricity using solar cells or for thermal applications like water heating, room heating, drying or desalination. Concentrated sunlight can also be used to generate power using solar cells or by way of heating water or other fluid to drive a motor or turbine.

Solar Generation
The use of radiation from the sun to substitute for electric power or natural gas heating.

Source-Specific Gas Sales Contract
A contract that commits the seller to deliver natural gas, usually within a stated maximum and minimum, from specific described and committed natural gas reserves or sources.

Solar Heating
Technologies or systems that take advantage of the heat energy coming from the sun. Solar thermal
collectors are used in solar hot water systems (often found in homes) and photovoltaic collectors are used in
solar electric systems.

Solar Module or Solar Panel
A collection of solar cells interconnected to form a solar panel or module.

Solar Altitude Angle
The angle between a line from a point on the earth's surface to the center of the solar disc, and a line extending horizontally from the point.

Solar Air Heater
A type of solar thermal system where air is heated in a collector and either transferred directly to the interior space or to a storage medium, such as a rock bin.

Solar Noon
The time of the day, at a specific location, when the sun reaches its highest, apparent point in the sky; equal to true or due, geographic south.

Solar One
A solar thermal electric central receiver power plant ("power tower") located in Barstow, California, and completed in i 981. The Solar One had a design capacity of 10,000 peak kilowatts, and was composed of a receiver located on the top of a tower surrounded by a field of reflectors. The concentrated sunlight created steam to drive a steam turbine and electric generator located on the ground.

Solar Pond
A body of water that contains brackish (highly saline) water that forms layers of differing salinity (stratifies) that absorb and trap solar energy. Solar ponds can be used to provide heat for industrial or agricultural processes, building heating and cooling, and to generate electricity.

Solar Power Satellite
A solar power station investigated by NASA that entailed a satellite in geosynchronous orbit that would consist of a very large array of solar photovoltaic modules that would convert solar generated electricity to microwaves and beam them to a fixed point on the earth.

Solar Panel
See Photovoltaic Module.

Solar Radiation
A general term for the visible and near visible (ultraviolet and near-infrared) electromagnetic radiation that is emitted by the sun. It has a spectral, or wavelength, distribution that corresponds to different energy levels; short wavelength radiation has a higher energy than long-wavelength radiation.

Solar Simulator
An apparatus that replicates the solar spectrum, and used for testing solar energy conversion devices.

Solar Space Heater
A solar energy system designed to provide heat to individual rooms in a building.

Solar Spectrum
The total distribution of electromagnetic radiation emanating from the sun. The different regions of the solar spectrum are described by their wavelength range. The visible region extends from about 390 to 780 nanometers (a nanometer is one billionth of one meter). About 99 percent of solar radiation is contained in a wavelength region from 300 nm (ultraviolet) to 3,000 nm (near-infrared). The combined radiation in the wavelength region from 280 nm to 4,000 nm is called the broadband, or total, solar radiation.

Solar Thermal Electric Systems
Solar energy conversion technologies that convert solar energy to electricity, by heating a working fluid to power a turbine that drives a generator. Examples of these systems include central receiver systems, parabolic dish, and solar trough.

Solar Thermal Parabolic Dishes
A solar thermal technology that uses a modular mirror system that approximates a parabola and incorporates two-axis tracking to focus the sunlight onto receivers located at the focal point of each dish. The mirror system typically is made from a number of mirror facets, either glass or polymer mirror, or can consist of a single stretched membrane using a polymer mirror. The concentrated sunlight may be used directly by a Stirling, Rankine, or Brayton cycle heat engine at the focal point of the receiver or to heat a working fluid that is piped to a central engine. The primary applications include remote electrification, water pumping, and grid-connected generation.

Solar Thermal Systems
Solar energy systems that collect or absorb solar energy for useful purposes. Can be used to generate high temperature heat (for electricity production and/or process heat), medium temperature heat (for process and space/water heating and electricity generation), and low temperature heat (for water and space heating and cooling).

Solar Time
The period marked by successive crossing of the earth's meridian by the sun; the hour angle of the sun at a point of observance (apparent time) is corrected to true (solar) time by taking into account the variation in the earth's orbit and rate of rotation. Solar time and local standard time are usually different for any specific location.

Solar Trough Systems (see also Parabolic Trough, above) – A type of solar thermal system where sunlight is concentrated by a curved reflector onto a pipe containing a working fluid that can be used for process heat or to produce electricity. The world's largest solar thermal electric power plants use solar trough technology. They are located in California, and have a combined electricity generating capacity of 240,000 kilowatts.

Solar Transmittance
The amount of solar energy that passes through a glazing material, expressed as a percentage.

Solar Two
Solar Two is a retrofit of the Solar One project (see above). It is demonstrating the technical feasibility and power potential of a solar power tower using advanced molten-salt technology to store energy. Solar Two retains several of the main components of Solar One, including the receiver tower, turbine, generator, and the 1,818 heliostats.

Solenoid
An electromechanical device composed of a coil of wire wound around a cylinder containing a bar or plunger, that when a current is applied to the coil, the electromotive force causes the plunger to move; a series of coils or wires used to produce a magnetic field.

Solenoid Valve
An automatic valve that is opened or closed by an electromagnet.

Solid Fuels
Any fuel that is in solid form, such as wood, peat, lignite, coal, and manufactured fuels such as pulverized coal, coke, charcoal, briquettes, pellets, etc.

Solidity
In reference to a wind energy conversion device, the ratio of rotor blade surface area to the frontal, swept area that the rotor passes through.

Split System Air Conditioner
An air conditioning system that comes in two to five pieces: one piece contains the compressor, condenser, and a fan; the others have an evaporator and a fan. The condenser, installed outside the house, connects to several evaporators, one in each room to be cooled, mounted inside the house. Each evaporator is individually controlled, allowing different rooms or zones to be cooled to varying degrees.

Spray Pyrolysis
A deposition process whereby heat is used to break molecules into

elemental sources that are then spray deposited on a substrate.

Spreader Stocker
A type of furnace in which fuel is spread, automatically or mechanically, across the furnace grate.

Sputtering
A process used to apply photovoltaic semi-conductor material to a substrate by a physical vapor deposition process where high-energy ions are used to bombard elemental sources of semiconductor material, which eject vapors of atoms that are then deposited in thin layers on a substrate.

Square Wave Inverter
A type of inverter that produces square wave output.; consists of a DC source, four switches, and the load. The switches are power semiconductors that can carry a large current and withstand a high voltage rating. The switches are turned on and off at a correct sequence, at a certain frequency. The square wave inverter is the simplest and the least expensive to purchase, but it produces the lowest quality of power.

Squirrel Cage Motors
This is another name for an induction motor. The motors consist of a rotor inside a stator. The rotor has laminated, thin flat steel discs, stacked with channels along the length. If the casting composed of bars and attached end rings were viewed without the laminations the casting would appear similar to a squirrel cage.

Staebler-Wronski effect
The tendency of the sunlight to electricity conversion efficiency of amorphous silicon photovoltaic devices to degrade (drop) upon initial exposure to light.

Stack
A smokestack or flue for exhausting the products of combustion from a combustion appliance.

Stack **(Heat)** Loss Sensible and latent heat contained in combustion gases and vapor emitted to the atmosphere.

Stagnation Temperature
A condition that can occur in a solar collector if the working fluid does not circulate when sun is shining on the collector.

Stall
In reference to a wind turbine, a condition when the rotor stops turning.

Stand-Alone Generator
A power source/generator that operates independently of or is not connected to an electric transmission and distribution network; used to meet a load(s) physically close to the generator.

Stand-Alone Inverter
An inverter that operates independent of or is not connected to an electric transmission and distribution network.

Stand-Alone System
An system that operates independent of or is not connected to an electric transmission and distribution network. Power systems that are not connected to an electric supply net work or grid. They usually generate power using local resources like solar, wind or diesel.

Standard Air
Air with a weight of 0.075 pounds per cubic foot with an equivalent density of dry air at a temperature of 86 degrees Fahrenheit and standard barometric pressure of 29.92 inches of mercury.

Standard Conditions
In refrigeration, an evaporating temperature of 5 degrees Fahrenheit (F), a condensing temperature of 86 degrees F., liquid temperature before expansion of 77 degrees F., and suction temperature of 12 degrees F.

Standard Cubic Foot
A column of gas at standard conditions of temperature and pressure (32 degrees Fahrenheit and one atmosphere).

Standard Industrial Classification (SIC) Code
Standardized codes used to classify businesses by type of activity they engage in.

Stand-by Heat Loses
A term used to describe heat energy lost from a water heater tank.

Stand-By Power
For the consumer, this is the electricity that is used by your TVs, stereos, and other electronic devices that use remote controls. When you press "off" to turn off your device, minimal power (dormant mode) is still being used to maintain the internal electronics in a ready, quick-response mode. This way, your device can be turned on with your remote control and be immediately ready to operate.

Static Pressure
The force per unit area acting on the surface of a solid boundary parallel to the flow.

Starting Surge
Power, often above an appliance's rated wattage, required to bring any appliance with a motor up to operating speed.

Starting Torque
The torque at the bottom of a speed (rpm) versus torque curve. The torque developed by the motor is a percentage of the full-load or rated torque. At this torque the speed, the rotational speed of the motor as a percentage of synchronous speed is zero. This torque is what is available to initially get the load moving and begin its acceleration.

Steam
Water in vapor form; used as the working fluid in steam turbines and heating systems.

Steam Boiler
A type of furnace in which fuel is burned and the heat is used to produce steam.

Steam Turbine
A device that converts high-pressure steam, produced in a boiler, into mechanical energy that can then be used to produce electricity by forcing blades in a cylinder to rotate and turn a generator shaft.

Stirling Engine
A heat engine of the reciprocating (piston) where the working gas and a heat source are independent. The working gas is compressed in one region of the engine and transferred to another region where it is expanded. The expanded gas is then returned to the first region for recompression. The working gas thus moves back and forth in a closed cycle.

Stoichiometry
Chemical reactions, typically associated with combustion processes; the balancing of chemical reactions by providing the exact proportions of reactant compounds to ensure a complete reaction; all the reactants are used up to produce a single set of products.

Stoichiometric Ratio
The ratio of chemical substances necessary for a reaction to occur completely.

Storage Capacity
The amount of energy an energy storage device or system can store.

Storage Hydropower
A hydropower facility that stores water in a reservoir during high-inflow

periods to augment water during low-inflow periods. Storage projects allow the flow releases and power production to be more flexible and dependable. Many hydropower project operations use a combination of approaches.

Storage Tank
The tank of a water heater.

Storage Water Heater
A water heater that releases hot water from the top of the tank when a hot water tap is opened. To replace that hot water, cold water enters the bottom of the tank to ensure a full tank.

Storm Door
An exterior door that protects the primary door.

Storm Windows
Glass, plastic panels, or plastic sheets that reduce air infiltration and some heat loss when attached to either the interior or exterior of existing windows.

Stranded Investment (Costs and Benefits)
An investment in a power plant or demand side management measures or programs, that become uneconomical due to increased competition in the electric power market. For example, an electric power plant may produce power that is more costly than what the market rate for electricity is, and the power plant owner may have to close the plant, even though the capital and financing costs of building the plant have not been recovered through prior sales of electricity from the plant. This is considered a Stranded Cost. Stranded Benefits are those power provider investments in measures or programs considered to benefit consumers by reducing energy consumption and/or providing environmental benefits that have to be curtailed due to increased competition and lower profit margins.

Stud
A popular term used for a length of wood or steel used in or for wall framing.

Substation
An electrical installation containing power conversion (and sometimes generation) equipment, such as transformers, compensators, and circuit breakers.

Substrate
The physical material upon which a photovoltaic cell is applied.

Sun Path Diagram

A circular projection of the sky vault onto a flat diagram used to determine solar positions and shading effects of landscape features on a solar energy system.

Sunspace

A room that faces south (in the northern hemisphere), or a small structure attached to the south side of a house.

Sun Tempered Building

A building that is elongated in the east-west direction, with the majority of the windows on the south side. The area of the windows is generally limited to about 7% of the total floor area. A sun-tempered design has no added thermal mass beyond what is already in the framing, wall board, and so on. Insulation levels are generally high.

Superconducting Magnetic Energy Storage (SMES)

SMES technology uses the superconducting characteristics of low-temperature materials to produce intense magnetic fields to store energy. SMES has been proposed as a storage option to support large-scale use of photovoltaics and wind as a means to smooth out fluctuations in power generation.

Superconductivity

The abrupt and large increase in electrical conductivity exhibited by some metals as the temperature approaches absolute zero.

Super Insulated Houses

A type of house that has massive amounts of insulation, airtight construction, and controlled ventilation without sacrificing comfort, health, or aesthetics.

Super Window

A popular term for highly insulating window with a heat loss so low it performs better than an insulated wall in winter, since the sunlight that it admits is greater than its heat loss over a 24 hour period.

Supplementary Heat

A heat source, such as a space heater, used to provide more heat than that provided by a primary heating source.

Supply Duct

The duct(s) of a forced air heating/cooling system through which heated or cooled air is supplied to rooms by the action of the fan of the central heating or cooling unit.

Supply Side
Technologies that pertain to the generation of electricity.

Surface Water Loop
In this type of closed-loop geofhermal heat pump installation, the fluid-filled plastic heat exchanger pipes are coiled into circles and submerged at least eight feet below the surface of a body of surface water, such as a pond or lake. The coils should only be placed in a water source that meets minimum volume, depth, and quality criteria.

Swamp Cooler
A popular term used for an evaporative cooling device.

Swept Area
In reference to a wind energy conversion device, the area through which the rotor blades spin, as seen when directly facing the center of the rotor blades.

Synchronous Generator
An electrical generator that runs at a constant speed and draws its excitation from a power source external or independent of the load or transmission network it is supplying.

Synchronous Inverter
An electrical inverter that inverts direct current electricity to alternating current electricity, and that uses another alternating current source, such as an electric power transmission and distribution network (grid), for voltage and frequency reference to provide power in phase and at the same frequency as the external power source.

Synchronous Motor
A type of motor designed to operate precisely at the synchronous speed with no slip in the full-load speeds (rpm).

System Mix
The proportion of electricity distributed by a power provider that is generated from available sources such as coal, natural gas, petroleum, nuclear, hydropower, wind, or geothermal.

Solar Array
A group of solar collectors or solar modules connected together.

Solar Azimuth
The angle between the sun's apparent position in the sky and true south, as measured on a horizontal plane.

Solar Cell
A solar photovoltaic device with a specified area.

Solar Collector
A device used to collect, absorb, and transfer solar energy to a working fluid. Flat plate collectors are the most common type of collectors used for solar water or pool heating systems. In the case of a photovoltaics system, the solar collector could be crystalline silicon panels or thin-film roof shingles, for example.

Solar Constant
The average amount of solar radiation that reaches the earth's upper atmosphere on a surface perpendicular to the sun's rays; equal to 1353 Watts per square meter or 492 Btu per square foot.

Solar Cooling
The use of solar thermal energy or solar electricity to power a cooling appliance. There are five basic types of solar cooling technologies: absorption cooling, which can use solar thermal energy to vaporize the refrigerant; desiccant cooling, which can use solar thermal energy to regenerate (dry) the desiccant; vapor compression cooling, which can use solar thermal energy to operate a Rankine-cycle heat engine; and evaporative coolers ("swamp" coolers), and heat-pumps and air conditioners that can by powered by solar photovoltaic systems.

Solar Declination
The apparent angle of the sun north or south of the earth's equatorial plane. The earth's rotation on its axis causes a daily change in the declination.

Solar Distillation
The process of distilling (purifying) water using solar energy. Water can be placed in an air tight solar collector with a sloped glazing material, and as it heats and evaporates, distilled water condenses on the collector glazing, and runs down where it can be collected in a tray.

Solar Energy
Electromagnetic energy transmitted from the sun (solar radiation). The amount that reaches the earth is equal to one billionth of total solar energy generated, or the equivalent of about 420 trillion kilowatt-hours.

Solar Energy Collector
See solar collector.

Solar Film
A window glazing coating, usually tinted bronze or gray, used to reduce building cooling loads, glare, and fabric fading.

Solar Fraction
The percentage of a building's seasonal energy requirements that can be met by a solar energy device(s) or system(s).

Solar Furnace
A device that achieves very high temperatures by the use of reflectors to focus and concentrate sunlight onto a small receiver.

Solar Gain
The amount of energy that a building absorbs due to solar energy striking its exterior and conducting to the interior or passing through windows and being absorbed by materials in the building.

Solar Irradiation
The amount of solar radiation, both direct and diffuse, received at any location.

Solarium
A glazed structure, such as greenhouse or "sunspace."

Solar Mass
A term used for materials used to absorb and store solar energy.

Solar Module (Panel)
A solar photovoltaic device that, produces a specified power output under defined test conditions, usually composed of groups of solar cells connected in series, in parallel, or in series-parallel combinations.

Solar Passive System
A means of capturing, storing and using heat from the sun.

Special Contracts
Any contract that provides a utility service under terms and conditions other than those listed in the utility's tariffs. For example, an electric utility may enter into an agreement with a large customer to provide electricity at a rate below the tariffed rate in order to prevent the customer from taking advantage of some other option that would result in the loss of the customer's load. This generally allows that customer to compete more effectively in their product market.

Special Protection System
A protection system designed to perform functions other than the isolation of electrical faults. Also called "remedial action scheme."

Specific Gravity
As applied to natural gas, specific gravity is the ratio of the weight of a

given volume to that of the same volume of air, both measured under the same conditions.

Speculate

To take on a position with the intent of increasing return. The individual or firm that speculates does not
use or supply the underlying commodity but is willing to assume some of the price risk associated with the commodity in order to earn a return. Speculators provide the market with liquidity.

Speculators

Those who use options to take on risk and the potential gains/losses associated with that risk.

Split-the-Savings

A method of pricing where the buyer and the seller agree to divide the difference between the seller's costs of producing power and the buyer's otherwise available purchase price of power.

Splitting Schedules

An interchange schedule where power is scheduled in from one source and out to multiple destinations.

Spill

Release of water from a reservoir over a spillway rather than putting it through turbines to produce electricity. A spillway is the overflow structure of the dam.

Spinning Reserve

The amount of unloaded generating capability of a participant connected to and synchronized with the interconnected system of the participants and ready to take load. Spinning Reserve allocation to any generator shall not exceed the amount of generation increase that can be realized in 10 minutes. Unused capacity available from units connected to and synchronized with the grid to serve additional demand. The spinning reserve must be under automatic governor control to instantly respond to system requirements.

Spot Market

A power market where goods are traded for immediate delivery.

Stability

The stability of a power system is its ability to develop restoring forces equal to or greater than the disturbing forces so as to maintain a state of equilibrium.

Stabilized Energy Conversion Efficiency
The long-term ratio of electrical output to light input.

Standard Conditions
The basic temperature and pressure for measurement of natural gas Volumes.

Standard Deviation
A measure of the volatility of an underlying instrument. It is a statistical quantity that measures the magnitude of the daily price change of that asset.

Standard Industrial Classification (SIC)
A set of codes developed by the Office of Management and Budget, which categorizes business into groups with similar economic activities.

Standard Metering Base
Standard conditions, plus agreed corrections, to which all natural gas volumes are corrected for purposes of comparison and payment.

Standard Options Contract
A contract that adheres to an established set of standards regarding the size of the contract, the strike prices, expiration dates and other conditions.

Standby Charge
A set unit fee payable at the outset by the recipient of a service based on total entitlement imposed on each unit of natural gas not purchased from, but transported by, the pipeline (similar to a "demand" charge). The charge is intended to recover fixed costs otherwise recoverable in the sales commodity charge.

Standby Facility
A facility that supports a utility system and is generally running under no load. It is available to replace or supplement a facility normally in service.

Standby Service
Support service that is available, as needed, to supplement a consumer, a utility system or to another utility to replace normally scheduled power that becomes unavailable. General term for an application in which the battery is maintained in a fully charged condition by trickle or float charging. Synonymous with 'Float Service'.

Start-Up
The windspeed at which a wind turbine rotor starts to rotate. It does not

necessarily produce any power until it reaches cut-in speed.

Stationary
With wind generator towers, a tower that does not tilt up and down. The tower must be climbed or accessed with a crane to install or service equipment at the top.

Stator
The part of a motor, generator or alternator that does not rotate. In permanent magnet alternators it holds the coils and laminates

Slag
A residue produced by the combustion of coal. This heat-fused material accumulates on the sides and bottom of a boiler and is removed periodically and disposed of according to environmental regulations.

Stator
The stationary part of a generator within which a rotor turns.

Socket
A connecting place or junction for electric wires, plugs and light bulbs.

Surge Suppressor
An electronic device that protects electric equipment from short-term, high-voltage flows of electricity such as lightning strikes.

Stand-alone photovoltaic power system
Autonomous system with storage batteries (see off-grid photovoltaic power system).

Standard test conditions (STC)
The testing conditions to measure photovoltaic cells or modules nominal output power. Irradiance level is 1 000 W/m², with the reference air mass 1,5 solar spectral irradiance distribution and cell or module junction temperature of 25°C.

Static Electricity
An unbalanced electric charge that is sitting on top of an insulator, not moving, as opposed to an electric current which is flowing along a conductor.

Static Pressure
Pressure produced by an unmoving column of water, (also: static head) There are no friction/head losses when water is not moving, so static pressure is determined only by the vertical height of the water column.

The static pressure on a 10ft. tall vertical pipe full of water would be the same as a 1000ft. long pipeline with 10ft. of head over its entire distance.

Station
A site that contains one or more power generating units.

Station Service
The electric supply for the ancillary equipment used to operate a generating station or substation.

Station Service Generator
A generator, usually found in hydroelectric plants, used to supply electric energy for station service equipment.

Steady State
A condition in which circuit values remain essentially constant after all initial fluctuating conditions have settled down.

Steady-State Variation
The effect of periodic and random deviations of instantaneous voltage or frequency on the mean steadystate value, at any constant load, the limit of such effect being expressed as a plus and minus percent of nominal value.

Steam Coal
Also known as "thermal coal," this is coal used in electric utility power plants, district steam heating plants and industrial steam boilers to produce electricity or process steam or both.

Steam Generation Plant
A thermal electric generating plant which creates steam to drive a turbine.

Steam Turbine
See TURBINE. A device that converts high-pressure steam, produced in a boiler, into mechanical energy that can then be used to produce electricity by forcing blades in a cylinder to rotate and turn a generator shaft.

Steam-Electric Plant (Conventional)
A plant in which the prime mover is a steam turbine. The steam used to drive the turbine is produced in a boiler where fossil fuels are burned.

Stirling Engine
An external combustion engine in which air is alternately heated and cooled to drive a piston up and down.

Stochastic
A principal momentum indicator or price oscillator used with natural gas futures, similar to the Relative Strength Index, although the calculation includes the lowest low and the highest high over a specific period.

Storage Energy
The energy equivalent of water stored in a reservoir above normal bottom elevation.

Storage Facility
Facility used for the storage of natural gas; usually a cavern carved out of natural salt domes or depleted natural gas reservoirs into which natural gas can be reinjected and produced with minimal loss.

Storage Reservoir
A reservoir which has space for retaining water from springtime snowmelts. Stored water is released as necessary for purposes such as power generation, fish passage and irrigation.

Storage Service
A service in which natural gas is received by the seller of the service and held for the account of the customer for redelivery at a later time. Storage services are typically utilized by customers to allow more even purchases or sales of natural gas throughout the year, despite variations in end-use demand. Storage service is also a critical element of the peak period deliverability of many interstate natural gas pipelines and distributors. Injection, withdrawal and holding fees are usually charged, and limits on rates, times of injection and withdrawal, and maximum volumes to be held are usually imposed.

Storage, Underground
The utilization of subsurface facilities for storing natural gas that has been transferred from its original location for the primary purposes of conservation, fuller utilization of pipeline facilities, and more effective and economic delivery to markets.

Straddle Plant
A natural gas processing plant constructed near a transmission pipeline downstream from the fields where the natural gas in the pipeline has been produced. Also called an "on-line" plant. Generally, the straddle plant does not purchase and resell natural gas, but provides only a processing service for the owner of the natural gas or of processing rights to the natural gas. Frequently, natural gas producers reserve processing rights when they sell natural gas, so they can have natural gas liquids removed from the gas stream by a straddle plant.

Straight Fixed Variable (SFV) Rate Design

A rate design method applied by the FERC on gas pipelines which allocates all fixed costs to the demand component and all variable costs to the commodity, or usage component.

Straight Gas Utility

A utility company that derives the major portion of its total sales revenues from natural gas operations.

Stranded Costs

Under FERC Order No. 636, costs associated with certain gas pipeline assets previously used to provide bundled sales service, such as gas in storage and capacity on upstream pipelines, can no longer be assigned to customers of the unbundled services.

Stranded Investment

An investment with a cost recovery schedule that was initially approved by regulatory action that subsequent regulatory action or market forces has rendered not practically recoverable. Costs that electric utilities are currently permitted to recover through their rates but whose recovery may be impeded or prevented by the advent of competition in the industry.

Streamflow

The rate at which water passes a given point in a stream, usually expressed in cubic feet per second (cfs).

Stress

An external force applied to a component or assembly that tends to damage or destroy it.

Subbituminous Coal

Young black coal with high moisture content of between 15 and 40 percent by weight. In the U.S. the most often cited example is the Power River Basin coal found in Wyoming and Montana. Heating value varies from 7,000 Btu/lb to slightly over 9,000 Btu/lb. This type of coal is considered by many to have the largest reserves by weight around the world. Countries such as Indonesia and Malaysia have much more subbituminous coal that bituminous coal. Sulfur value is typically quire low, and ash is also usually low. Volatile matter is usually high, and can exceed 40% of the weight of the cal "as received."

Substation

An electrical control centre between a power station and your home where transformers lower electricity's voltage. Facility equipment that switches, changes or regulates electric voltage. Location where high voltage transmission lines connect to switchgear and step-down transformers to produce lower voltages at lower power levels for local distribution networks. An assemblage of equipment within a fenced area that switches, changes or regulates voltage in electric transmission and distribution systems. Among other things, substations are used to increase the voltage of electricity so that it can be transported efficiently over long distances and reduce the voltage so that it can be delivered in a practical and economical manner to homes and businesses. An electrical station where the high voltage electrical current from the transmission grid is reduced so that it is suitable for supply to customers.

Submetering
The practice of remetering purchased energy beyond the customer's utility meter, generally done when natural gas or electricity is distributed to building tenants through privately-owned or rented meters.

Subsidization
The imposition of costs on one customer or class of customers that are attributable to services provided to other customers or classes of customers, who therefore pay less than the appropriate actual costs for the services they receive.

Suction Head
The vertical distance from the surface of the water source to the center of the pump (when the pump is located above the water level). Additional energy in a reaction turbine hydro system, created by the draught tube channeling outlet water. Inlet pressure, from the water 'pushing' on the turbine runner as it enters, creates ~80% of the energy in a reaction system. Suction head, from the vacuum created by the closed outlet system, 'pulls' on the runner as the water exits the system, adding up to ~20% additional power output to the system.

Sulfur
One of the elements present in varying quantities in coal and fuel oil (residual oil) which contributes to environmental degradation when coal or oil is burned. In terms of sulfur content by weight, coal is generally classified as low (less than or equal to 1 percent), medium (greater than 1 percent and less than or equal to 3 percent), and high (greater than 3 percent). Sulfur content is measured as a percent by weight of coal on an "as received" or a "dry" (moisture- free, usually part of a laboratory analysis) basis.

Summer Valley
The depression that occurs in the summer months in the daily load of a natural gas distribution system or pipeline.

Sunk Cost
In economics, a sunk cost is a cost that has already been incurred, and

therefore cannot be avoided by any strategy going forward.

Surface Mine

Also known as a "strip mine," this refers to a mine where the coal seam lies sufficiently close to the surface to extract the coal by removing the overburden to uncover the seam, sweeping the seam clean of sand and other adulterating materials, and excavating the coal for shipment to utility, industrial and metallurgical facilities.

Superconductor

A material that becomes a perfect conductor of electricity when chilled to cold temperatures. Developments beginning in 1986 have raised the threshold temperature to levels which, in the near future, may provide wires capable of conducting large electric currents without line loss. Almost all substances have some resistance to electrical currents and this causes the loss of some of the electrical power generated. Only a superconducting wire could prevent such line losses because a current that is started in a superconductor can flow forever.

Superconductivity

The flow of electric current without resistance in certain metals and alloys at temperatures near absolute
zero. Perpetual motion on an atomic scale; the conduction of electricity without the slightest power loss -perfect conductivity.

Supervisory Control and Data Acquisition (SCADA)

A system of remote control and telemetry used to monitor and control the transmission system.

Supplemental Regulation Service

A method of providing regulation service in which the control area providing the regulation service receives a signal representing all or a portion of the other control area's ACE.

Supply-Side

Activities conducted on the utility's side of the customer meter. Activities designed to supply electric power to customers, rather than meeting load though energy efficiency measures or on site generation on the customer side of the meter.

Surge

A short duration high voltage condition. A surge lasts for several cycles where a transient lasts less than one half cycle. Often confused with "transient". A sharp transient increase of current, voltage or power flow in an electric circuit or across an electric system.

Surge Arrester

A device which protects lines and equipment against voltage surges caused by lightning or abnormal system conditions which can damage cable or equipment insulation. The surge arrester is connected from the line to ground to provide a conducting path. This limits the voltage on lines or equipment and dissipates excess energy harmlessly.

Surplus Energy

Energy generating capability that is beyond the immediate needs of the producing system. This energy may be sold on an interruptible basis or as firm power.

Suspension

The authority of the FERC under the Natural Gas Act to accept a rate filing, to go into effect as early as one month (absent waiver) or as late as five months, subject to refund.

Sustained Orderly Development

A condition in which a growing and stable market is identified by orders that are placed on a reliable schedule. The orders increase in magnitude as previous deliveries and engineering and field experience lead to further reductions in costs. The reliability of these orders can be projected many years into the future, on the basis of long term contracts, to minimize market risks and investor exposure.

Swap

A portfolio of forward contracts. A swap is almost identical to a sequence of forward contracts (commitment to buy (long) or sell (short) an underlying asset at a prespecified price and time), and its close relative the future, at different maturity dates. One of the advantages of swaps is that a market maker can tailor a swap to fit the needs of a particular counterparty, whereas standardization is the key to the success of exchange-traded instruments.

Swaption

An option that has embedded in it the ability of a counterparty to terminate the swap according to some prespecified terms, generally with no penalty for the counterparty. An option to enter into a swap contract. A receiver's swaption is the right to be a fixed rate receiver and a payer's swaption is the right to be a fixed rate payer.

Swing Supply

A supply of natural gas that is the last to be taken and the first to be curtailed by the customer. Swing supply serves the variation in the customer's demand.

Swing Supply Service
A service in which the supply being offered will be the last to be purchased by the customer if there is additional demand and the first to be curtailed by the customer if there is any reduction in demand.

Switch
A device for making, breaking or changing the connections in an electric circuit.

Switch Gear
A group of switches, relays, circuit breakers, etc. Used to control distribution of power to other distribution equipment and large loads.

Switching Station
Facility equipment used to tie together two or more electric circuits through switches. The switches are selectively arranged to permit a circuit to be disconnected, or to change the electric connection between the circuits. An assemblage of equipment for the sole purpose of tying together two or more electric circuits through switches or circuit breakers, selectively arranged to permit a circuit to be disconnected in an emergency, or to change the electric connections between the circuits. A type of substation.

Synchronism
Expresses the condition across an open circuit wherein the voltage sine wave on one side matches the voltage sine wave on the other side in frequency and amplitude without phase angle difference.

Synchronization
Maintaining a constant phase relationship between AC signals.

Synchronize
Process of connecting two previously separated alternating current Apparatuses after matching frequency, voltage, phase angles, etc.

Synchronous
A piece of rotating equipment whose electrical output is at the same frequency and time relationship as the power grid.Events that have the same period or which occur at the same time. For instance, a synchronous transfer mechanism for a standby power generator transfers power to or from the utility in phase. In other words, the voltage waveform of the generator and of the utility are in phase and the waveforms occur at the same time and interval during the transfer.

Synchronous Motor
An AC motor whose speed is exactly proportional to the power input frequency.

System

The entire generating, transmitting and distributing facilities of an electric company. Physically connected generation, transmission, and distribution facilities operated as an integrated unit under one central management, or operating supervision. A combination of generation transmission and distribution components comprising an electric utility or group of utilities.

Systems; Balance of Systems

Solar electric systems include the photovoltaic array and the other components that allow these solar panels to be used in homes and commercial facilities where a regulated DC power supply or an AC power supply is required. Components used in solar electric systems include; wire and disconnect devices, charge regulators, inverters, metering, and grounding components.

System Integration (of new technologies)

The successful integration of a new technology into the electric utility system by analyzing the technology's system effects and resolving any negative impacts that might result from its broader use.

System Load Factor

The average hourly quantity of electricity available during the year expressed as a percentage of the maximum demand at the end of the year.

System Capacity

The maximum power capability of a system. For example, a utility system might have a rated capacity of 5000 megawatts, or might sell 50 megawatts of capacity.

System Lambda

The marginal, variable production cost of electricity at a given level of system output.

System Operator

A person authorized to operate or supervise the operation of the bulk electric system.

System Personnel

Those people who have the capability to affect system operations and who must abide by the authority vested in the System Operator. May include power plant operators, system maintenance personnel, power schedulers, power marketers, etc.

System Impact Study

An assessment by the transmission provider of: (i) the adequacy of the transmission system to accommodate a transmission request for either Firm Point-to-Point Transmission Service or Network Integration Transmission Service; and (ii) whether any additional costs may be incurred in order to provide transmission service.

T

Tail
The proper term is actually Vane, but Tail is commonly used.

Tail Boom
A strut that holds the tail (Vane) to the wind generator frame.

Tail Race
The channel or pipe carrying water from a hydro turbine outlet back to the stream/river it was diverted from.

Take-or-Pay Clause
A contract provision obligating the buyer to pay for a certain minimum quantity of product, whether or not the buyer actually takes that quantity during the stated period.

Take-or-Pay Quantity
Under a take-or-pay clause, the minimum amount of product that the buyer is obligated to pay for whether or not the buyer actually takes that amount of product, usually stated in terms of an absolute quantity, or a percentage of total contract quantity, over a specific period of time, usually a year.

Take-or-Pay Surcharge
A surcharge to an interstate pipeline's sales and transportation rates permitted by FERC, designed to recover the pipeline's costs of settling its historic take-or-pay liabilities.

TAP
A connection point brought out of a transformer winding to permit changing the turns ratio.

TAP Switcher
A voltage regulator which uses power semiconductors, rated at line voltage and current, to switch taps of a transformer thereby changing the turns ratio and adjusting output voltage.

Tape Wound
Cores made by rolling strips of alloy iron into a toroidal shape. The

metal strips have a precisely controlled thickness which are coted with a very thin insulation material to prevent the metal in the layers to make contact with each other. The finished cores have an outside coating to protect the metal layers and they are offered in a variety of material mixes. Tape wound cores are capable of storing high amounts of energy and contain a high permeability. Their major disadvantage is that they are relatively expensive when compared to other core types (Also see Toroidal Inductor)

Tape Wound Cores(CoEv)
Cores made by rolling strips of alloy iron into a toroidal shape. The metal strips have a precisely controlled thickness, which are coated with a very thin insulating material to prevent the metal in the layers to make contact with each other. The finished cores have an outside coating to protect the metal layers and they are offered in a variety of material mixes. Tape wound cores are capable of storing high amounts of energy and contain a high permeability. Their major disadvantage is that they are relatively expensive when compared to other core types.

Tariff
A document filed by a regulated entity with either a federal or state commission. It lists the rates the regulated entity will charge to provide service to its customers as well as the terms and conditions that it will follow in providing service.

Telecommunications Transformers
Also referred to as broadband transformers, these are transformers specialized for connecting a piece of equipment to the phone line or telephone network. Its function is to isolate the equipment from the phone line, improve common mode noise rejection, and match different impedances.

Telecommuter
Person who performs work at home while linked to the office by means of a telecommunications-equipped computer system.

Telemetry
(From telemetering) Measurement with the aid of intermediate means that permit the measurement to be interpreted at a distance from the primary detector. A site telemetry system supplies the intermediate means of communication for all major environmental units at the site. Data from these units can then be interpreted by a computer. Site telemetry differs from central monitoring in that it uses the distributed processing power of monitored equipment from a variety of manufacturers.

Telemetering
Process by which measurable electrical quantities from substations and

generating stations are transmitted through telecommunication to a remote location.

Temperature Coefficient

The relative change of the quantity considered divided by the temperatures producing it.

Temperature Coefficient Of Inductance

Tc of L)Is the value of inductance change as a function of temperature exposure, normally expressed in parts per million per degrees Celsius. This is a calculation comparing inductance at a reference temperature (25 degrees C, room ambient) to the extremes and other temperatures within operating range. Can be called Percent Delta L. or Temperature Stability: the lower the change the better for most applications.

Temperature Factor

The fractional change in initial permeability over a temperature range divided by the initial permeability

Temperature Range

The ambient temperature range of the air (or other medium) surrounding a Poly Switch device under normal operating conditions.

Temperature Rise

The increase in surface temperature of a component in air due to the power dissipation in the component. The power dissipation for an inductor includes both copper and core losses.

Temperature, Maximum Ambient Operating

The highest ambient temperature at which a circuit is expected to operate.

Tenor

The maturity of a swap transaction.

Terawatt hours (TWh)

1 x 109 kilowatt hours; one thousand Gigawatt hours.

Term Swap

Swaps often involve longer maturities than can generally be found on futures or option contracts traded on organized exchanges. Term swap usually involves maturities greater than three years.

Terra- watt Hour

A unit of energy equal to one million kilowatt-hours, ITWh is equivalent to the total electricity typically used by 250,000 homes in one year.

Tertiary Recovery

Enhanced methods for the recovery of oil and natural gas that require a means for displacing the oil or natural gas from the reservoir rock, modifying the properties of the fluids in the reservoir and/or the reservoir rock to cause movement of the oil or natural gas in an efficient manner and providing the energy and drive mechanism to force its flow to a production well.

Tesla

The MKSA (SI) unit for magnetic flux density, defined by FaradayOs Law. A Tesla represents a volt-second per square meter per turn. One Tesla is equal to 10,000 Gauss.

Test Frequency

Is the industry/military standard for testing a range of inductances. It is not intended as the application frequency. Expressed in megahertz (MHz) or kilohertz (KHz)

Test Period

In a pipeline rate case, a test period is used to determine the cost of service upon which the pipeline's rates will be based. A test period consists of a base period of twelve consecutive months of recent actual operational experience, adjusted for changes in revenues and costs that are known and are measurable with reasonable accuracy at the time of the rate filing and which will become effective within nine months after the last month of actual data utilized in the rate filing.

Test, Passive Aging

A test described in RaychemOs PS300 publication in which the resistance of a PolySwitch device at room temperature is measured before and after aging at an elevated temperature (e.g., 70jC or 85 jC) for an extended time (e.g., 1000 hours).

Test, Solvent Resistance

A test described in RaychemOs PS300 publication to test the durability of the markings on PolySwitch devices when exposed to various solvents.

THD: Total Harmonic Distortion

A means of determining the distortion of a signal by measuring the energy of multiple frequency components other than the fundamental (in this case usually 50 Hz).

Therm

A unit of heating value equivalent to 100,000 British thermal units (Btu) (0.1 MMBtu).

Thermal

A term used to identify a type of electric generating station, capacity, capability, or output in which the source of energy for the prime mover is heat.

Thermal Conductivity

Given materials ability to conduct heat, which is the time rate for heat transfer (via conduction) across a unit material thickness of 1 meter and when the temperature differential of the two opposite faces is 1 degree K.

Thermal Derating

The change in the hold current and trip current of a PolySwitch device that takes place as there is a change in the ambient temperature of the air (or other medium) surrounding the device. An increase in ambient temperature decreases the hold current (and the trip current). A decrease in ambient temperature increases the trip current (and the hold current).

Thermal Efficiency

Efficiency with which heat energy contained in fuel is converted into electrical energy. For fossil fuel stations this is calculated by expressing electricity produced as a percentage of total energy content of the fuel consumed. For nuclear stations this is calculated using quantity of heat released as a result of fission inside the reactor.

Thermal Energy Storage

Storage of energy produced during one period that is used for heating or cooling during a later period. For example, chilled water may be produced electrically and later used to cool buildings, or solar energy may be used to produce hot water during the day that is used for heating at night. Other types of thermal storage might use ground, rock, or other materials to store energy.

Thermal Gasket

Flexible pad or wafer with a very low thermal resistance that is put between a power module baseplate and heat sink to ensure high thermal conductivity across the junction

Thermal Generation

The production of electricity from plants that convert heat energy into electrical energy. The heat in thermal plants can be produced from a number of sources such as coal, oil, gas or nuclear fuel.

Thermal Sources Of Electricity

These include coal, oil, natural gas, nuclear, landfill gas, municipal solid Electricity waste and other waste product, straw, coke oven gas and blast furnace gas.

Three Phase Power

Three separate outputs from a single source with a phase differential of 120 electrical degrees between any two adjacent voltages or currents. Mathematical calculations with three-phase power must allow for the additional power delivered by the third phase. Remember, both single phase and three phase have the same phase to phase voltages, therefore you must utilize the square root of 3 in your calculations. For example, KVA equals volts times amps for DC and for single phase. For three phase the formula is volts times the square root of three times amps. An electric circuit that consists of three separate currents delivered at one-third cycle intervals by means of a three-wire circuit; typically used to power large industrial motors that operate at 200 volts or higher.

Three-Phase Power Supply

Electric energy that is transmitted by three or four wires to the customer. Relatively high voltage customers usually receive three-phase power.

Thermal Joint Compound

A fluid or paste spread between the mating surfaces of a power device baseplate and a heat sink or system chassis.

Thermal Protection

Feature that shuts the converter down if the internal tempurature exceeds preset limits. Also called thermal shutdown.

Thermal Resistance

Measure of a given materials opposition to the flow of heat. Units are in degrees C/W.

Thermal Resistivity

Measure of a materials ability to impede the flow of heat. Typically given in degrees C T/W, where T is the material thickness and W is the power flowing through the material in watts.

Thermal Shock Test

A test in which the resistance of a PolySwitch device at room temperature is measured before and after a temperature cycling treatment (e.g., cycled 10 times between B55jC and +125 jC).

Thrust

In a wind generator, wind forces pushing back against the rotor. Wind generator bearings must be designed to handle thrust or else they will fail.

Thrust Bearing

A bearing that is designed to handle axial forces along the centerline of the shaft. In a wind generator, this is the force of the wind pushing back against the blades.

Tidal Power

The power available from the rise and fall of ocean tides. A tidal power plant works on the principal of a dam or barrage that captures water in a basin at the peak of a tidal flow, then directs the water through a hydroelectric turbines as the tide ebbs.

Tie Line

Circuit which connects two or more control areas or systems of a power system.

Tiered Rates

A rate design which divides customer use into different tiers, or blocks, with different prices charged for each.

Tight Pool

A group of utilities who dedicate their generating and transmission resources for joint economic dispatch. Usually costs and revenues are divided after the fact and no individual pool member is responsible for the procurement of individual power supplies.

Tilt-Up

A tower that is hinged at the base and tilted up into position using a gin pole and winch or vehicle. Wind turbines on tilt-up towers can be serviced on the ground, with no climbing required.

Tip

The end of a wind generator blade farthest from the hub.

Tip Speed Ratio

The ratio of how much faster than the windspeed that the blade tips are moving.

Time Error

The integral of frequency error. Generally utilized as a measure of regulating performance for frequency regulation. Time error can be measured as the error between a clock synchronized to the electrical system and the astronomical time kept by the National Bureau of Standards.

Time Error Correction

An offset to the interconnection's frequency to correct for the time error that accumulates on electric clocks.

Time-of-Use (TOU) Rates or Pricing
A rate design imposing higher charges during periods of the day when relatively higher peak demands are experienced. Rate design imposing higher charges during periods of the day when relatively higher peak demands are experienced and lower charges during low demand periods.

Three-Terminal Regulator
Regulator packaged in a standard 3-terminal transistor package. These devices can be a switching type or a linear shunt or series regulator.

Time-to-Trip
The time needed, from the onset of a fault current, to trip a PolySwitch device. For any particular type of PolySwitch device, trip time depends upon the size of the fault current and the ambient temperature. The higher the fault current and/or the higher the temperature, the shorter the trip time.

Time Value
The dollar amount by which the premium of an option exceeds the intrinsic value of an option.

Tipple
A surface processing structure for cleaning and sizing coal and automatically loading it onto rail cars or trucks for movement to market.

Tolerable Zone
The Tolerable Zone covers a band of voltage values above and below the Preferred Zone. In the Tolerable Zone, the customer's equipment may be expected to operate satisfactorily although the performance may perhaps be less than warranted by the manufacturer.

Tolling Arrangement
An arrangement whereby a party moves fuel to a power generator and receives kilowatt hours (kWh) in return for a pre-established fee.

Tolling Fee
A fee paid for use of electric generation assets used to convert fuel to power.

Toroid
A core that has a donut shaped surface. Toroidal cores are available in many magnetic core materials. Characteristics of toroidal inductors include self-shielding due to a closed magnetic path, efficient energy transfer, high coupling between windings, and early saturation.

Toroidal Inductor

An inductor constructed by placing a winding(s) on a core that has a donut shaped surface. Toroidal cores are available in many magnetic core materials within the four basic types: Ferrite, Powdered iron, Alloy and High Flux, and Tape Wound. Characteristics of toroidal inductors include: self shielding (closed magnetic path), efficient energy transfer, high coupling between windings and early saturation.

Total Harmonic Distortion (THD)

The square root of the sum of the squares of the RMS harmonic voltages or currents divided by the RMS fundamental voltage or current. Can also be calculated in the same way for only even harmonics or odd harmonics.

Tower

A structure that supports a wind generator, usually high in the air.

Tracking

For a multiple output converter the parameter that gives the change in one output voltage caused by a change in the voltage level or load on another output.

Tracking array

Some solar array structures are designed to mechanically track the movement of the sun so that the solar panels always face the sun. Tracking arrays cost more than fixed array structures, but produce more solar output from the system.

Trailing Edge

The edge of a blade that faces away from the direction of rotation.

Transco

The term for that portion of a functionally disaggregated electric utility's business that involves the bulk transmission of power that is operated separately from any other power functions the utility might own or operate.

Transducer

A device that senses one form of energy and converts it to another, i.e., temperature to voltage (for monitoring).

Transfer Switch

A switch used to transfer a load between a UPS and its bypass source.

Transformer

An electrical device for changing the voltage of alternating current. An electric device, without continuously moving parts, in which electromagnetic induction transforms electric energy from one or more other circuits at the same frequency, usually with changes of value of voltage and current. Raises or lowers the voltage of alternating current. An electromagnetic device for changing the voltage of alternating electricity. A passive device that changes voltage, current, or impedance to the required parameters. This is usually done by placing two or more windings around a soft magnetic core. Applying a voltage to the primary winding will produce a magnetic field in the core, and in turn induce a voltage in the secondary winding(s). A device used to raise or lower voltage in electric distribution or transmission lines. A step-up transformer raises voltage and a step-down transformer lowers voltage

Transient/Spike
A high amplitude, short duration pulse superimposed on the normal voltage wave form or ground line. Spike or step change in a converter paramenter. Commonly used in describing input line and output load characteristics. A high-voltage, extremely short and fast electrical pulse. These pulses can destroy electronic equipment instantly or over a period of time.

Transient Recovery Time
Time required for a converter output to return to within specified limits following a step change in output load current. Expressed as a percentage of rated value.

Transient Response
The ability of a power conditioner to respond to a change. Transient step load response is the ability of a power conditioner to maintain a constant output voltage when sudden load (current) changes arc made.

Transient Suppression
The use of special devices to minimize the effects of transients in electronic circuits. Transient suppression devices include the metal oxide varistor (MOV), semiconductor transient voltage suppressor (TVS) and gas tube.

Transition Costs
Costs associated with the change of an industry from a regulated, bundled service to a competitive open-access service, including "Stranded Costs."

Transmission
The network of high voltage lines, transformers and switches used to move electrical power from generators to the distribution system. Also utilized to interconnect different utility systems and independent power producers together into a synchronized network. Transmission is considered to end when the energy is transformed for distribution to the

consumer. The process of transporting electric energy in bulk from a source of supply to other power systems, eg. substations. It is done at high voltage to reduce loss. The network of high-voltage lines, transformers and switches used to move electrical power from generators to the distribution system. The transportation of electricity over high-voltage power lines. The definition of high-voltage varies from one utility to another. PG&E defines all power lines and substations that operate at 50,000 volts (50 kV) or higher as transmission lines. At Alameda Power & Telecom and in Southern California, only power lines and substations that operate at more than 150,000 volts (150 kV) are part of the transmission system. Power lines and substations that operate at lower voltages than transmission are part of electric distribution. The process of transporting electric energy in bulk on high voltage lines from the generating facility to the local distribution company for delivery to retail customers.

Transmission Access
The ability of third parties to make use of transmission facilities owned by others (wheeling utilities) to deliver power to another utility.

Transmission Company
Company which obtains the major portion of its natural gas operating revenues from the operation of a natural gas transmission system and/or from mainline sales to industrial customers.

Transmission Dependent Utility
A utility that relies on its neighboring utilities to transmit to it the power it buys from its suppliers. A utility without its own generation sources, dependent on another utility's transmission system to get its purchased power supplies.

Transmission Grid
An interconnected system of electric transmission lines and associated equipment for the transfer of electric energy in bulk between points of supply and points of demand.

Transmission (Trunk) Line
Pipeline transporting natural gas from principal supply areas to distribution centers, large volume customers or other transmission lines. Transmission lines generally have a linear configuration, may be quite large in diameter, operate at relatively high pressure, and traverse long distances. Wires or cables through which high voltage electricity is carried from a power station.

Transmission Line
The conductors used to carry electrical energy from one location to another.

Transmission Loading Relief (TLR)
When a transmission operator must curtail transmission to prevent the grid from collapse

Transmission Loss
The power lost in transmission between one point and another. It is measured as the difference between the net power passing the first point and the net power passing the second point.

Transmission Reliability Margin
The transmission transfer capability that is required to ensure that interconnections are secure under a reasonable range of system conditions

Transmission System (Electric)
An interconnected group of electric transmission lines and associated equipment for moving or transferring electric energy in bulk between points of supply and points at which it is transformed for delivery over the distribution system lines to consumers, or is delivered to other electric systems. The facilities owned, controlled or operated by the transmission provider that are used to provide transmission service.

Transverse Mode Noise
(Normal mode)- An undesirable voltage which appears from line to line of a power line.

Transmission Must Run (TMR)
Generation that was introduced to the Alberta market to support the over-burdened transmission system caused by the expanding demand of the southern region of the province.

Transmission Voltage
Voltage levels utilized for bulk transmission systems: generally 69 KV - 750 KV AC or DC.

Transportation Contract
A contract setting forth the terms and conditions applicable to gas or electric transportation service.

Transporter
The pipeline company that transports natural gas for a shipper.

Treating Plant
Facility that treats raw natural gas to remove undesirable impurities such as carbon dioxide, hydrogen sulfide and water vapor. Treating plants may be owned by producers, independent treaters or transmission pipeline companies.

Triac
An electronic device that provides switching action for either polarity of an applied voltage and can be controlled from a single gate. Usually composed of two SCR's connected back to back.

Trickle Charge
Continuous charging by means of a small current designed to compensate for self discharge in a battery which is isolated from any load. For valve regulated batteries, constant voltage charging is common.

Trunk Lines
See PIPELINE SYSTEM.

TTL
Transistor-Transistor Logic. Electronic circuitry that defines a binary logic state when components are in saturation or cutoff.

Trash Rack
A mesh or set of bars at the inlet of a hydro system that catches leaves, branches and other debris, and prevents it from obstructing or damaging the turbine.

Trip
Switching of a PolySwitch device from a low resistance to a high resistance. In its low-resistance state, the device permits normal currents to flow in a circuit. Occurrence of a fault drives the device to its high-resistance (or OtrippedO) state, and this reduces the current in the circuit to a low level.

Trip Current
The smallest steady state current that, if passed through a PolySwitch device, will cause the device to trip, under specified conditions.

Trip Cycle
The tripping and resetting of a PolySwitch device under specified conditions.

Trip Cycle Life
The number of trip cycles that a PolySwitch device will undergo without failure, with failure being defined in a specified way.

Trip Time
The time needed, from the onset of a fault current, to trip a PolySwitch device. For any particular type of PolySwitch device, trip time depends upon the size of the fault current and the ambient temperature. The higher the fault current and/or the higher the temperature, the shorter the trip time.

TtT

The time needed, from the onset of a fault current, to trip a PolySwitch device. For any particular type of PolySwitch device, trip time depends upon the size of the fault current and the ambient temperature. The higher the fault current and/or the higher the temperature, the shorter the trip time.

Turbine

The part of a generating unit usually consisting of a series of curved vanes or blades on a central spindle,
which is spun by the force of water, steam or hot gas to drive an electric generator. Turbines convert the kinetic energy of such fluids to mechanical energy through the principles of impulse and reaction, or a measure of the two. Has blades which can be pushed by water, steam, gas or wind to spin a shaft. When attached to a generator, the spinning shaft helps to drive the generator to make electricity. Device that converts the flow of a fluid (air, steam, water, or hot gases) into mechanical motion for generating electricity.

Turgo Turbine

An impulse turbine that can provide higher power output in some high head hydro sites than a Pelton style. The Turgo runner design allows for more efficient escape of'used' water, and a larger water jet, for improved power production in sites with high enough flow rates. Turgo runners are generally more expensive than Pelton style, due to more difficult manufacturing processes.

Turn Ratio

The ratio of the primary voltage (or turns) to the secondary voltage (or turns)

Twist

In a wind generator blade, the difference in Pitch between the blade root and the blade tip. Generally, the twist allows more Pitch at the blade root for easier Startup, and less Pitch at the tip for better high-speed performance

Twisted Pair

Cable consisting of two 18 to 24 AWG (American Wire Gauge) solid copper strands twisted around each other. The twisting provides a measure of protection from electromagnetic and radio-frequency interference.

Two Part Rate

A charge for energy consisting of a demand component and an energy or commodity component.

TYPES OF ELECTRIC SERVICE FIRM

The delivery of electricity by a company on a continuous basis. Residential and smaller commercial customers generally use this service.

INTERRUPTIBLE

- The delivery of electricity to a customer that may be interrupted by the local distribution company generally because of system supply or capacity limitations.

Tankless Water Heater

A water heater that heats water before it is directly distributed for end use as required; a demand water heater.

Task Lighting

Any light source designed specifically to direct light a task or work performed by a person or machine.

Temperature Coefficient (of a solar photovoltaic cell)

The amount that the voltage, current, and/or power output of a solar cell changes due to a change in the cell temperature.

Temperature Humidity Index

An index that combines sensible temperature and air humidity to arrive at a number that closely responds to the effective temperature; used to relate temperature and humidity to levels of comfort.

Temperature/Pressure Relief Valve

A component of a water heating system that opens at a designated temperature or pressure to prevent a possible tank, radiator, or delivery pipe rupture.

Temperature Zones

Individual rooms or zones in a building where temperature is controlled separately from other rooms or zones.

Tempering Valve

A valve used to mix heated water with cold in a heating system to provide a desired water temperature for end use.

Termite Shield

A construction element that inhibits termites from entering building foundations and walls.

Therm

A unit of heat containing 100,000 British thermal units (Btu).

Thermal Balance Point

The point or outdoor temperature where the heating capacity of a heat pump matches the heating requirements of a building.

Thermal Capacitance
The ability of a material to absorb and store heat for use later.

Thermal Efficiency
A measure of the efficiency of converting a fuel to energy and useful work; useful work and energy output divided by higher heating value of input fuel times 100 (for percent).

Thermal Energy
The energy developed through the use of heat energy.

Thermal Energy Storage
The storage of heat energy during power provider off-peak times at night, for use during the next day without incurring daytime peak electric rates.

Thermal Envelope Houses
An architectural design (also known as the double envelope house), sometimes called a "housc-within-a-house," that employs a double envelope with a continuous airspace of at least 6 to 12 inches on the north wall, south wall, roof, and floor, achieved by building inner and outer walls, a crawl space or sub-basemenl below the floor, and a shallow attic space below the weather roof. The east and west walls are single, conventional walls. A buffer zone of solar-heated, circulating air warms the inner envelope of the house. The south-facing airspace may double as a sunspace or greenhouse.

Thermal
Mass Materials that store heat.

Thermal Storage Walls (Masonry or Water)
A thermal storage wall is a south-facing wall that is glazed on the outside. Solar heat strikes the glazing and is absorbed into the wall, which conducts the heat into the room over time. The walls are at least 8 in thick. Generally, the thicker the wall, the less the indoor temperature fluctuates.

Thermal Resistance (R-Value)
This designates the resistance of a material to heat conduction. The greater the R-value the larger the number.

Thermocouple
A device consisting of two dissimilar conductors with their ends connected together. When the two junctions are at different temperatures, a small voltage is generated.

Thermodynamic Cycle
An idealized process in which a working fluid (water, air, ammonia, etc) successively changes its state (from a liquid to a gas and back to a liquid) for the purpose of producing useful work or energy, or transferring energy.

Thermodynamics
A study of the transformation of energy from one form to another, and its practical application, (see Law(s) of Thermodynamics above).

Thermoelectric Conversion
The conversion of heat into electricity by the use of thermocouples.

Thermography
A building energy auditing technique for locating areas of low insulation in a building envelope by means of a thermographic scanner.

Thermophotovoltaic Cell
A device where sunlight concentrated onto a absorber heats it to a high temperature, and the thermal radiation emitted by the absorber is used as the energy source for a photovoltaic cell that is designed to maximize conversion efficiency at the wavelength of the thermal radiation.

Thermopile
A large number of thermocouples connected in series.

Thermosiphon System
This passive solar hot water system consists relies on warm water rising, a phenomenon known as natural convection, to circulate water through the collectors and to the tank. In this type of installation, the tank must be above the collector. As water in the collector heats, it becomes lighter and rises naturally into the tank above. Meanwhile, cooler water in the tank flows down pipes to the bottom of the collector, causing circulation throughout the system. The storage tank is attached to the top of the collector so that thermosiphoning can occur.

Thermosiphon
The natural, convective movement of air or water due to differences in temperature. In solar passive design a thermosyphon collector can be constructed and attached to a house to deliver heat to the home by the continuous pattern of the convective loop (or thermosyphon).

Thermostat
A device used to control temperatures; used to control the operation of heating and cooling devices by turning the device on or off when a specified temperature is reached.

Thin-Film
A layer of semiconductor material, such as copper indium diselenide or gallium arsenide, a few microns or less in thickness, used to make solar photovoltaic cells.

Three-phase Current
Alternating current in which three separate pulses are present, identical in frequency and voltage, but separated 120 degrees in phase.

Tidal Power
The power available from the rise and fall of ocean tides. A tidal power plant works on the principal of a dam or barrage that captures water in a basin at the peak of a tidal flow, then directs the water through a hydroelectric turbine as the tide ebbs.

Tilt Angle (of a Solar Collector or Module)
The angle at which a solar collector or module is set to face the sun relative to a horizontal position. The tilt angle can be set or adjusted to maximize seasonal or annual energy collection.

Time-of-Use (TOU) Rates
The pricing of electricity based on the estimated cost of electricity during a particular time block. Time-of-use rates are usually divided into three or four time blocks per twenty-four hour period (on-peak, mid-peak, off-peak and sometimes super off-peak) and by seasons of the year (summer and winter). Real-time pricing differs from TOU rates in that it is based on actual (as opposed to forecasted) prices which may fluctuate many times a day and are weather-sensitive, rather than varying with a fixed schedule.

Timer
A device that can be set to automatically turn appliances (lights) off and on at set times.

Time of Use (TOU)
Rates that vary by the time of day that the electricity is used, with higher rates being charged during hours of peak system usage. Consumers may potentially lower their costs by shifting their usage to "non-peak" hours when electricity is available at a lower rate. In most cases, this requires a special meter.

Timer (Water Heater)
This device can automatically turn the heater off at night and on in the morning.

Tip Speed Ratio
In reference to a wind energy conversion device's blades, the difference between the rotational speed of the tip of the blade and the actual velocity of the wind.

Ton (of Air Conditioning)
A unit of air cooling capacity; 12,000 Btu per hour.

Topping-cycle
A means to increase the thermal efficiency of a steam electric generating system by increasing temperatures and interposing a device, such as a gas turbine, between the heat source and the conventional steam-turbine generator to convert some of the additional heat energy into electricity.

Torque (Motor)
The turning or twisting force generated by an electrical motor in order for it to operate.

Total Harmonic Distortion
The measure of closeness in shape between a waveform and it's fundamental component.

Total Heat
The sum of the sensible and latent heat in a substance or fluid above a base point, usually 32 degrees Fahrenheit.

Total Incident Radiation
The total radiation incident on a specific surface area over a time interval.

Total Internal Reflection
The trapping of light by refraction and reflection at critical angles inside a semiconductor device so that it cannot escape the device and must be eventually absorbed by the semiconductor.

Tracking Solar Array
A solar energy array that follows the path of the sun to maximize the solar radiation incident on the PV surface. The two most common orientations are (1) one axis where the array tracks the sun east to west and (2) two-axis tracking where the array points directly at the sun at all times. Tracking arrays use both the direct and diffuse sunlight. Two-axis tracking arrays capture the maximum possible daily energy.

Trailing Edge
The part of a wind energy conversion device blade, or airfoil, that is the last to contact the wind.

Transformer
An electromagnetic device that changes the voltage of alternating current electricity. It consists of an induction coil having a primary and secondary winding and a closed iron core.

Transmission
The process of sending or moving electricity from one point to another; usually defines that part of an electric power provider's electric power lines from the power plant buss to the last transformer before the customer's connection. The process of transporting electricity from a generation company to an electric company over high-voltage power lines.

Transmission and Distribution Losses
The losses that result from inherent resistance in electrical conductors and transformation inefficiencies in distribution transformers in a transmission and distribution network.

Transmission Lines
Transmit high-voltage electricity from the transformer to the electric distribution system.

Traveling Grate
A furnace grate that moves fuel through the combustion chamber.

Trellis
An architectural feature used to shade exterior walls; usually made of a lattice of metal or wood; often covered by vines to provide additional summertime shading.

Trickle (Solar) Collector
A type of solar thermal collector in which a heat transfer fluid drips out of header pipe at the top of the collector, runs down the collector absorber and into a tray at the bottom where it drains to a storage tank.

Triple Pane (Window)
This represents three layers of glazing in a window with an airspace between the middle glass and the exterior and interior panes.

Trombe Wall
A wall with high thermal mass used to store solar energy passively in a solar home. The wall absorbs solar energy and transfers it to the space behind the wall by means of radiation and by convection currents moving through spaces under, in front of, and on top of the wall. *

True Power
The actual power rating that is developed by a motor before losses occur.

True South
The direction, at any point on the earth that is geographically in the northern hemisphere, facing toward the South Pole of the earth. Essentially a line extending from the point on the horizon to the highest point that the sun reaches on any day (solar noon) in the sky.

Turnkey price
Price of an installed photovoltaic system excluding VAT/TVA/sales taxes, operation and maintenance costs but including installation costs. For an off-grid photovoltaic system, the prices associated with storage battery maintenance/replacement are excluded. If additional costs are incurred for reasons not directly related to the photovoltaic system, these are excluded. For example if extra costs are incurred fitting PV modules to a factory roof because special precautions are required to avoid disrupting production, these extra costs are not included. Equally the additional transport costs of installing a telecommunication systems in a remote area are not included.

Tube (Fluorescent Light)
A fluorescent lamp that has a tubular shape.

Tube-In-Plate-Absorber
A type of solar thermal collector where the heat transfer fluid flows through tubes formed in the absorber plate.*

Tube-Type Collector
A type of solar thermal collector that has tubes (pipes) that the heat transfer fluid flows through that are connected to a flat absorber plate.

Tungsten Halogen Lamp
A type of incandescent lamp that contains a halogen gas in the bulb, which reduces the filament evaporation rate increasing the lamp life. The high operating temperature and need for special fixtures limits their use to commercial applications and for use in projector lamps and spotlights.

Turbine
A device for converting the flow of a fluid (air, steam, water, or hot gases) into mechanical motion.

Turn Down Ratio
The ratio of a boiler's or gasifier's maximum output to its minimum output.

Two-Tank Solar System
A solar thermal system that has one tank for storing solar heated water

to preheat the water in a conventional water heater.

Two-Axis Tracking
A solar array tracking system capable of rotating independently about two axes (e.g., vertical and horizontal).

U

Ultimate Customer
A customer that purchases energy for consumption and not for resale.

Unavailable
State in which a unit is not capable of operation because of the failure of a component, external restriction, testing, work being performed or some adverse condition.

Unbundled Services
The selling and pricing of energy services separately as opposed to offering services "bundled" into packages with a single price for the whole package. With unbundling, separate fees are charged for each service, based upon only the costs of providing that service (i.e., transportation, storage, generation, production, etc.). The selling and pricing of services separately as opposed to offering services "bundled" into packages with a single price for the whole package.

Unbundling
Separating (spinning off) the generation, transmission, distribution and customer service functions of an electric utility; separating a customer's bill into its individual components.Electric service is traditionally provided on a bundled basis, meaning that generation, transmission and distribution services are provided as a single package. By unbundling, the packaged offering of the various services that make up traditional utility service would be separated into discreet, separately priced components.

Underlying or Underlying Instrument
The security, commodity or financial instrument that the option conveys the right to buy (in the case of a call) or to sell (in the case of a put).

Undershoot
Transient change in a converter output voltage that does not meet the lower limit of the voltage accuracy specificiation. Typically occurs at converter turn on/off or with some step change in output load or input line. Also see Voltage Accuracy.

Undervoltage
Negative change in amplitude of a voltage.

Undue Discrimination
A subjective standard for determining illegal rates or service under the Natural Gas Act and the Federal Power Act, which is applied on a case by case basis.

Uniform System of Accounts
Prescribed financial rules and regulations established by the Federal Energy Regulatory Commission for utilities subject to its jurisdiction under the authority granted by the Federal Power Act.

Unit Commitment
Determining the generators that must be operated to meet daily demand

Unit Train
A combination of coal cars, typically open top hopper cars, of 100 or more, which are kept together as a unit, moving coal from one mine to one customer, often being dedicated to the movement of coal from one mine to one power plant.

Universal Service
Electric service sufficient for basic needs (an evolving bundle of basic services) available to virtually all members of the population regardless of income.

Uplift
The additional expense from operating more expensive generating units to meet local demand; also called congestion costs

UPS
Uninterruptible Power Source.

Upstream Pipeline
The pipeline delivering natural gas to another pipeline at an interconnection point where the second pipeline is closer to the consumer.

Usage Charge
A component of a utility's rate structure charged on a per unit of energy basis.

USB
Universal Serial Bus interoperability standard that defines the electrical power and signal transfer requirements in computing and multi-media applications. USB power requirements define a supply and output

voltage of 5V, with output currents rated at 0.5A for self-powered equipment and 0.1A output for bus-powered equipment.

Used and Useful
The traditional test for whether a utility asset may be included in rate base, self-defined and subjective.

Useful Thermal Output
The thermal energy made available for use in any industrial or commercial process, or used in any heating or cooling application; i.e., total thermal energy made available for processes and applications other than electrical generation.

Utility
A regulated entity which exhibits the characteristics of a natural monopoly. For the purposes of electric industry restructuring, "utility" refers to the regulated, vertically integrated electric company. "Transmission utility" refers to the regulated owner/operator of the transmission system only. "Distribution utility" refers to the regulated owner/operator of the distribution system which serves retail customers.

Utility Plant
All equipment used for the generation, transmission, and distribution of electricity, or an account in which record is kept of this equipment. Includes Plant in Service, Purchased or Sold, in Process of Reclassification, Leased to Others, Held for Future Use, Under Construction, and Acquisition Adjustments and Adjustment Accounts, without deduction of Accumulated Provision for Depreciation and Amortization.

Utilization Factor
A ratio of the maximum demand of a system or part of a system to its rated capacity.

Utility Grade Relays
Relays which meet IEEE standards C37.90, C37.90.1, and C37.90.2.

Ultimate Analysis
A procedure for determining the primary elements in a substance (carbon, hydrogen, oxygen, nitrogen, sulfur, and ash).

Ultraviolet
Electromagnetic radiation in the wavelength range of 4 to 400 nanometers.

Unglazed Solar Collector
A solar thermal collector that has an absorber that does not have a glazed

covering. Solar swimming pool heater systems usually use unglazed collectors because they circulate relatively large volumes of water through the collector and capture nearly 80 percent of the solar energy available.

Underground Home
A house built into the ground or slope of a hill, or which has most or all exterior surfaces covered with earth.

Unitary Air Conditioner
An air conditioner consisting of one or more assemblies that move, clean, cool, and dehumidify air.

Unvented Heater
A combustion heating appliance that vents the combustion by-products directly into the heated space. The latest models have oxygen-sensors that shut off the unit when the oxygen level in the room falls below a safe level.

Useful Heat
Heat stored above room temperature (in a solar heating system).

Utility
A regulated entity which exhibits the characteristics of a natural monopoly (also referred to as a power provider). For the purposes of electric industry restructuring, "utility" refers to the regulated, vertically-integrated electric company. "Transmission utility" refers to the regulated owner/operator of the transmission system only. "Distribution utility" refers to the regulated owner/operator of the distribution system which serves retail customers.

U-Value (sec Coefficient of Heat Transmission)
The reciprocal of R-Value. The lower the number, the greater the heat transfer resistance (insulating) characteristics of the material.

V

VAC
Volts of alternating current.

Vacuum Evaporation
The deposition of thin films of semiconductor material by the evaporation of elemental sources in a vacuum.

Valence Band
The highest energy band in a semiconductor that can be filled with electrons.

Valley-Filling
Demand-side management programs that seek to increase off-peak electricity consumption without necessarily reducing on-peak demands.

Value of Service
A utility pricing concept in which the usefulness or necessity of a service to a customer group replaces or supplements cost factors as a major influence on the rates charged to the group. In ratemaking, this means that the price charged reflects the service's value to the customer rather than its cost to the producer. Value of service need not equal the cost of service.

Vane
A large, flat piece of material used to align a wind turbine rotor correctly into the wind. Usually mounted vertically on the tail boom. Sometimes called a Tail. *See also: Furling Tail; Tail, Tail Boom*

Vapor
The gaseous state of a substance.

Vapor Retarder
A material that retards the movement of water vapor through a building element (walls, ceilings) and prevents insulation and structural wood from becoming damp and metals from corroding. Often applied to insulation batts or separately in the form of treated papers, plastic sheets, and metallic foils.

VAR
Voltage-Ampere-Reactive. A measure of reactive power. The unit of measure of the power that maintains the constant variation of the electromagnetic fields associated with alternating-current circuits

Variable Cost
The total costs incurred to produce energy, excluding fixed costs which are incurred regardless of whether the resource is operating. Variable costs usually include fuel, increased maintenance and additional labor.

Variable Pitch
A type of wind turbine rotor where the attack angle of the blades can be adjusted either automatically or manually

Variable-Speed Wind Turbines
Turbines in which the rotor speed increases and decreases with changing wind speed, producing electricity with a variable frequency.

Varistor
A voltage-dependant variable resistor. Normally used to protect sensative

equipment from power spikes or lightning strikes by shunting the energy to ground.

Valve Regulated Cells

A cell which is closed under normal conditions but which has an arrangement which allows the escape of gases if the internal pressure exceeds a predetermined value. Electrolyte is not normally added to a sealed valve regulated cell.

VDC

Volts of direct current.

Velocity

The distance travelled in a certain direction per unit of time. Velocity differs from speed in that the direction of motion is also specified.

Vent

A component of a heating or ventilation appliance used to conduct fresh air into, or waste air or combustion gases out of, an appliance or interior space.

Vent Damper –

A device mounted in the vent connector that closes the vent when the heating unit is not firing. This traps heat inside the heating system and house rather than letting it draft up and out the vent system.

Vented Heater

A type of combustion heating appliance in which the combustion gases are vented to the outside, either with a fan (forced) or by natural convection.

Ventilation

The process of moving air (changing) into and out of an interior space either by natural or mechanically induced (forced) means.

Ventilation Air

That portion of supply air that is drawn from outside, plus any recirculated air that has been treated to maintain a desired air quality.

Vent Pipe

A tube in which combustion gases from a combustion appliance are vented out of the appliance to the outdoors.

Venture Capital

Funds available to invest in new or unproven business enterprises.

Vertical-Axis Wind Turbine (VAWT)
A type of wind turbine in which the axis of rotation is perpendicular to the wind stream and the ground.

Vertical Ground Loop
In this type of closed-loop geothermal heat pump installation, the fluid-filled plastic heat exchanger pipes are laid out in a plane perpendicular to the ground surface. For a vertical system, holes (approximately four inches in diameter) are drilled about 20 feet apart and 100 to 400 feet deep. Into these holes go two pipes that are connected at the bottom with a U-bend to form a loop. The vertical loops are connected with horizontal pipe (i.e., manifold), placed in trenches, and connected to the heat pump in the building. Large commercial buildings and schools often use vertical systems because the land area required for horizontal ground loops would be prohibitive. Vertical loops are also used where the soil is too shallow for trenching, or for existing buildings, as they minimize the disturbance to landscaping.

Vertical Integration
An arrangement whereby the same company owns all the different aspects of making, selling and delivering a product or service. In the electric industry, it refers to the historically common arrangement whereby a utility would own its own generating plants, transmission system and distribution lines to pro

Vertically Integrated Utility
A utility that owns and controls generation, transmission and distribution components vide all aspects of electric service.

Vertical Spread
A spread that involves options with different strike prices, but identical expiration dates.

Virtual Direct Access
A form of partial deregulation of the electric industry whereby the utility remains the sole retail supplier to customers on a pool basis but the customers have the right to enter into bilateral contracts for differences from the pool prices.

Visible Light Transmittance
The amount of visible light that passes through the glazing material of a window, expressed as a percentage.

Visible Radiation
The visible portion of the electromagnetic spectrum with wavelengths from 0.4 to 0.76 microns

Vmax

The highest voltage that can safely be dropped across a PolySwitch device in its tripped state under specified fault conditions.

Volatility

A measurement of the price fluctuation of an underlying instrument that takes place over a certain period of time.

Volt

A unit of electrical pressure which forces electrical charges to move through a wire or other conductors. The voltage in an electric circuit pushes electrons around the circuit. The unit of measurement of electromotive force. It is equivalent to the force required to produce a current of one ampere through a resistance of one ohm. The unit of measure for electrical potential. A unit of electrical force equal to that amount of electromotive force that will cause a steady current of one ampere to flow through a resistance of one ohm. Generally measured in kilovolts or kV. Typical transmission level voltages are 115 kV, 230 kV and 500 kV.

Volt-Ampere (VA)

In an a.c. circuit, a measure of apparent power, given by: VA-EI, where E is the potential in volts; I is the
curernt in amperes; and VA is apparent power in volt-amperes

Voltage

The force that makes electricity flow; the unit of measure of electric potential .A measure of the force or "push" given the electrons in an electrical circuit; a measure of electrical potential. One volt produces one amp of current when acting against a resistance of one ohm. The amount of electromotive force, measured in volts, that exists between two points.

Voltage of a Circuit

The electric pressure of a circuit in an electric system measured in volts. It is generally a nominal rating based on the maximum normal effective difference of potential between any two conductors of the circuit.

Voltage Regulator

An electrical device that regulates voltage on distribution lines. It automatically raises and lowers the voltage to maintain required voltage levels for service.

Volt-Ampere

A unit of electrical measurement equal to the product of a volt and an ampere.

Volumetric Wires Charge
A fee for using the transmission or distribution system that is based on the volume of electricity that is transmitted

VOM
Volt ohm-meter.

Volumetric Rate
See RATE, VOLUMETRIC.

Voltage
Electric potential or potential difference expressed in volts. Electromotive force or potential difference, usually expressed in volts. Electrical pressure, the force which causes current to flow through a conductor. Voltage must be expressed as a difference of potential between two points since it is a relational term. Connecting both voltmeter leads to the same point will show no voltage present although the voltage between that point and ground may be hundred or thousands of volts. This is why most nominal voltages are expressed as "phase to phase" or "phase to neutral". The unit of measurement is "volts". The electrical symbol is "e".

Volt-Microsecond Constant
The product of the voltage applied across the winding and the time for the magnetizing current to reach 1.5 times the linear extrapolation of the current waveform. This constant is a measure of the energy handling capability of a transformer or inductor. It is dependent upon the core area, core material, number of turns, and the duty cycle of the applied pulse.

Voltage Balance
For a multiple output converter, the percentage difference in voltage level of two outputs with opposite polarities and equal nominal values.

Voltage Control
The control of transmission voltage adjustments in generator reactive output and transformer taps, and by switching capacitors and inductors on the transmission and distribution systems.

Voltage, Maximum
The highest voltage that can safely be dropped across a PolySwitch device in its tripped state under specified fault conditions.
Synonyms: Maximum Device Voltage,Maximum Interrupt Voltage, Vmax

Voltage, Maximum Operating
The maximum voltage across a PolySwitch device under a typical fault

condition. In many circuits, this is the voltage of the power source in the circuit. It may be possible to use a PolySwitch device at a higher voltage, but each such use must be individually qualified.

Voltage Reduction
Any intentional reduction of system voltage by 3 percent or greater for reasons of maintaining the continuity of service of the bulk electric power supply system.

Voltage Regulation
The ability of a power conditioner to maintain a stable output voltage when input voltage fluctuates.

Voltage Regulator
An electrical device that regulates voltage on distribution lines. It automatically raises and lowers the voltage to maintain required voltage levels for service.

Voltage Support
A small remote generator located on a transmission system to provide voltage within tolerance limits to the customer. If the voltage delivered is outside of the tolerance levels, appliances will not run efficiently.

Volt-Ampere
A unit of apparent power in an alternating-current circuit.

Volume Resistivilty (Core)
The ability of a core to resist the flow of electrical current either through the bulk of the material or on its surface. The unit of the volume resistivity is Ohm-cm. Core volume resistivity becomes an issue in inductor designs where the leads/terminals come in contact with the core material. This type includes axial and radial inductors that have leads epoxied into the core. As for core materials, high permeability ferrites present the most concern as their volume resistivity is typically the lowest. %0aUnder certian conditions, a low resistive path can be realized between two inductor terminals if theyare in contact with a low resistivity core. The inductor, under these condidtions, will lose its higher impedance characteristics.

Volumetric Wires Charge
A fee for using the transmission or distribution system that is based on the volume of electricity that is transmitted

W

Wafer
A thin sheet of semiconductor (photovoltaic material) made by cutting it from a single crystal or ingot.

Wall
A vertical structural element that holds up a roof, encloses part or all of a room, or stands by itself to hold back soil.

Wall Orientation
The geographical direction that the primary or largest exterior wall of a building faces.

Warmup Drift
See Drift

Water Jacket
A heat exchanger element enclosed in a boiler. Water is circulated with a pump through the jacket where it picks up heat from the combustion chamber after which the heated water circulates to heat distribution devices. A water jacket is also an enclosed water-filled chamber in a tankless coiled water heater. When a faucet is turned on water flows into the water heater heat exchanger. The water in the chamber is heated and transfers heat to the cooler water in the heat exchanger and is sent through the hot water outlet to the appropriate faucet.

Water Source Heat Pump
A type of (geothermal) heat pump that uses well (ground) or surface water as a heat source. Water has a more stable seasonal temperature than air thus making for a more efficient heat source.

Water Turbine
A turbine that uses water pressure to rotate its blades; the primary types are the Pelton wheel, for high heads (pressure); the Francis turbine, for low to medium heads; and the Kaplan for a wide range of heads. Primarily used to power an electric generator.

Water Wall
An interior wall made of water filled containers for absorbing and storing solar energy.

Water Wheel
A wheel that is designed to use the weight and/or force of moving water to turn it, primarily to operate machinery or grind grain.

Watt

The rate of energy transfer equivalent to one ampere under an electrical pressure of one volt. One watt equals 1/746 horsepower, or one joule per second. It is the product of Voltage and Current (amperage). The electrical unit of power. The rate of energy transfer equivalent to one ampere flowing under a pressure of one volt at unity power factor. Watts are a basic unit of measure of electric power, or the rate of doing electric work. Light bulbs and appliances are rated by the amount of electric power they consume measured in watts. For instance, a 100-watt light bulb on a 110-volt electric circuit uses 0.9 amps of current to produce 100 watts of work. A comparison with other measures of work is that one horsepower equal 746-watts. Unit of electric power — equal to l/746th of 1 horse-power -that is usually expressed in kilowatts (kW or thousands of watts) and megawatts (MW or millions of watts). SI unit of power. Symbol is W. In this website it is understood power under standard test conditions (STC). Also written Wp (peak watt) by PV professionals to mean peak power at STC. Multiples like kW (one thousand watts = 1 000 W) or MW (one million watts = 1 000 000 W) are also used.

Watt-hour

A unit of electricity consumption of one Watt over the period of one hour. A unit of work or energy equivalent to the power of one watt operating for one hour. The amount of electricity used by one watt in one hour eg. A 100 watt light bulb will use 100 watt-hours of electricity each hour it is used. An electrical energy unit of measure equal to one watt of power supplied to, or taken from, an electric circuit steadily for one hour. Examples - kilowatt hour (kWh) and megawatt hour (MWh). The basic unit of measure for consumption of electric energy. One watt-hour is one watt of electricity used for a period of one hour.

Wattmeter

A device for measuring power consumption.

Wave Form

The shape of the phase power at a certain frequency and amplitude.

Wavelength

The distance between similar points on successive waves.

Wave Power

The concept of capturing and converting the energy available in the motion of ocean waves to energy.

WB1
Web-based Intranets

Weatherization
Caulking and weatherstripping to reduce air infiltration and exfiltration into/out of a building.

Weatherstripping
A material used to seal gaps around windows and exterior doors.

Weir
A low dam over which a river flows, but which allows nearly all water to be diverted to a water turbine if the water level drops below its height. Helps insure year-round power production in areas with highly variable water levels.

Wheeling
The use of transmission facilities of one utility system to transmit power to another utility system, or between customer facilities within a single utility system or between systems. The use of the transmission facilities of one system to transmit power for another system. Wheeling Wheeling can apply to either wholesale or retail service. Moving electricity from the generating facility to the customer over one or more separately owned electric transmission and distribution systems.
The process of transmitting electricity over one or more separately owned electric transmission and distribution systems. (See Wholesale and Retail Wheeling.)

Wheeling Service
The movement of electricity from one system to another over transmission facilities of intervening systems. Wheeling service contracts can be established between two or more systems.

Whole House Fan
A mechanical/electrical device used to pull air out of an interior space; usually located in the highest location of a building, in the ceiling, and venting to the attic or directly to the outside.

Wholesale Wheeling
The wheeling of electric power in amounts and at prices that generally have been negotiated in long term contracts between the power provider and a distributor or very large power customer.

Wind Energy
Energy available from the movement of the wind across a landscape caused by the heating of the atmosphere, earth, and oceans by the sun.

The kinetic energy of wind converted into mechanical energy by wind turbines (i.e., blades rotating from a hub) that drive generators to produce electricity.

Wind Energy Conversion System (WECS) or Device
An apparatus for converting the energy available in the wind to mechanical energy that can be used to power machinery (grain mills, water pumps) and to operate an electrical generator.

Wind Generator
A device that captures the force of the wind to provide rotational motion to produce power with an alternator or generator. *See also: Alternator, Generator, Wind Turbine*

Windmill
A device that uses wind power to mill grain into flour. But informally used as a synonym for wind generator or wind turbine, and to describe machines that pump water with wind power. *See also: Wind Turbine*

Window
A generic term for a glazed opening that allows daylight to enter into a building and can be opened for ventilation.

Windpower Curve
A graph representing the relationship between the power available from the wind and the wind speed. The power from the wind increases proportionally with the cube of the wind speed.

Wind Power Plant
A group of wind turbines interconnected to a common power provider system through a system of transformers, distribution lines, and (usually) one substation. Operation, control, and maintenance functions are often centralized through a network of computerized monitoring systems, supplemented by visual inspection. This is a term commonly used in the United States. In Europe, it is called a generating station.

Windpower Profile
The change in the power available in the wind due to changes in the wind speed or velocity profile; the windpower profile is proportional to the cube of the wind speed profile.

Wind Resource Assessment
The process of characterizing the wind resource, and its energy potential, for a specific site or geographical area.

Wind Rose
A diagram that indicates the average percentage of time that the wind

blows from different directions, on a monthly or annual basis.

Wind Speed
The rate of flow of the wind undisturbed by obstacles.

Wind Speed Duration Curve
A graph that indicates the distribution of wind speeds as a function of the cumulative number of hours that the wind speed exceeds a given wind speed in a year.

Wind Speed Frequency Curve
A curve that indicates the number of hours per year that specific wind speeds occur.

Wind Speed Profile
A profile of how the wind speed changes with height above the surface of the ground or water.

Wind Turbine
A term used for a wind energy conversion device that produces electricity; typically having one, two, or three blades.

Wind Turbine Generators
Devices which are designed to convert wind energy into electrical energy. A device that converts the kinetic energy in the wind into electrical energy

Winding Factor (K)
The ratio of the total area of copper wire inside the center hole of a toroid to the window area of the toroid.

Window Area (Wa)
The area in and around a magnetic core which can be used for the placement of windings.

Wind Turbine
A machine that captures the force of the wind. Called a Wind Generator when used to produce electricity. Called a Windmill when used to crush grain or pump water. *See also: Wind Generator, Windmill*

Windward
Toward the direction from which the wind blows.

Wind Turbine
A term used for a wind energy conversion device that produces electricity. These typically have between one and three blades.

Wires Company
Entity that operates an electrical transmission system as a common carrier but does not own generating facilities or distribution networks

Wind Turbine Rated Capacity
The amount of power a wind turbine can produce at its rated wind speed, e.g., 100 kW at 20 mph. The rated wind speed generally corresponds to the point at which the conversion efficiency is near its maximum. Because of the variability of the wind, the amount of energy a wind turbine actually produces is
a function of the capacity factor (e.g., a wind turbine produces 20% to 35% of its rated capacity over a year).

Wind Velocity
The wind speed and direction in an undisturbed flow.

Wingwall
A building structural element that is built onto a building's exterior along the inner edges of all the windows, and extending from the ground to the eaves. Wingwalls help ventilate rooms that have only one exterior wall which leads to poor cross ventilation. Wingwalls cause fluctuations in the natural wind direction to create moderate pressure differences across the windows. They are only effective on the windward side of the building.

Wire (Electrical)
A generic term for an electrical conductor.

Withstand Voltage
Maximum voltage level that can be applied between circuits or components without causing a breakdown. Also see Breakdown Voltage and Isolation.

Work
The transfer of force from one body or system to another. Work is performed by a force moving an object.

Wood Stove
A wood-burning appliance for space and/or water heating and/or cooking.

Working Fluid
A fluid used to absorb and transfer heat energy.

Wound Rotor Motors
A type of motor that has a rotor with electrical windings connected

through slip rings to the external power circuit. An external resistance controller in the rotor circuit allows the performance of the motor to be tailored to the needs of the system and to be changed with relative ease to accommodate system changes or to vary the speed of the motor.

Wye or "Y" Connected Circuit (Star Connected)
A three-phase circuit in which windings of all three phases have one common connection. A wye connection refers to a polyphase electrical supply where the source transformer has the conductors connected to the terminals in a physical arrangement resembling a Y. Each point of the Y represents the connection of a hot conductor. The angular displacement between each point of the Y is 120 degrees. The center point is the common return point for the neutral conductor.

X

xDSL
Refers to the various flavors of DSL (Digital Subscriber Loop). All encompassing term.

Y

Yaw
The rotation of a horizontal axis wind turbine around its tower or vertical axis.Rotation parallel to the ground. A wind generator Yaws to face winds coming from different directions.

Yaw Axis
Vertical axis through the center of gravity.

Yurt
An octagonal shaped shelter that originated in Mongolia, and traditionally made from leather or canvas for easy transportation.

Z

Zener Diode

A diode that maintains a relatively constant voltage when the reverse voltage across it is increased passed a specific point, called the zener voltage.

Zero Signal Reference
A connection point, bus, or conductor used as one side of a signal circuit.

It may or may not be designated as ground. Is sometimes referred to as circuit common.

Zero Voltage Switching

Technique in which the power switch in a converter turns on and off when there is a zero voltage across it. This minimized switching transient noise output from the converter.

Zone

An area within the interior space of a building, such as an individual room(s), to be cooled, heated, or ventilated. A zone has its own thermostat to control the flow of conditioned air into the space.

Zoning

The combining of rooms in a structure according to similar heating and cooling patterns. Zoning requires using more than one thermostat to control heating, cooling, and ventilation equipment.

DBL
7+9.5

Cyder Tech Bill No 132/137/CT/P dt 17/7/06